ADOLF HITLER

THE CURIOUS AND MACABRE ANECDOTES

PATRICK DELAFORCE

FONTHILL

Fonthill Media Limited
Fonthill Media LLC
www.fonthillmedia.com
office@fonthillmedia.com

This edition published in the United Kingdom 2012

British Library Cataloguing in Publication Data:
A catalogue record for this book is available from the British Library

Copyright © Patrick Delaforce 2012

ISBN 978-1-78155-073-1 (print)
ISBN 978-1-78155-158-5 (e-book)

Typeset in 9.5pt on 13pt Sabon LT
Printed and bound in England

Connect with us
 facebook.com/fonthillmedia twitter.com/fonthillmedia

Introduction

One of the greatest mysteries of the twentieth century was how a motley collection of not very intelligent German street brawlers, led and totally dominated by one man, could by brutal war take most of Europe and threaten the rest of the world. Adolf Hitler (1889-1945), an Austrian 'misfit', a loner without much education, no family genes of note and no political or martial background created the infamous Third Reich by sheer determination, confidence, will power and luck.

Whilst in Landsberg prison in 1923-24, guilty of a premature, badly planned 'putsch' to seize power, he composed a long, boring diatribe, which he called *Mein Kampf* (*My Struggle*) and which sold seven million copies. It told the world, *inter alia*, of his step-by-step ruthless plans to seize power and smash and grab much of Europe and Russia to obtain *lebensraum* – more living space – for 80 million Germans. The royalties from the book made him a millionaire. The non-German politicians who read *Mein Kampf* could not possibly envisage a 34-year-old rabble-rouser actually clawing his way to power and ultimately causing 50 million deaths.

Although, stony broke in Vienna, his vapid, prolific watercolour paintings were sold by Jewish merchants, and he himself was not sure whether his mother's father was a Jew, he soon developed a manic compulsion to destroy all the Jews in Germany, indeed in Europe. He and his terrible cohorts, Himmler, Goebbels, Heydrich and Eichmann controlled thirty extermination centres to implement the 'Final Solution' – the wholesale destruction of European Jewry. In *Mein Kampf* Hitler set out his belief in the superiority of Aryan and Nordic races and that there was an international conspiracy of Jews, who were even using Bolshevism, particularly Russian Bolshevism, to achieve world domination.

The power of his personality, drive, zeal, iron will, eternal optimism and promises of peace had an immense impact. In the early 1930s he convinced his National Socialist German Workers' Party (all other parties had been outlawed) and his supporters that the new Germany, Nazi Germany, under his leadership as Führer (leader) was great, was strong and had a manifest destiny, even though there would be sacrifices along the way. In April 1939, Hitler wrote to the American President Roosevelt 'I took over a state which was faced by complete ruin, thanks to its trust in the promises of the rest of the world ... I have conquered chaos in Germany [after the Weimar Republic], re-established order and enormously increased production ... I have succeeded in finding useful work for the seven million unemployed ...'

And it is true that in terms of social reform, there was much that was good – or at least beneficial to the (non-Jewish) German population. There are many examples of Hitler's social reforms: vast improvements in workers' conditions at work and at home; benevolent farming laws; laws for the reduction of unemployment; the establishment of chambers of culture; the building of autobahns; the Volkswagen; workers' recreation facilities; the 'Strength through joy' movement; and holiday courses. Through Goebbels, Hitler controlled all the media in Germany and with his compelling oratory simply brainwashed the German people over a twelve-year period. His people regarded him as 'The Messiah', the German women adored him, and the men, including the other Nazi leaders, feared him.

He was to become hated and feared throughout the world, and seen by many as an embodiment of evil. His beliefs, his policies, his actions were vile, horrible and – yes – evil ... but as an individual, he can be seen not as awe-inspiring but as repellent, ridiculous, pathetic, pompous, even laughable – as well as hateful. Much of this book is devoted to the background and the little details that made up this twisted individual: Hitler's schooling, academic reports, masters and choir singing; the 'loner' down-and-out in Vienna; his thwarted ambition to be a painter; his service in the Great War; his leather shorts; his *Kampf*, the first crude, amateurish, post-war efforts at demagogue politics; his loyalty to his early street thugs; his love affairs; the men and women he surrounded himself with, including two of the Mitford girls and the Duke and Duchess of Windsor; his diet; his blue eyes; the occasional brutal plot and conspiracy; and those strange final weeks in the bunker beneath the garden of the Reich Chancellery in Berlin.

Hitler once said, 'The victor in war is he who commits the fewest number of mistakes and who has, also, a blind faith in victory.' He was arrogant and ruthless – and he certainly had blind faith in victory until the dramatic events in the bunker in late April 1945 when the Russian shells were falling around him, and marriage to Eva Braun, the firing of Himmler and Goering, and suicide were imminent.

But for four astonishing mistakes, Hitler's Third Reich would have been extended into the twenty-first century!

*   *   *   *   *

When the British Expeditionary Force was encircled at Dunkirk in 1940, if Hitler had deployed *all* the resources then massing on the frontiers with Russia, there is not much doubt that he would have succeeded with Operation Sealion and over-run the United Kingdom. He hoped, however, that peace feelers would be successful and he could keep England neutralized, so Operation Barbarossa was given top priority.

*　　*　　*　　*　　*

In *Mein Kampf* Hitler decreed that most of Russia, with its 'Jewish' Bolshevism, its oilfields, and its *lebensraum*, should be conquered. Operation Barbarossa might have succeeded if it had been launched on 15 May 1941 instead of 22 June, which would have given a further five weeks of Blitzkrieg weather. Hitler could have created a defensive wall to keep Stalin's demoralized armies at bay after the short brutal Polish campaign. A keen military historian, Hitler should have heeded the fate of Napoleon's ill-judged disastrous campaign against Russia. Another dictator who thought he could rule Europe.

*　　*　　*　　*　　*

There was absolutely no necessity for Adolf Hitler to declare war on the USA on 11 December 1941. It was a gesture of solidarity with Japan (who had not invaded Russia as he had hoped). As a veteran of the Great War, Hitler must have appreciated the vital role the American army had played in 1918, and known that not in a hundred years could the Third Reich have conquered the USA. The declaration of war was a real *folie de grandeur*.

*　　*　　*　　*　　*

The brilliant German physicists of the 1920s and 1930s had developed considerable atomic nuclear knowledge and plans. Because Hitler detested Jews and many of the physicists were Jews, he thought 'nuclear power' was a Jewish conspiracy and refrained from financial backing.

*　　*　　*　　*　　*

So, Hitler's Third Reich lasted twelve years, not the thousand he predicted. By these mistakes Hitler and his brilliant military machine were doomed. Instead, Götterdämmerung!

The Author

Patrick Delaforce was educated at Winchester College. During the Second World War, aged 17, he was in Churchill's Home Guard and witnessed the London Blitz of 1940 and 1941. Later he served as a troop leader in Normandy with the Royal Horse Artillery of the 11th Armoured Division. Hitler's Wehrmacht blew him up with their mines in Holland, and he was again wounded by a rifle grenade on the banks of the River Elbe.

He was with the first battle group into Bergen-Belsen concentration camp in April 1945, was twice mentioned in despatches, and was awarded the Bronze Cross of Orange-Nassau. In autumn 1945 he served on a War Crimes Tribunal in Hamburg and tried many concentration camp guards. Finally, he was an official British Army of the Rhine witness when Mr Albert Pierrepoint, the British hangman, executed 13 convicted war criminals in Hameln on 13 December 1945. After leaving the army, he worked as a port wine shipper and ran an advertising agency in New York, before becoming a professional writer, mainly on historical and military subjects. 40 books by him have been published with 100 editions (including in Russia). Fonthill Media are publishing six of his titles.

Note on Sources

The number in small type at the end of most of the entries refers to the numbered bibliography, and this lists the main source. Occasionally two or three specific sources are noted. Some entries are made up from a variety of sources, in which case they are not numbered at all.

Note on Accents and Spellings

In line with contemporary convention, the use of accents, mainly the German umlaut, has not been used in people's names. For example, the accent 'ö' has been substituted with 'oe' and the accent 'ü' has been substituted with 'ue'. For place names and most other purposes the umlaut has been retained. Where a German city has an accepted English name version, for example Munich and Nuremberg, the English name has been used. Names such as 'Rudolph' and 'Adolph' have been changed to 'Rudolf' and 'Adolf' for consistency.

ADOLF HITLER
The Curious and Macabre Anecdotes

The Young Choirboy

A customs official called Alois Schicklgruber for a variety of reasons changed his name in January 1877 to Alois Hitler. Photographs show him in uniform with glittering buttons; a portly man with the cautious face of a minor official, he moved house eleven times in twenty-five years and married three times. Adolf Hitler was born on 20 April 1889 in Braunau am Inn, the fourth child of the third marriage. For centuries the small farmers in the Waldviertel between the River Danube and the Bohemian border from villages called Spital, Walterschlag, Weitra, Dollersheim and Strones produced families named Hüttler, Hiedler or Hitler who were probably of Czech origin. The young Adolf's family moved to Gross-Schönau in Lower Austria, then to Passau, then to Linz. In 1895 Alois bought a 10-acre farm near Lambach. In the famous old Benedictine monastery there, the 6-year-old Adolf Hitler served as church acolyte and choirboy. He recalled 'the opportunity to intoxicate myself with the solemn splendour of the brilliant church festivals'. Ten years later, at his mother's wish, Hitler was confirmed. Klara hoped her son would become a monk. His restless father sold the farm and bought a house outside Linz, in Leonding, and retired on a pension, aged 58.

Above, left and right: Alois and Klara Hitler.
Below: Hitler in the autumn of 1889 when just a few months old.

Young Hitler at school, third row, far left.

'Very Painful Adolescence'

The Hitler family – Alois junior, Angela, Adolf, Edmund and sister Paula, plus a cook and a maid – was a comfortable, middle-class establishment, which also included Adolf's ill-tempered, hunchbacked aunt Johanna. Alois had been promoted in 1892 to be a Higher Collector of Customs – a provincial civil servant who was status-conscious, humourless, thrifty and very bad-tempered. He smoked too much, drank quite a lot, and his passion was bee-keeping. In *Mein Kampf* Hitler commented that his adolescence had been 'very painful'. As part of the Hitler 'myth' he said that his harsh, over-strict father, Alois, beat him frequently with his belt. Alois was humourless and reputedly mocked his son's aspirations to be an artist. There is little doubt that Hitler adored his mother, Klara, but hated his father. After the Anschluss in 1938 when Austria was conquered, Hitler ordered the Wehrmacht to turn the village of Döllersheim into an army training camp. In doing so the tanks destroyed his father's birthplace and his grandmother's grave. Hitler sometimes told his guests at table that he knew nothing about family histories. 'There were relations of mine of whose existence I was quite unaware until I became Reich Chancellor. I am a completely non-family man with no sense of the clan spirit. I belong solely to the community of my nation. I have to think twice before I can remember my cousins or my aunts. To me the whole thing is uninteresting and futile.'[35]

Young Hitler aged about ten.

Fatherly Love?

Hitler spoke to his secretary, Christa Schroeder, about his parents.

'I never loved my father but feared him. He was prone to rages and would resort to violence. My poor mother would then always be afraid for me. When I read Karl May he wrote that it was a sign of bravery to hide one's pain, I decided that when he beat me the next time I would make no sound. When it happened – I knew my mother was standing anxiously at the door – I counted every stroke out loud. Mother thought I had gone mad when I reported to her with a beaming smile, "Thirty-two strokes father gave me" From that day I never needed to repeat the experiment, for my father never beat me again.'

Making the Girls Laugh

In 1901, the 12-year-old schoolboy in the Linz Realschule wagered his classmates that he could make the girls in his class laugh during a religious service. Whenever they glanced at him he won the bet by brushing his non-existent moustache.

The Lost Soul

Religious instruction in Austrian schools was given by priests. Fifty years after he left school Hitler could recall details of how he teased Father Schwarz at his Realschule in the Herrengasse.

'I was the eternal asker of questions. Since I was completely master of the material, I was unassailable. I always had the best marks. On the other hand I was less impeccable under the heading of Behaviour.'

He asked embarrassing questions and the exasperated priest asked him if he said his prayers in the morning, at mid-day and at night. 'No, sir, I don't say prayers. Besides I don't see how God could be interested in the prayers of a secondary schoolboy.'

Schwarz, however, was insistent. 'In your heart you should have ideals for our beloved country, our beloved house of Hapsburg. Whoever does not love the Imperial family does not love the Church and whoever does not love the Church, does not love God. So sit down, Hitler.' And 'one day my mother came to the school and Father Schwarz took the opportunity to pounce on her and explain that I was a lost soul.'

The Very Young Political Revolutionary

When Hitler, aged 34, composed *Mein Kampf* in Landsberg prison he wrote of his schoolboy life and activities. He claimed that his 'habit of historical thinking that he had learned at school' and 'world history' study gave him 'an inexhaustible source of understanding ... for politics'. 'Thus at an early age I had become a political revolutionary and I became an artistice revolutionary at an equally early age.' At the age of twelve he saw a theatre performance of *Wilhelm Tell*, and aged thirteen, his first opera, *Lohengrin*. 'My youthful enthusiasm for the master of Bayreuth knew no bounds.'

The Violent Schoolboy Orator

In *Mein Kampf* Hitler wrote, 'All my playing about in the open, the long walk to school [Lambach, a market village in Upper Austria], my association with extremely "husky" boys which caused my mother bitter anguish, made me the very opposite of a stay-at-home ... even then my oratorical talent was being developed with more or less *violent* arguments with my schoolmates. I had become a little ringleader; at school I learned easily and at that time very well, but was otherwise hard to handle.' But his school reports (*see p. 14*) are rather second-rate!

Hitler the Poet (1)

Lodging with a family in Steyr, Austria, aged 15, Hitler spent much of his time drawing, painting and reading. He also wrote a rather deranged poem which is now in the Bundesarchiv Koblenz. Some of the wording is not decipherable. Translated, it reads:

> The people sit there in a ventilated house
> Filling themselves with beer and wine
> Eating and drinking ecstatically
> (–) out then on all fours.
> There they climb high mountain peaks
> (–) with faces full of pride
> And fall down like acrobats somersaulting
> And cannot find balance
> Then, sad, they return home
> And quite forget the time
> Then he sees (–), his wife, poor man,
> Who cures his injuries with a good hiding.

The budding painter illustrated his poem with a man being beaten by a buxom woman![68]

Shooting Rats in Steyr

Steyr, a small town 30 miles south of Linz, was according to Hitler 'an unpleasant town – the opposite of Linz which was full of national spirit. Steyr was black and red – the clergy and Marxism.' He lodged at No. 9, Grunmarkt, in a little room overlooking the courtyard. His school companion was Gustav, and Petronella, the rather nice 33-year-old landlady, was very fond of the two lads and sided with them against her older husband. She stuffed their pockets with dainties. One of the young Adolf's hobbies was shooting rats with an airgun from their bedroom.

Sozzled in Steyr

After his final examinations, Hitler celebrated with a great party.

'I had obtained my certificate, next day I was to leave Steyr and return to my mother. My comrades and I secretly gathered over a quart of local wine.

I've completely forgotten what happened that night. I was woken at dawn by a milkwoman on the road from Steyr to Karsten. I was in a lamentable state when I got back to Petronella's house.'

Totally drunk, the 16-year-old had used his certificate as toilet paper and thrown it away!

'Since I had drunk away all my money, she [Petronella] carried her kindness so far as to lend me five gulden. I am still humiliated [1942]. I made a promise that I would never get drunk again, and I've kept my word.'[61]

The Young War-Monger

'Rummaging through my father's library I came across various books of a military nature, among them a popular edition of the Franco-Prussian War of 1870-71. It consisted of two issues of an illustrated periodical from those years, which now became my favourite reading. It was not long before the great heroic struggle had become my greatest inner experience. From then on I became more and more enthusiastic about everything that was in any way connected with war, or for that matter with soldiering.' So the Franco-Prussian War set the young Adolf on a long, long trail of military adventures. His contempt for France probably ensued from the same moment.[32]

Hitler's Teachers

Dr Leopold Poetsch, an ardent German nationalist and a town councillor of Linz, taught the young Adolf Hitler his history, and made a deep impression on him. 'There we sat, often aflame with enthusiasm sometimes even moved to tears. The national fervour which we felt in our small way was used by him as an instrument in our education. It was because I had such a professor that history became my favourite subject.' Certainly Hitler told his table

Ludwig Wittgenstein (bottom left in photograph) and Adolf Hitler (top right) both attended the Linz Realschule, a state school of about 300 students, and were there at the same time from 1903 to 1904.

companions dozens of historical titbits – he had an astonishing memory for trivia of every possible kind. He thought his school teachers were absolute tyrants. 'They had no sympathy with youth. Their one object was to stuff our brains and to turn us into erudite apes like themselves. If any pupil showed the slightest trace of originality, they persecuted him relentlessly.' The physics master, Koenig, was a 'real fool'. His pupils made cruel fun of the tubby little priest who taught divinity. Hitler's French teacher had 'a frowsty beard, greasy and dirty, yellow collar, a most repellent creature [he was] furious because I learnt not a word of French.'[61]

Education, Education, Education!

Hitler's school report for the fourth class of the Staatsrealschule in Steyr, issued on 16 September 1905, reads:

	FIRST SEMESTER	SECOND SEMESTER
Moral conduct	Satisfactory	Satisfactory
Diligence	Unequal	Adequate
Religion	Adequate	Satisfactory
German language	Inadequate	Adequate
Geography & History	Adequate	Satisfactory
Mathematics	Inadequate	Satisfactory
Chemistry	Adequate	Adequate
Geometry	Adequate	Adequate
Freehand drawing	Laudable	Excellent
Gymnastics	Excellent	Excellent
Stenography	Inadequate	–
Singing	–	Satisfactory
Written work	Displeasing	Displeasing
Physics	Satisfactory	Adequate

The 17-year-old was obviously lazy (see Diligence), but performed very well in his art classes (Freehand drawing). There are two surprises. Hitler as an adult detested physical exercise, rarely walked and certainly played no sports, so 'Excellent' in gymnastics is surprising. And his devotion to his history teacher, Dr Poetsch is not reflected in his school grades.[29]

'Notoriously Cantankerous'

Dr Eduard Huemer gave this description of the young schoolboy: 'I can recall the gaunt, pale-faced youth pretty well [written in 1923]. He had definite talent, though in a narrow field. But he lacked self-discipline, being notoriously cantankerous, wilful, arrogant and bad-tempered. He had obvious difficulty in fitting in at school. Moreover he was lazy. His enthusiasm for hard work evaporated all too quickly. He reacted with ill-concealed hostility to advice or reproof. At the same time he demanded of his fellow pupils their unqualified subservience, fancying himself in the role of leader.'

'Wholly to Art'

His widowed mother moved into an apartment in Linz which she shared with the inadequate, arrogant 16-year-old dreamer, who for a time devoted himself 'wholly to art'. He sketched, painted, drew plans for museums, a bridge over the River Danube, theatres and indeed the total rebuilding of Linz. Briefly he took piano lessons and got bored. He became a *boulevardier* fop with a black, ivory-topped cane and visited concerts, theatres, a musical club, a library club and a wax museum. He was a drifter in a dream world, with just one friend, August Kubizek, known as 'Gustl', who was a decorator's son. He described himself as a 'loner'.

Hitler as Playwright

In 1906 Hitler, busy doing nothing very much whilst in Linz, was allowed to use a well-equipped library owned by the father of a friend (a government official). He discovered Richard Wagner's prose writings, including *Jews in Music* and *Decay and Regeneration*. He also went to a meeting for 'persons physically separated' since neither religious nor civil divorce existed in Austria, and became a member of this organization. 'Seized with virtuous indignation' since 'men, models of ignominy whose wives, by law could never separate from them', young Adolf Hitler decided to write a play on the subject. 'Since my writing was illegible, I dictated the play to my sister, pacing up and down in my room. The play was divided into a number of scenes. I displayed a lofty, burning imagination. At the time I was fifteen years old. My sister said to me, "You know Adolf, your play can't be acted." I couldn't persuade her that she was mistaken.' His sister, Elli, 'went on strike. That was the end of my masterpiece.'[61]

The Artist Manqué

Hitler tried hard to attend the Academy of Fine Arts in Vienna. When he registered with the Vienna police it was as a 'student', then as a 'painter' and 'studying to be a writer'. To gain admission to the Academy's school of painting he had to submit a number of his drawings. If they were considered to be reasonable, the candidate then had to take an examination in drawing held each year in October. He was refused entry on two occasions.

<u>1907/8</u> 'Composition exercises in drawing. First day "expulsion from paradise". Second day "episode from the deluge". The following took the test with insufficient results, or were not admitted. Adolf Hitler, Braunau a. Inn, April 20 1889, German Catholic. Father civil servant. 4 classes in Realschule. Few heads. Test drawing unsatisfactory.'

<u>1908, October</u> 'The following gentlemen performed their test drawings with insufficient success or were not admitted to the test. No. 24, Adolf Hitler, Braunau a. Inn, Twentieth of April 1889, German Catholic civil servant. 4 Realschulein. Not admitted to the test.'

The drawings he brought to the test were regarded by the examiners as being inadequate – hence no test. Hitler's version was that he appealed and was told that he should apply for admission to the Architectural School, but as Hitler had no high school diploma he could not apply.[29]

Tobacco

In March 1942, reminiscing with his friend Heinrich Hoffmann, Hitler said: 'I experienced such poverty in Vienna. I spent long months without ever having the smallest hot meal. I lived on milk and dry bread. But I spent thirty kreuzers a day on my cigarettes. I smoked between twenty-five and forty of them a day. At that time a kreuzer meant more to me than ten thousand marks today. One day I reflected that with five kreuzers I could buy some butter to put on my bread. I threw my cigarettes into the Danube and since that day I've never smoked again ... So many men whom I've known have died of excessive use of tobacco. My father, first of all. Then Dietrich Eckhart, Troost. Soon it'll be your turn Hoffmann.'

The Impoverished Orphan?

On 29 November 1921, aged 31, Hitler supplied a memoir of his early life to the archivist of the NSDAP, the Nazi party: 'I was orphaned with no father

One of Hitler's paintings.

or mother at seventeen and left without any financial support. My total cash at the time of the trip to Vienna was about 80 kronen. I was therefore forced immediately to earn my bread as a common labourer. I went, as a not yet eighteen year old, as a worker's helper on construction jobs and had in the course of two years experienced almost all types of work of the common daily wage earner ... After indescribable effort I succeeded to educate myself so well as a painter that I, through this activity from my twentieth year on, was able to make out in this work even if at first scantily. I became an architectural draftsman and architectural painter and was practically completely independent by my twenty-first year. In 1912 I went in this capacity to Munich.' Once the young Hitler shovelled snow from the pavement in front of the Vienna Opera House and tried for a porter's job in Vienna's Westbahnhof railway station. He certainly painted prolifically, including landscapes with houses and churches, but he was certainly not a qualified architectural draftsman. In the period 1907-9 he spent money on opera tickets, kid gloves and ivory-handled canes. In 1908 his aunt Johanna Poelzl loaned him 924 kronen, and after his mother's death in December 1907 he received a further 652 kronen; he also received 25 kronen a month of his orphan's pension. Therefore his *unearned* income was about 80 kronen a month – equivalent to a young schoolteacher's salary. A painting sold each day brought in 5 kronen and he shared the proceeds from his paintings 50-50 with Reinhold Hanische. So his real abject poverty in the winter of 1909-10 can only be put down to very poor budgeting![27]

Hitler the Painter (1)

Reinhold Hanisch was a tramp who became Hitler's only friend in the charity ward at Meidling, a Vienna suburb. Hanisch vividly described the young Adolf as wearing a frock coat and a greasy black derby hat, from which his hair hung over his coat collar; a thick ruff of fluffy beard encircled his chin. He would hang around night shelters, living on the bread and soup he got there and discussing politics, often getting into heated arguments. Hanisch persuaded Hitler to move into a hostel for men, where he stayed for a seven-month period in 1909-10; they were not only blue and white collar workers, and some craftsmen, but the flotsam of society, gamblers, money lenders, beggars, bankrupt businessmen and discharged army officers. Hanisch was registered in the false name of Fritz Walter. He persuaded the apathetic young painter actually to do some work and the pair went into partnership on a fifty-fifty basis. Hitler did paint sketches and watercolours at the rate of one per day, which Hanisch sold in the streets and bars of Vienna. The pair of near down-and-outs could not clothes themselves properly but they were no longer cold and hungry. Amongst their many Jewish friends was a Hungarian art dealer, Josef Neumann, who not only bought Hitler's paintings but also introduced him to three other dealers.[29] Hitler also copied postcards and lithographs of Viennese scenes and produced a poster advertising a hair tonic, another for a bed-feathers shop and another for an anti-perspirant powder sold under the brand name 'Teddy'. Yet another was for a toilet soap, a mountain of soap bars in front of the majestic St Stephan's Cathedral. The untalented, lonely young 22-year-old fell out with Hanisch over a Hellenic masterpiece on German soil, a painting of the Vienna Parliament building. Hitler thought it was worth 50 crowns, Hanisch sold it for 10 and Hitler had his friend arrested, instituted legal proceeding and at the trial on 11 August 1910, Hanisch was sentenced to seven days in jail.

Hitler the Painter (2)

Hanisch left the men's hostel in Vienna and Hitler soon made friends with Josef Greiner. They shared interests in painting, music and the occult. Hitler's painting technique now improved without any formal art training. He had a natural ability and was fluent in pencil and charcoal studies, excellent as a landscape water colourist, and indeed in oils. It was his network of Jewish art dealers who bought most of his work. When he moved from Vienna to Munich, he stayed with the Popp family and continued to paint, but sales were less successful – no Jewish art dealers! He continued to draw and paint throughout the Great War until his paints and artwork were stolen.[24]

Hitler's First Love

Apart from his mother who spoiled him and whom he adored, Hitler's first love, aged 17, was Stephanie Isak, a tall blonde girl who lived in the same suburb of Linz as he did. The young Galahad wrote a string of romantic poems to her, but unfortunately she was heavily chaperoned by her mother. Stephanie was Jewish and she married a soldier, Lieutenant Jansten. Hitler told his great friend, August (Gustl) Kubizek, that he wanted to kidnap the girl and then because she continued to ignore him, he planned a joint suicide pact by jumping in the River Danube![44]

Wieland the Smith

August Kubizek, Hitler's childhood friend and a music student, influenced him greatly. They devised ambitious architectural designs and visited the opera together. Wagner's early opera *Rienzi* about a humble medieval Roman citizen who became a city leader inspired Hitler to write dramas based on old German sagas and an opera called *Wieland the smith*, a Wagnerian pastiche. Kubizek later recounted all their adventures together in his book *The Young Hitler I Knew*.[44]

Hitler the Painter (3)

As Albert Speer's great architectural talents impressed the Führer so honours and presents were given. 'With a few shy words [he] gave me one of the watercolours he had done in his youth. A Gothic Church done in 1909, it is executed in an extremely precise, patient and pedantic style. No personal impulses can be felt in it, not a stroke has any verve. But it is not only the brush strokes that lack all character. By its choice of subject, the flat colours, the conventional perspective, the picture seems a candid witness to this early period of Hitler. All his watercolours from the same time have this quality and even the watercolours done while he was an orderly in the First World War lack distinctiveness. He still thought well enough of the modest watercolours of his youth to give them away occasionally as a special distinction.'

He went on making drawings and architectural sketches until the mid-1930s using red and blue pencil.

Speer had very high standards and was the only cultured man amongst Hitler's coterie, so his assessment of his Führer's daubs is predictably rather damning.[58]

Hitler the Painter (4)

In 1983 Doctor August Priesack, a Munich art authority, and the US collector Billy F. Price jointly published a catalogue of Hitler paintings. Many of the so-called 'Hitler' paintings are forgeries by a German artist named Konrad Kujau.

An auction of twenty-one paintings and two sketches by Adolf Hitler realized £118,000 in September 2006. The collection was discovered in 1986 in a Belgian farmhouse, and was painted by Hitler sixty years before. *The Church of Preux-au-Bois* sold for £10,500, *Church at Louvignies* for £6,000, *A Row of Cottages* for £5,500 and a double-sided watercolour canvas depicting an airfield on one side and landscape on the reverse went for £3,500.

The Marquess of Bath has a collection of thirty of Hitler's paintings at Longleat and there is another collection (A. P. Price HU63413) at the Imperial War Museum, London. One of these is entitled *Church and Village of Ardoye in Flanders, summer of 1917*.

Down and Almost Out in Vienna

The Männerheim (men's home) on Meldmanstrasse in a northern suburb of Vienna was Hitler's abode from February 1910 to May 1913. His monthly rental in the respectable hostel for men was 12 kronen. His output of paintings was sold to Samuel Morgenstern, a frame maker, Jacob Alternberg and other worthy Jewish dealers. An eye-witness at the hostel described Hitler as 'wearing a knee-length "bicycle coat" of indeterminate colour, an old, grey, soft hat with the ribbon missing, hair down to his shoulders and an unruly beard. He owned no shirt, his coat was worn through at the elbows, the soles of his shoes were patched with paper.' On his twenty-fourth birthday, 20 April 1913, Hitler became eligible to receive his outstanding share of his father's inheritance. With this sum of 820 kronen he left Vienna for Munich, where he registered as a 'stateless person', describing himself as a writer.[27]

Chez Mr Popp, the Tailor

Hitler arrived in Munich on 26 May 1913, aged 24, with his father's legacy to fund him. He lived in a room rented from Mr Josef Popp, a tailor on the Schleissheimerstrasse, in the Swabing artists' quarter. His rent was only 20 marks a month and kind Mr Popp, a rather smart couturier, subsidized Hitler's clothing. So the 'down and out' described his Munich period as 'the happiest and most contented of my life'. He continued to paint and sold two paintings

Hitler in the crowd cheering the outbreak of war, August 1914. This photograph was used for propaganda purposes by the Party and its genuineness is questionable.

to Herr Heilmann, a friendly local baker, for 10-20 marks each; he sold a small oil painting and had commissions for two watercolours from Doctor Schirmer; and a Herr Würsler bought an oil painting for 25 marks. The fifteen months of comfortable, mildly profitable time spent in Munich came to an end on the outbreak of the Great War. On 16 August 1914 Hitler joined the 1st Bavarian Infantry Regiment.[32]

The Great War: 'No Leadership Qualities'

On 5 February 1914 Hitler appeared before an Army Draft Board in Salzburg and the result of his physical examination was: 'Unfit for military and auxiliary service; too weak. Incapable of bearing arms.' He returned to Munich where he was seen among the cheering crowds in the Odeonsplatz when war was declared on 1 August. 'Thus my heart, like that of a million others overflowed with proud joy.' He wrote a petition to the King of Bavaria, volunteering to serve in a Bavarian regiment, despite being an Austrian citizen. He joined the 16th Bavarian Reserve Infantry regiment commanded by Colonel List and wrote that it was 'the greatest and most unforgettable time of my earthly existence'. Private first class Hitler was employed as a runner or messenger (a Meldeganger) between regimental HQ and the front line troops. In December 1914 he received the Iron Cross Second Class, in May 1918 he was awarded a regimental certificate for bravery, and on 4 August 1918 the Iron Cross First Class, which was rarely given to very junior 'other ranks'. These decorations were recommended by the Jewish regimental adjutant, Hugo Gutmann, who later reported 'we could discover no leadership qualities in him'. In October

Hitler in his formal
battalion uniform,
c. 1915.

1916 he was lightly wounded at Le Barque and sent to Beelitz hospital near
Berlin, where he convalesced for six months. He fought with the List regiment
in Flanders, in the battles of Arras, Chemin des Dames, Montdidier-Nyons,
Soissons and Reims. In March 1917 he was promoted to Lance Corporal. In
October 1918 south of Ypres he was under fire from British gas shells and
temporarily blinded and was sent back to Pasewalk hospital in Pomerania,
near Stettin. His two closest comrades were Ernst Schmidt and Heinrich
Bachman. Rudolf Hess also served with the same regiment. Hitler was still a
'loner' but brave and conscientious.

The Great War: 'Cold-Blooded Courage'

In the archives of the town of Marbach, Germany, is an account by Alexander
Moritz Frey, a private soldier in the List Regiment. Frey first met Hitler in 1915
and wrote: 'A pale, tall man tumbled down into the cellar after the first shells
of the daily evening attacks had begun to fall, fear and rage glowing in his eyes.

At that time he looked tall because he was so thin. A full moustache which had to be trimmed later because of the new gas masks, covered the ugly slit of his mouth.' His commanding officer wrote: 'As a dispatch runner he has shown cold-blooded courage and exemplary boldness under conditions of great peril, when all the communication lines were cut, the untiring and fearless activity of Hitler made it possible for important messages to go through.'

Foxl – Hitler's First Dog

Corporal Adolf Hitler, on duty in the Great War at Fromelles, owned a dog called Foxl. 'It was crazy how fond I was of the beast. Nobody could touch me without Foxl's instantly becoming furious. Everybody in the trenches loved him. During marches he would run all around us, observing everthing, not missing a thing. I used to share everything with him. In the evening he used to live beside me.' In January 1915 Foxl had appeared chasing a rat in Hitler's trench. 'With exemplary patience (he didn't understand a word of German) I gradually got him used to me.' Foxl was English, possibly a fox terrier, who had wandered across No Mans Land. 'I taught him everything: how to jump over obstacles; how to climb up a ladder and down again. The essential thing is that a dog should always sleep beside its master.' Foxl went through the battles of the Somme and Arras, but eventually, between Colmar and Harpsheim, he was stolen from a train by a railway employee.[61]

Hitler with two comrades, Ernst Schmidt and Max Amann. With them is Hitler's English terrier, Fuchsl (Foxl).

Hitler with more comrades and Foxl, probably taken at about the same time.

Hitler the Poet (2)

In the trench warfare of 1915 Hitler wrote (translated):

> I often go on chilly nights
> To the oak of Woden in the quiet woods
> Weaving a union by the use of dark powers
> The Moon shapes runic letters with its magic spell
> And all who are full of pride in daylight's hours
> Are humbled by its magic formula!
> They draw their swords of shining steel – but instead of fighting
> They freeze into solid stalagmites
> So are the false parted from the true souls
> I reach into a nest of words
> And hand out gifts to the good and just
> And my formula brings them blessings and riches!

Great War Paintings

When Hitler enlisted in the army in autumn 1914, he registered his profession as 'artist' along with others, Wilhelm Kuh, Alexander Weiss and Max Martens. The British Army had the equivalent of the London Artists Rifles of the Great War.

A photograph taken in France, 1916. From left to right: Sperl, Georg Wimmer, Josef Inkofer, Lausamer, Max Mund, Hitler and in the foreground, Balthasar Brandmayer.

Hitler painted at the front for three years, in the area occupied by the Bavarian Reserve Infantry Regiment 16 'List'. His complete military service record was compiled in July 1937 for the Nazi Party Archives. It included details of his two injuries and his two citations for bravery: an Iron Cross Second Class in 1914 and an Iron Cross First Class (the highest military award for an NCO) in 1918.

His earliest surviving painting is 'Sunken Road near Wytschaete', depicting a vacant trench running through a war-ravaged forest, with butchered trees representing the four out of eight deaths in his message-running unit. Other paintings are of a ruined monastery at Messines, the first aid Dressing Station at Fromelles, and his farmhouse billet in Fournes, with his messenger bicycle against the outside wall.

Berlin – 'Capital of the World'

In September 1916 Hitler's regiment RIR 16, all 3,600 of them, marched to Haubourdin and entrained to Iwuy. There they exchanged their spiked *pickelhauben* for steel helmets, marched to Cambrai, then to Frémicourt, and on 1 October went into the Somme battle. Between the towns of Bapaume and Le Barque, at Wytschaete, the regiment's log notes 250 dead, 855 wounded and 90 taken prisoner. Hitler was wounded in the leg by shrapnel and was taken to a field hospital at Hermies, then by train to a Red Cross military hospital near Potsdam, 40 miles south-west of Berlin. For the first time he was able to visit the 'capital city of Prussia. I got to know the museums and collections ... whoever enters the Reich Chancellory should feel he is standing before the masters of the world.' He foresaw the day when 'Berlin would emerge as the capital of the world.'

Hitler (back row, second from right) at Beelitz Military Hospital, 26 October 1916. This is an original Hoffmann photograph and all the men are shown in their First World War field-hospital uniforms.

The Tatterdemalion Ballet Dancers

'When we went into the line in 1916 south of Bapaume the heat was intolerable. As we marched through the streets there was not a house, not a tree to be seen: everything had been destroyed and even the grass was burnt. It was a veritable wilderness ... The soldier has a boundless affection for the ground on which he has shed his blood. Marching along the roads was a misery for us poor old infantrymen; again and again we were driven off the road by the bloody gunners and again and again we had to dive into the swamps to save our skins.' Towards the end of the war Hitler and his comrades had to cut up their greatcoats to make puttees. 'We looked like a bunch of tatterdemalion ballet dancers!'

In the Great War Adolf Hitler was a brave frontline soldier. He was awarded the Iron Cross, Second Class, a Military Cross (Third Class with Swords), the Regimental Award for Outstanding Bravery, the Medal for the Wounded and the Service Medal, Third Class. Thereafter on appropriate occasions he would wear only the Iron Cross, First Class, awarded in August 1918, proving his heroism without doubt.[61]

Right: Hitler *c.* 1916.

Below: Hindenburg, the Kaiser and Ludendorff during the First World War.

Gas, Blindness and a Vision

On 13 October 1918 in the final British offensive of the Great War, Hitler was blinded in a gas attack. 'On a hill south of Wervick we came that evening into several hours of drumfire with gas shells which continued all night. By midnight a number of us passed out, a few of our comrades forever.' He was sent to a lazarette near Pasewalk in East Prussia, and gradually regained his eyesight. In November when he heard the news of the German capitulation he was struck with a second attack of blindness. He claimed he had received a quasi-mystical vision in which he was instructed to save Germany from the traitors and Jews who had stabbed the heroic armed forces in the back and brought about defeat.

The Little Soldier

Churchill wrote after the Führer's death: 'As Hitler lay sightless and helpless in hospital during the winter of 1918 his own personal failure seemed merged in the disaster of the whole German people. The shock of defeat, the collapse of law and order, the triumph of the French, caused this convalescent regimental orderly an agony which consumed his being ... the downfall of Germany seemed to him inexplicable by ordinary processes. Somewhere there had been a gigantic and monstrous betrayal. Lonely and spent, within himself the little soldier pondered and speculated upon the possible course of the catastrophe.'

Hitler the Communist

Shortly after leaving hospital the corporal returned to Munich on 21 November 1918. The barracks to which he returned were run by soldiers' councils. The Soviet Republic of Bavaria, a revolutionary blend of Social Democrats and the radical Independent Social Democrats were led by Kurt Eisner (1867-1919). A Munich theatre critic, this Jewish Marxist journalist and very left-wing Socialist appealed to Hitler as he flirted with Communism.

As a member of the 7th Company, 1st Reserve Battalion of the Bavarian 2nd Infantry Regiment, Hitler was made *vertrauensmann* or representative. His duties included co-operation with the propaganda department of the revolutionary SPD/USPD regime. On 13 April the Communist Räterepublik had been proclaimed and the Munich soldiers' councils held elections to ensure that the Munich garrison stood loyally behind the 'Red Republic'. As Deputy Battalion Representative Corporal Hitler was a supporter of a Communist 'republic'. Many of his friends – 'Sepp' Dietrich, Julius Schreck, Hermann Esser, Gottfried Feder and Balthaser Brandmayer – supported the establishment of a republic. On 3 May 1919 the 'Red Army' was savagely destroyed and Munich 'liberated' with a death roll of 606 by the 'White Army' of Prussian and Württemberg troops. Nevertheless, for a brief period Hitler was a Communist![20/39]

The Polar Star

Dietrich Eckart had a profound influence on the young Hitler, although he was twenty-one years older. He was a journalist, poet, playwright, a violent nationalist, a racist Jew-baiter, a Bavarian, bohemian bon viveur, fond of the Munich wine cellars, beer, food and, above all talk. He owned a provocative news sheet 'Auf Gut Deutsch', had translated *Peer Gynt*, loved Schopenhauer,

Dietrich Eckhart (1868-1923). Eckhart was involved in the Beer Hall Putsch and died of a heart attack shortly afterwards.

and introduced the young, naïve Hitler to the Obersalzburg coterie: Dr Emil Gansser, Hermann Esser, Anton Drexler and the Bechsteins. More importantly, Eckart lent Hitler books and corrected his social styles of speaking and writing. He bought Hitler his first trench coat and took him on his first aeroplane ride and to his first theatre production in Berlin. Eckhart published Hitler's first essays and shaped his emotional and intellectual world. Later he was the first person to call Hitler 'Führer' in public. Hitler wrote: 'We often spent agreeable evenings in the Deutsche Haus Café. Dietrich Eckhart – he shone in our eyes like the polar star. What others wrote was so flat. When he admonished someone it was with so much wit. At that time I was intellectually a child still on the bottle.' An alcoholic, Eckart was imprisoned with Hitler in Landsberg, but died in December 1923.

Hitler's First Conspiracy

In March 1920 various Freikorps, private armies of ex-soldiers, including the Ehrardt Brigade marched on Berlin to protest against the government's acceptance of the Versailles Treaty. A right-wing journalist, Wolfgang Kapp, was proclaimed Chancellor and the Freikorps warriors announced the end of the liberal Weimar government. Hitler wanted a higher profile for the German Workers Party and with his poetic friend Dietrich Eckart (1868-1923) visited

Ernst Julius Guenther Roehm (1887-1934).

Berlin to join in the Kapp putsch. On arrival they found a general workers' strike protesting against Kapp, who panicked and fled. In Berlin the two would-be conspirators met General Ludendorff and von Kahr, the Bavarian leader. Hitler made the first of his many speeches to the 'Gymnastic and Sports Division', which later became the more colourful SA under Captain Ernst Roehm. Of course there was pandemonium and brawling, Hitler was arrested for a breach of the peace and was imprisoned for five weeks. His first public address after being released was a violent attack on the Jews, on the Communists, on the Social Democrats and on the financial markets. The very dangerous rabble-rouser was on his way.[20]

The 'Machine-Gun King'

Hitler first met Ernst Roehm (1887-1934), a tough, brutal, much-decorated war hero, in 1920. Roehm had founded the secret Iron Fist Society for radical right-wing officers, which Hitler joined. Then Roehm persuaded Hitler to investigate and infiltrate the German Workers Party (DAP). Impressed by Hitler's raw intensity Roehm joined the DAP (as it was then) as member number 623. He helped fund Hitler and introduced him to influential officers and politicians in the early 1920s. Roehm's nickname was 'the machine-gun king' as he had 'acquired' quantities of weapons from various paramilitary groups. Short, overweight, scarred, with flushed cheeks, this swaggering, bellicose regular officer became Hitler's firm friend, although Roehm was a homosexual. They addressed each other as 'Du' – a familiar greeting. In December 1920 Roehm and Dietrich Eckart persuaded General von Epp (1866-1947) to raise 60,000 marks from the army's secret funds to buy control of the Thule Society's newspaper, *Volkischer Beobachter*, as a mouthpiece for the DAP. Hitler and Roehm remained close friends in the stormy years of struggle 1921-23 and in 1931 Roehm became head of the SA, which by 1934 boasted 4,500,000 members.

The German Workers Party

In 1919 Anton Drexler, a Bavarian idealist, set up a committee of independent workers, with an anti-foreigner and anti-semitic policy. Hitler joined the German Workers Party on 12 September as the seventh member of their committee. Drexler, Gottfried Feder (1883-1941) and Hitler drew up a twenty-five-point programme, which was adopted on 1 April 1920. Point 1 required the union of all Germans in a Greater Germany, Point 2 demanded the abrogation of the Versailles Treaty, Point 4 required that Jews should be denied political or social office and those who had entered the Reich after August 1914 should be expelled.

This was the first major step in Hitler's career; in 1921 he assumed leadership of the party and Drexler was completely bypassed. Under Hitler's control the party became the NSDAP, Nationalsozialistische Deutsche Arbeiterpartei (National Socialist German Workers Party), or more simply the Nazi party. It was the first important stage in Hitler's transformation from an unemployed ex-soldier into a nascent political firebrand. It was also the terrible moment in his life when the anti-semitism virus took hold of him and never left him. One of the Hitler myths is that during his hospital convalescence in 1919, he had visions of 'Jewish-Bolshevik' conspiracies – which was, of course, nonsense.

Sturm Abteilung (SA)

In 1920 Hitler created a paramilitary organization ostensibly to keep order – shock troops – recruited from ex-service and ex-Freikorps men. Ernst Roehm,

Hitler in his comfortable *lederhosen* with Helene and Edwin Bechstein *c*. 1921.

a tough, scar-faced soldier of fortune was their first commander. Initially they were used to provoke trouble and beat up other parties' meetings, particularly the Communists. Emil Maurice (Hitler's valet) and Johann Klintzsch were key members. On 5 October 1921 it became officially the Sturm Abteilung (SA or Storm Section of the National Socialist Movement). In 1921 and 1922 Hitler sent the SA into action in Munich and Coburg.

For Hitler the SA had primarily a political function, to be an instrument of political intimidation, but with brutal independent *condottieri* such as Roehm, Heines and von Heydebreck, it was difficult to control. Indeed Roehm led a breakaway party called The Frontbann.

Two key officers in the SA as it grew rapidly were Rudolf Hess, who had served with Hitler in 1914, and Hermann Goering, the swaggering, boisterous, brave ex-member of the Richthofen Fighter Squadron. 'I liked him. I made him head of my SA. He's the only one of its heads who ran the SA properly. I gave him a dishevelled rabble. In a very short time he had organized a division of eleven thousand men.'

Hitler's Piano Player

Ernst 'Putzi' Hanfstaengl (1887-1976) was one of the more engaging characters in Hitler's entourage. A Harvard-educated son of rich art dealers from Munich he had great talent for piano playing and sang all the fashionable society songs at evening soirées. Rather a clown, tall, eccentric, incoherent and highstrung, he was popular with foreign journalists. When Hitler was wounded in the abortive 1923 putsch he sought refuge with Putzi and his beautiful wife. A thousand-dollar loan helped fund Hitler's nascent political career. Putzi was an inveterate gossip and he told too many people how Goering and Goebbels disliked each other and that they both hated Julius Streicher. Putzi could always soothe Hitler's moods by playing Wagner, Beethoven, Liszt or Brahms, and by singing and telling jokes. He claimed in November 1922, shortly after meeting Hitler for the first time, that the chant of *Sieg Heil* and the accompanying arm movement that became a feature of Nazi rallies was a direct copy of the technique used by American football cheerleaders, which he had taught Hitler. Putzi's time at Harvard University, Boston led him to produce the suggestion that the Nazis should use American college-style music at political rallies to *excite* the crowds in contrast with the drab respectability of the other parties.[14]

The Piano Player's Wife (1)

Dietrich Eckhart, poet and occultist, was responsible for Hitler's entrée into Bavarian society. He was a very close friend who advised Hitler to remain a bachelor in order to attract women's support for the Nazi party. Helene Bechstein, who was married to the famous piano manufacturer, introduced Hitler to many society ladies and they taught the naïve and gauche young man how to behave in polite society.

So he met Ernst (Putzi) Hanfstaengl (qv), who became his 'piano player', and Helene, his strikingly beautiful American wife – a tall, most attractive brunette. In Putzi's book *Hitler, the Missing Years*, Helene admitted that Hitler was attracted to her but she did not reciprocate and thought that he had no interest in sex at all. Nevertheless Hitler plucked up courage and asked Helene, a happily married woman, to share her life with him. Taken by surprise, she declined and told him he ought to get married. Dolefully he explained that marriage was not an option for him. He was dedicated to his country. In spite of her rejection he remained good friends with the piano player and his wife.[28]

The Piano Player's Wife (2)

Helene Hanfstaengel recalled how in 1922 she first met Hitler: 'He was at the time a slim, shy young man with a faraway look in his very blue eyes. He was dressed almost shabbily – a cheap white shirt, black tie, a worn dark blue suit, with which he wore an incongruous dark brown leather vest, a beige-coloured trench coat, much the worse for wear, cheap black shoes and a soft, old greyish hat. His appearance was quite pathetic.' Hitler was besotted with her. He once went down on his knees to her to proclaim his love, and for many years he sent her flowers on her birthday. He was kind to young Egon, her son, and after he became Chancellor in 1933 invited them both to stay at Haus Wachenfeld, before it became the Berghof. Egon, then twelve, admired Hitler's collection of 64 Wild West novels by Karl May. Hitler talked to Egon about motorcars, engines, the size and performance of various ships, and technical things of interest to a young boy. Eventually Helene divorced Putzi in 1936 and Hitler was noticeably pleased. She escaped from Germany in 1938 and returned to her native America.

The Complete Hanswurst

The purchase and development of the Nazi newspaper *Volkischer Beobachter* was vital for Hitler's nascent party. Putzi Hanfstaengl received a dollar windfall from New York and lent, or rather thought he lent, a thousand dollars (a fortune in Weimar marks) in March 1922 for the purchase of two American rotary presses, which could turn the newspaper into a daily. The loan was for two months, interest free. Putzi never got his money back even though the paper doubled in size in a large-format edition. Moreover Putzi hired a cartoonist to design the masthead and devised the paper's slogan, *Arbeit und Brot* (work and bread). His arch-enemy Alfred Rosenberg was appointed the editor. Hitler appreciated his piano-player friend who now attended the Monday evening Stammtisch at the Café Neumaier on the corner of Petersplatz. Hitler took his supposedly rich 'American' friend on fundraising visits to the wealthy Munich and Berlin bourgeoisie, but the early Nazi supporters were jealous of Putzi's influence on their leader. Count von Treuberg urged Hitler to break completely with Putzi, saying 'Hanfstaengl is a complete *hanswurst* (clown)'. But Putzi certainly sang and played music for his supper. That made Hitler happy.[14]

Amann and the Profitable Eher Verlag

Hitler made friends with his comrades in the four years of frontline soldiering with the 1st Bavarian Infantry Regiment. Not with the Jewish Leutnant Hugo Gutmann, who recommended Hitler for the Iron Cross First class, but with Leutnant Fritz Wiedemann, who became his adjutant in 1935-39, and most certainly with tough Max Amann, his sergeant, who became his literary agent, his publisher, his financial adviser and almost, but not quite, a friend. On 17 December 1920 control of Eher Verlag, the publisher of the *Volkischer Beobachter*, a rather rundown newspaper that was printed twice a week with a circulation of 7,000, passed to Anton Drexler, the nominal president of the Deutsche Arbeitpartie (DAP). In the next few years Hitler and Amann with help from the printer Adolf Muller, a Nazi supporter, turned the paper around to become a daily in the 'American' format of 21 inches by 18 inches with 16 pages, and it had a circulation of 20,000-30,000 in 1923. Hitler gave every appearance of being its new owner and it became *the* Nazi newspaper. Under Amann's shrewd management the paper cleared all its debts and became highly profitable. By 1933 it was still a Munich paper with a circulation of 127,000. That year saw editions printed simultaneously in Berlin and Vienna. By 1941 it had reached 1,200,000 with huge advertising revenues. Amann and Hitler earned immense sums and the former channelled Hitler's share into Switzerland and the Netherlands. Also Amann published *Mein Kampf* for his Führer.[63]

Hitler's Boon Companions

At the Osteria Italiana in Munich (which is still there), described by Henriette von Schiriah as 'a cool, small winery with a little courtyard painted in Pompeian red' and '... a temple (an alcove with two columns in front of it) which was kept reserved for Hitler. But his regular table was the least comfortable at the back, in a corner.'

From the early 1920s Hitler's boon companions were Heinrich Hoffmann, photographer and Eva Braun's boss; Ernst Hanfstaengl; Adolf Wagner, later the powerful Gauleiter of Upper Bavaria; Julius Schaub, adjutant; Christian Weber, described as a pot-bellied former horse trader; and Hermann Esser, founder member of NSDAP, who was dubbed by Goebbels 'the little Hitler'. Later came the ubiquitous Martin Bormann; Otto Dietrich, press chief of NSDAP; Joseph 'Sepp' Dietrich; Max Amann; and Wilhelm Bruckner, Hitler's chief adjutant since 1930.

A typical meal would be spaghetti with a little muscat wine, tomato sauce on the side, then nuts and apples – strictly vegetarian.

Hitler's Photographer and Court Jester

Heinrich Hoffmann (1885-1957) was the son of a successful photographer and learned his craft in his father's business. In the Great War he served as a photographer in the Bavarian Army and published his first book of photographs in 1919, from which he made a lot of money. Two years later he became Hitler's personal photographer and Hoffman and his family in Munich introduced Hitler to society and encouraged him in his art collecting. Eva Braun worked in his studio, where she first met Hitler. Hoffman introduced Hitler to Doctor Theodor Morell (1890-1948), who for nine years treated him with various cranky 'cures'.

A slightly later photograph *c.* 1930 showing Anton Drexler and Rudolf Hess to Hitler's left.

Hitler in February 1942 spoke to his merry dinner companions, 'I know three people who when they're together never stop laughing. Hoffmann, Amann and Goebbels ... I'm very fond of Hoffman. He's a man who always makes fun of me. He's a "dead-pan" humorist and he never fails to find a victim.' Kurt Ludecke, writing in 1938, noted, 'Hoffman was an ideal companion, humorous and amusing, a good story-teller with plenty of what the Germans call "mother-wit". At Haus Wachenfeld, Kannenberg with his accordian and Hoffmann are said to be a team that can make Hitler laugh himself sick. I found plenty of horse-sense behind his jester's mask and we had a rollicking time.' Hoffmann was elected to the Reichstag in 1933, was made a professor and earned a fortune from the sales of a series of excellent photographs. He published a book of photographs taken by Eva Braun and her sister.[63]

'Hitler is Germany: Germany is Hitler'

Rudolf Hess (1894-1987) served in Hitler's Bavarian regiment in the Great War, a brave, disciplined and intensely patriotic young officer. Wounded in 1917 he transferred to the Luftwaffe and after the war joined the Thule Society. Founded during the war for the study of old Germanic literature it was devoted to extreme mysticism, the occult and nationalism. The swastika was one of the society's mystic symbols. Nazi members included Eckhart, Drexler, Frank, Rosenberg and Hess. In 1919 Hess joined Epp's Freikorps and proved to be a reckless, brutal street fighter. In May 1920 he heard Hitler speak at a DAP meeting in Munich and returned home to tell his future wife, Ilse Pröm, 'A man – I've heard a man: he's unknown, I've forgotten his name. But if anyone can free us from Versailles, then it's this man. This unknown man will restore our honour!' Hess formed a 100-strong SA troop amongst Munich fellow students in 1921. The months he spent with Hitler cemented their relationship. He became Hitler's most intimate and trusted confidant and earned the nicknames 'Fraulein Hess' or 'Frau Hitler'. He was fiercely heterosexual and guarded Hitler's interests with a ferocious jealousy. The perfect backroom boy, he controlled the NSDAP organization and revelled in the Nazi uniforms, parades and bands. He too could deliver powerful rabble-rousing speeches. By 1932 he was a SS ObergruppenFührer and Chairman of the Central Political Commission of the Nazi party and Hitler named him to follow Goering in the leadership succession. A tall, dark-browed, intensely proud man, he burned with a religious fervour for his leader and believed that 'Hitler is Germany: Germany is Hitler'.

Café Heck and Café Neumaier

Heinrich Hoffmann, Hitler's photographer, wrote about two Munich cafés, not restaurants, where Hitler held court drinking steins of beer, cups of coffee or eating snacks his gang had brought with them! Café Heck in Galerienstrasse was perhaps his favourite. He had a reserved table amongst the middle-class bourgeoisie of Munich, to which came members of the NSDAP (National Socialist German Workers Party), young Rudolf Hess (qv), the Baltic German, Alfred Rosenberg, Max von Scheubner-Richter and, of course, Putzi Hangstaengl. On Monday evenings a rather sordid group met at the old-fashioned Café Neumaier on the Viktualienmarkt. These were the surviving 'du' friends: Esser, Weber, Eckhart, Gottfried Feder and Hitler's bodyguard, Ulrich Graf. But ex-sergeant Amann (qv) who became boss of the Nazi press empire, Hess and Rosenberg were the most influential. Of course they discussed politics or listened to their leader chuntering away about art, architecture or his Great War experiences. At the end of the evening a Praetorian guard of Weber, Graf, Amann and a lieutenant Klintzch escorted Hitler to his appartment in Thierschstrasse.[39]

Heinrich Himmler with his older brother Gerhard in 1918.

Hitler's 'Tough 'Uns'

Heinrich Himmler, a brilliant organizer and a devoted follower of Hitler, who had briefly been a chicken farmer, was appointed Deputy Reichsführer of the Schutzstaffel (SS) in September 1927. Born in Landshut, Bavaria in 1900, Himmler became perhaps the most evil man in Europe. Hitler told his supper companions on 3 January 1942, 'There are always circumstances in which elite troops are called for. In 1922/23 I created the "Adolf Hitler Shock Troops". They were made up of men who were ready for revolution and knew that one day or another, things would come to hard knocks. When I came out of Landsberg [prison, to which he was sentenced after the Munich putsch had failed] everything was broken up and scattered in sometimes rival hands. I needed a bodyguard, even a restricted one. Men enlisted without restriction, even to march against their own brothers. Only twenty men to a city (on condition that one could count on them absolutely) rather than a suspect mass. It was [Emil] Maurice, [Julius] Schreck and [Erhard] Heiden who formed in Munich the first group of "tough 'uns" and were thus the origin of the SS. But it was with Himmler that the SS became that extraordinary body of men, devoted to an idea, loyal unto death. I see in Himmler our Ignatius de Loyola. With intelligence and obstinacy, against wind and tide, he forged this instrument ... The SS knows that its job is to set an example, to be and not to seem, and that all eyes are upon it.'[61]

The leather shorts.

The 'Unpadded Skeleton' and Leather Shorts

Friedelind Wagner, the composer's grand-daughter, recalled the young Hitler 'in Bavarian leather breeches, short, thick woollen socks, a red-blue-checked shirt and a short blue jacket that bagged about his unpadded skeleton! His sharp cheekbones stuck out over hollow, pasty cheeks and above them was a pair of unnaturally bright-blue eyes. There was a half-starved look about him, but something else too, a sort of fanatical look.' He did own a decent blue suit and rather surprisingly a dinner jacket and tails in which to go to the opera. Before he became famous he was much attached to Bavarian-style leather short trousers. 'The healthiest clothing without any doubt is leather shorts, shoes and stockings. Having to change into long trousers was always a misery to me. Even with a temperature of ten below zero I used to go about in leather shorts. The feeling of freedom they give you is wonderful. Abandoning my shorts was one of the biggest sacrifices I had to make. I only did it for the sake of North Germany. Quite a number of the young people of today [August 1942] wear shorts all the year around. In the future I shall have an SS Highland Brigade in leather shorts!'

Nevertheless, after Hitler became Chancellor in 1933 he was rarely, if ever, photographed in leather shorts – not *comme il faut* for a Führer![61]

Hitler *c.* 1922 with fashionable knitted tie and button-studded shirt; probably through the influence of his admirers Carola Hoffman and Helene Bechstein.

The Moustache Dialogue

The little black moustaches of Adolf Hitler and Charlie Chaplin must have been the most famous in the world in the mid-twentieth century. In the Munich and Bavarian dialect that type of moustache was called a *Rotzbremse* or 'snot brake'! Putzi Hanfstaengl told Hitler shortly after meeting him that he should grow his moustache right across his mouth, 'Look at portraits by Holbein and Van Dyke; the old masters would never have dreamed of such an ugly fashion'. To which Hitler answered, 'Don't worry about my moustache, If it is not the fashion now, it will be later, because *I* wear it.' And so it turned out.[14]

'So – Oder – So' (Hitler's No.1 Adage)

Hitler used this little catchphrase to mean 'Whatever it takes to get this thing done', if necessary using generosity or kindness, but also perhaps brutality, deceit or bribery.

The Failed Munich Beer Cellar Putsch, Stage 1

Inspired by Mussolini's successful 'march on Rome' in 1922 – his takeover of the Italian state – the 34-year-old Hitler decided in the autumn of 1923 that with rocketing inflation the German economy was on the verge of collapse. A successful putsch seizing control of Bavaria with a powerful force mainly of SA under Hermann Goering and Ernest Roehm's Reichskriegsflagge (the paramilitary wing of the Nazi party) starting in Munich might destroy the government. On Thursday 8 November the fanatical Hitler in a long, black overcoat headed a motley rabble of armed SA men who burst into Munich's Burgerbraukeller. He leapt onto a chair, fired his pistol upwards and shouted, 'A national revolution in Munich has just broken out. The whole city is at this moment occupied by our troops. The hall is surrounded by 600 men.' This was blatantly untrue! Roehm's men had at the same time surrounded the War Ministry. Heinrich Himmler's first foray into Nazi activities was as flag-bearer to Roehm. He posed dramatically for the press photographers. Hitler took Gustav von Kahr, the Bavarian State Commissioner, prisoner and then promised him a top job in his 'new' Germany. He made a notable speech to the beer cellar political crowd, then waited for General Erich Ludendorff to arrive. The Great War hero then persuaded von Kahr and the Bavarian ministers to agree to join Hitler's putsch. So far so good!

Gustav von Kahr talking to Erich von Ludendorff.

Hitler, Alfred Rosenberg (left) and Friedrich Weber of the *Freikorps Oberland* during the Munich Beer Hall Putsch.

The Munich Beer Cellar Putsch, Stage 2

The key to most political putsches is to secure control of the communication system. Hitler, Goering and Roehm were of course, amateurs and failed to control the telephone exchange and lines. That was the first major mistake. The second mistake was to trust von Kahr and the local army commander, who broke their promise to join the plotters. Hitler was dumbfounded to find his key hostage had disappeared. The next day there was a pitched battle. Hitler, Ludendorff, Roehm and Goering led 2,000 followers into the Odeons-Platz in the centre of Munich where state police and army confronted them. It was a battle – a fracas perhaps – in which three police and fourteen Nazis were killed. Goering was wounded and Hitler tripped over. General Ludendorff hit the ground at the first volley, was promptly arrested and then claimed he was an innocent bystander! Hitler was given shelter for a few days by his friends the Hanfstaengls where the beautiful Helene Hanfstaengl discouraged him from committing suicide.

The London *Times* correspondent reporting the incident described Hitler as 'a little man ... unshaven with disorderly hair and so hoarse that he could hardly speak'.

In spite of its failure the pathetic Munich beer cellar putsch became part of Nazi mythology.[3/20]

At the Ludendorff trial, February 1924, from left to right: Counsel Holt, Weber (in uniform), Roder (in uniform), Ludendorff and Hitler.

The Stiff Left Shoulder

During the putsch of 9 November 1923 Hitler fell on the pavement, dislocating his left shoulder. Dr Walter Schultze, the leader of the SA medical corps could not persuade Hitler to have it x-rayed with remedial action afterwards. He feared that he would be bumped off in the hospital. The shoulder was therefore never properly fixed, and remained stiff for ever afterwards. For Hitler clothing was purely functional. He hated to try on new clothes. Since he made lively hand and arm movements to emphasise points he was making in his speeches and also needed to salute frequently, he had an aversion to close fitting jackets or coats and his tailor had to shape all his uniforms and suits accordingly.

Hitler's Trial for Treason

For twenty-four days from 26 February 1924 Hitler and nine others were accused of high treason in a courtroom in the Infantry School in the Blutenburgstrasse, Munich. Two of Hitler's loyal supporters, Generals Ludendorff and Von Lossow, had taken part in the Munich 'putsch' of 8-9 November 1923. At his trial Von Lossow testified against Hitler, whose leadership had transformed the Bavarian political scene. The trial was front page news in every German newspaper, as Hitler took full responsibility for leading the SA [Sturm Abteilung] stormtroopers and Kampfbund in the ill-fated putsch. He dominated the court. 'It is not you gentlemen who pass judgement on us. That judgement is spoken by the eternal court of history ... That court will not ask us "Did you commit high treason, or did you not?" That court will judge us ... as Germans who wanted only the good of their own people and Fatherland; who wanted to fight and die ... You may pronounce us guilty a thousand times over ...' Ludendorff was acquitted and Hitler was given the minimum sentence of five years' imprisonment.

Hitler at home in the Landsberg Prison.

Landsberg Prison is on a hill outside the town of Landsberg am Lech in the southwest of Bavaria, about 40 miles west of Munich and 22 miles south of Augsburg.

School of Higher Education

As soon as Hitler arrived in the Landsberg prison nursing his dislocated shoulder and broken upper arm, he was so dispirited that he went on hunger strike. Anton Drexler and the pretty wives, Helene Hanfstaengl and Helene Bechstein, together persuaded him to lead a normal life. Hitler's party had been declared illegal and his storm troopers and some of the other leaders went underground. He now read voraciously – Nietzsche, Marx, Treitschke, Bismarck and various political, racist and occult works. He received favoured treatment, held court, was showered with gifts and dictated *Mein Kampf*, initially to his chauffeur, Emil Maurice and then to Rudolf Hess who joined him as a volunteer prisoner! A certain Xaver Schwarz, a treasurer of the Munich city council, volunteered his services and started to work wonders on the depleted NSDAP finances. He had as many visitors as he liked and Landsberg became his 'school of higher education'. The other 40 prisoners and all the guards fell under his spell and his thirty-fifth birthday on 20 April found his cell swamped with flowers and gifts. The dining room where he presided was decorated with a huge Nazi swastika banner. His war record counted in his favour and the Bavarian Supreme Court released him on 19 December 1924.[20/63]

Hitler with Emil Maurice, Hermann Kriebel and Rudolf Hess in the Landsberg Prison.

Lebensraum and Geopolitics

In Landsberg prison Hess introduced Hitler to Karl Haushofer (1869-1946), the Professor of Geopolitics at Munich University. Haushofer greatly assisted with and perhaps influenced Hitler's writings in *Mein Kampf*, particularly about occult training, political affairs and *lebensraum* ('living space'). Haushofer, a retired general, believed that a nation's ability to grow and prosper depended largely on living space. He also was the exponent on the idea and theory of geopolitics, which saw the oceanic power of the British Empire being superseded by Germany's continental power. Nevertheless he believed in the *complementary* nature of German and British power. So the title of Hitler's tome *Four and a Half years of Struggle against Lies, Stupidity and Cowardice* was shortened by Max Amann to 'My Struggle' *Mein Kampf*. Hitler came out of Landsberg with two key ideas which dominated most of the rest of his life: that *lebensraum* was essential for Nazi Germany; and that Germany and England should live and work together, one on land, the other with its oceans.[53]

Hermann Kriebel with Hitler and Emil Maurice. Kriebel was convicted with Hitler in 1924 following the Beer Hall Putsch and served his sentence in the Landsberg Prison.

Mein Kampf – *'Lies, Stupidity and Cowardice'*

In Landsberg prison, 40 miles west of Munich, Hitler held court from room No.7 on the first floor which he shared with Rudolf Hess, Friedrich Weber and Colonel Hermann Kriebel. Forty other captured National Socialists were in prison with Hitler. They had a comfortable easy life with good food, a garden and as many newspapers and books as they wished. From July 1924 Hitler started to dictate *Mein Kampf,* taken down by Hess and Emil Maurice. After leaving prison Hitler went to finish his book in Berchtesgaden: 'I lived there like a fighting cock. I was very fond of visiting the Dreimäderl Haus where there were always pretty girls.'

Max Amann was the tough, rude Bavarian sergeant-major regimental clerk in the List regiment, well known to Hitler, who became business manager of the Nazi party's paper and of the Party's publishing house, which eventually published *Mein Kampf.* Additional input and editing to Hitler's book was made by Muller, the printer, Putzi Hafstaengel, Joseph Stolzing-Czerny, music critic of the *Volkisher Beobachter*, and Bernard Stempfle, once editor of the Bavarian *Miesbacher Anzeiger.* All the elements of National Socialist ideology are contained in the book: nationalism, anti-bolshevism, anti-semitism, the purity of the Aryan race, 'lebensraum'– the need for more space, to be obtained by a continental war of conquest. There was a clear warning to the world from the 35-year-old prisoner who had considerable influence but as yet no power. The first volume was published in summer 1925; it was 400 pages long and cost 12 Reichsmarks. The second volume appeared in 1926. By 1940 six million copies had been sold. The edition published in the USA was called *My Battle*, in Italy it was entitled *La Mia Battaglia* and in Spain *Mi Lucha*. Royalties from *Mein Kampf* kept Hitler solvent from 1925 to 1929, these averaged 15,000 Reichsmarks annually.

The release from
Landsburg Prison,
20 December 1924.

The Reluctant War-Leader

After his release from Landsberg prison Hitler spent what little money he had on books, particularly Prussian and Austrian military history to be found in the antiquarian bookstores near the Café Heck. This led to the purchase of almanacs of military equipment and particularly weaponry from English, French and Russian sources. These included Hiegle's 1935 *Handbook of Tanks*, Weyer's *Handbook of War Fleets*, von Zeppelin's *The Conquest of the Air*. The great architects of war such as Julius Caesar, Frederick the Great (twelve different histories), von Clausewitz, von Bulow, von Stein Schlieffen and many others. Eventually Hitler owned over 7,000 volumes about military matters.

Corporal Hitler had been a brave company runner and messenger but he had never fired a gun in anger. There was no soldiering tradition in his family. All very curious.

In October 1941 Hitler told his dinner companion, ReichsFührer SS Himmler: 'A war-leader is what I am against my own will. If I apply my mind to military problems that's because for the moment I know that nobody would succeed better at this than I can.'

Churchill on Mein Kampf: 'The New Koran of Faith and War'

'The thirteen months in the Landsberg fortress enabled him to complete in outline *Mein Kampf*, a treatise on his political philosophy inscribed to the dead of the recent putsch. When eventually he came to power there was no book which deserved more careful study from the rulers, political and military of the Allied Powers. All was there – the programme of German resurrection; the

Hitler on a ferry at the Baltic coast.

technique of party propaganda; the plan for combating Marxism; the concept of a National Socialist state; the rightful position of Germany at the summit of the world.

'Here was the new Koran of faith and war – turgid, verbose, shapeless, but pregnant with its message.'

Hitler's 'Granite Pillars'

Winston Churchill described the main thesis of *Mein Kampf*. 'Man is a fighting animal. The German nation being a community of fighters is a fighting unit ... A country or race which ceases to fight is doomed. The fighting capacity of a race depends on its purity ... Pacifism is the greatest sin for it means the surrender of the fight for its existence. The masses must be mobilised ... Will and determination are the prime qualities.

Only brute force can ensure the survival of the race ... The new Reich must gather all the scattered German elements in Europe.

Above all things the German army must be taught to believe in its own invincibility.'

Hitler's Russian Philosopher

Alfred Rosenberg (1893-1946) was born in Russian Estonia and fought in the Russian Army in the Great War. He went to Munich as a refugee after the Russian revolution in 1918. Because of his anti-semitic and anti-communist writing he joined the Thule Gesellschaft right-wing nationalistic club. He organized the 'Fighting League for German Culture', a union for lawyers, physicians and teachers; became editor of the *Volkischer Beobachter*; joined

An intriguing photograph, presumably in an aeroplane *c.* 1925. All appear in good spirits apart from Hitler. With him are Julius Schreck, Julius Schaub, Ernst 'Putzi' Hanfstaengl, Joseph 'Sepp' Dietrich and Wilhelm Brueckner.

the Nazi party; and marched with Hitler and Ludendorff in the 1923 beer hall putsch, but ran like a rabbit when the shooting started! Hitler obviously thought much of him and made him Party leader whilst he was in prison. In 1930 Rosenberg published *The Myth of the Twentieth Century*, which with *Mein Kampf*, was regarded as being essential Nazi thinking. Hitler's opinion was that Rosenberg with his Russian-speaking background was an expert on Bolshevism, but not a manager. William Shirer, the American journalist, thought that what Rosenberg 'lacked in repulsiveness he made up in befuddlement'. The official Nazi 'philosopher' was tedious, muddled, verbose and plain stupid. In 1933 Hitler put him in charge of the Party's foreign affairs department and then, typically, allowed von Ribbentrop to compete with his own Foreign Bureau! Many of his enemies in the Nazi party, particularly Goebbels and Strasser, accused Rosenberg of having Jewish blood. He bought paintings and sculptures on behalf of Hitler for the Munich Art Gallery and for Hitler's 'dream' museum planned for Linz. His task force helped to loot European art treasures from 1940 and the next year Hitler made him Minister for the captured Russian territories. He was quite useless of course, but he could speak Russian!

Hitler's Secret Bank Account

In 1921, 1922 and certainly in 1923 Hitler visited Switzerland. On 5 August 1943 he told his dinner companions, 'In 1923 I was in Switzerland and I remember a meal in Zurich at which the number of courses completely flabbergasted me.' He was there either with Max Amann or with Dr Emil Gansser, to raise funds for the support of his NSDAP party. Hitler returned from one trip to Zurich with a steamer trunk stuffed with Swiss francs and American dollars. Sales of *Mein Kampf* arranged by Max Amann outside Germany had been distinctly profitable.[66/61/51]

The Hitler Song Book

Putzi Hanfstaengl dropped into Hitler's modest flat, caught sight of a beat-up old piano in the hallway and casually played a Bach prelude. Hitler then asked him if he knew any Wagner. So out came 'Die Meistersinger von Nürnberg' to Hitler's amazement and excitement and he said, 'You must play for me often. There is nothing like that to get me into tune before I have to face the public'. After that Putzi, who was a good fluent pianist with a wide-ranging repertoire, would often play for two hours at a stretch. Putzi recalled, 'I must have played from Tristan and Isolde hundreds of times and he couldn't have enough of it. It did him good physically. The music brought Hitler the relaxation he sought.' In 1924 Putzi published a 'Hitler Song Book' which included titles like 'Hitler Lied' (Hitler Song), 'Deutsche Voran' (Germans First) and 'Die Hitler-Medizin' (Hitler Medicine). Putzi knew how to compose catchy tunes and songs which went down well at Nazi party rallies – he was Hitler's court musician.[14]

Hitler's Tubby Printer (1)

Dietrich Eckart (1868-1923), an early friend of Hitler's and a nationalist poet, introduced Hitler to Adolf Mueller who had been a supporter of the Nazi party since its inception. Opposite the photographic studios of Heinrich Hoffmann was the printing plant of M. Mueller u. Sohn at Schellingstrasse 39, Munich. Adolf Mueller, small, stout and almost stone deaf was to quote Eckart 'as black as the devil and more cunning than the cunningest peasant but he's the best printer I've known in my life and also the most generous man'. With help from the ubiquitous Max Amann, a shareholder of Mueller's, the tubby printer secured the contract for all the Nazi party material including books and the *Volkischer Beobachter*. In the early 1920s Mueller taught Hitler how to drive.

Hitler conducts a meeting of the
Nazi leadership at Schellingstrasse
50 in 1925. At the head of the table
from right to left: Heinrich Himmler,
Gregor Strasser, Adolf Hitler, Franz
X. Schwarz, Walter Buch and Baldur
Benedikt von Schirach.

Until the November 1923 putsch business had been good and the two Adolfs
were friends, indeed it was Mueller and Amann who came to greet and collect
Hitler from the Landsberg prison. In the critical time after Hitler's release from
prison it was Mueller who advanced cash and printed Hitler's newspaper and
book on credit. By 1928 Mueller was a very wealthy man with a luxurious
house at St Quirin on the shores of Te Gernsee south of Munich. Hitler and the
NSDAP leaders used Mueller's house for conferences and after his niece Geli's
suicide in September 1931 a distraught Hitler took refuge with Mueller.

'Dogs of Fascists': Hitler's Salute

'The military salute is not a fortunate gesture. I imposed the German salute
for the following reason. I'd given orders at the beginning that in the Army
I should <u>not</u> be greeted with the German salute ... On parade when mounted
officers give the military salute what a wretched figure they cut! The raised
arm of the German salute that has quite a different style! I made it the salute
of the party long after the Duce [Mussolini] had adopted it. In the days of
Frederick the Great [Hitler's hero] people still saluted with their hats, with
pompous gestures. In the Middle Ages the serfs humbly doffed their bonnets,
while the noblemen gave the German salute. It was in the Ratskeller at Bremen
about the year 1921 that I first saw this style – a survival of an ancient custom
signifying "See, I have no weapon in my hand!" I introduced the salute into the
Party at our first meeting in Weimar. The SS at once gave it a soldierly style. It's
from that moment that our opponents honoured us with the epithet "dogs of
Fascists".'

Hitler's photographer friend, Heinrich Hoffman, was of course on hand (4
July 1926) and Hitler's 'new' salute became international news.

The Nazis meet in the Munich *Buergerbraukeller*. From left to right: Franz X. Schwarz, Hermann Esser, [an unknown indistinct person in shadow], Hitler and Franz Ritter Von Epp, [an unknown para-military] and half off the photograph, Gregor Strasser. *c.* 1927.

Wenn Schon, Denn Schon (Hitler Adage No. 2)

This catchphrase was used. Often meaning 'If you do something, then do it without hesitation or consideration, fully, vigorously, ruthlessly – and Now.'

Bavarian Ladies

Emil Maurice, Hitler's chauffeur and for many years a good friend, visited life classes with Hitler to gaze at the naked women models posing for artists. They would visit nightclubs and even pick up girls on the streets. Hitler would bring a woman back to his room and always presented her with flowers. The sister of one of his drivers – Jenny Haug, who habitually carried a gun with her as an extra bodyguard – was in love with Hitler. Putzi Hanfstaengl wrote that Hitler had a collection of pornographic books, most of them written by Jewish authors, and Hitler was fascinated by the Berlin lady boxers!

There is evidence that Hitler had an affair with a 16-year-old girl who ran a boutique with her older sister. Before long she became his mistress, but it was the same story. She wanted marriage, perhaps to Hitler, or at least to someone she loved. Poor besotted Mitzi, jealous of Hitler's attentions elsewhere, tried to hang herself, but was saved from death by her brother in law. However, by this time Hitler was involved with his niece.[25/28]

Hitler's Tubby Printer (2)

Hitler said that Adolf Mueller's first words to him were, '"To prevent any misunderstanding from arising let it be clearly understood that, where there's no payment, there's no printing either." Mueller would only accept orders for pamphlets against cash payment. He refused dubious orders by saying that his

A Nazi rally in 1928 with a slightly slimmer Hermann Goering in the foreground.

workmen fed themselves not on political convictions, but on the pay he gave them. When one visited him, Mueller never ceased to groan. Nevertheless he grew fatter and fatter. He printed more and more. He constantly bought new machines but his leitmotiv was "I can't get along on these rates. I'm ruining myself" ... His press is equipped in the most modern style. He's a real genius in the party.'

Whenever Mueller upped his printing rates, Hitler would throw a tantrum but as Mueller was stone deaf, it had no effect at all. Despite his girth he was a determined Lothario with a divorced wife, several mistresses and many bastards. Hitler knew that Mueller was very generous and that on each new arrival he gave the mother 5,000 marks. His working week was two days supervising his printing works, two days with his divorced wife and two days with his mistress of the moment. As Hitler said of him, 'That Mueller, he's quite a fellow.'[61]

The Great Air Ace Joins Hitler – Cheaply

Hermann Goering (1893-1946) was born in Rosenheim, Bavaria to minor gentry. He fought in the Great War, initially in the infantry and then as a brilliant fighter pilot. He became a hero, gained twenty-two victories, earned the 'Pour le mérite' medal and commanded the famous Richthofen squadron. After the war he flew a Fokker monoplane at air displays and as a dashing, 26-year-old lieutenant, met his first wife, Carin, who was five years older than him. He attended the Munich university to study political science and history. At a mass demonstration in Königsplatz in November 1922 he first met Hitler – intense, pale with his small moustache, slouch hat and carrying a dog whip. Soon at the Monday evening court at the Café Neumaier, Goering and Carin were listening to Hitler at his regular table. One phrase struck Goering forcibly – it was useless, Hitler said, to have empty threats and protests about the Versailles Peace Treaty and the extradition of the German Army commanders. 'You've got to have bayonets to back up threats.' The next day Goering, after consultation with Carin, offered his services to Hitler, who was delighted. 'Splendid, a war ace with the "Pour le Mérite" – imagine it! Excellent propaganda! Moreover he has money and doesn't cost me a cent.' He said all this to his close supporter Kurt Luedecke. In return Hitler 'promised' Goering he would become leader of the Reich![53]

A formal portrait photograph by
Heinrich Hoffman

The Moustache Dialogue (2): The Big Nose

Ada Klein worked on the Nazi party paper *Volkischer Beobachter* with Alfred
Rosenberg, as editor in the early 1930s. She knew the youngish Hitler quite
well and he once told her: 'Many people say I should shave off my moustache
but that is impossible. Imagine my face without a moustache', and he then
held his hand below his nose like a plate. 'My nose is much too big. I need the
moustache to relieve the effect.'

Christa Schroeder, another favourite secretary, believed he should have
grown a beard to hide his mouth.

Hitler on Religion – An Abbot Perhaps?

In his original manuscript of *Mein Kampf* Hitler wrote of his early wish to
become an abbot as his 'highest and most desirable ideal'. His friends and
family witnessed his early obsession with Roman Catholicism. His beautiful
friend Helene Hanfstaengl remembered that he spoke extensively of his early
devotion to Roman Catholicism, and how he used to drape a tablecloth over
his shoulders, stand on a kitchen stool and deliver sermons to his assembled
siblings. His sister Paula recalled her brother telling her: 'I believe the good
Lord holds a protective hand over me'. In his huge library he had 400 books,
mainly about the Catholic Church. And in *Hitler's Table Talk 1941-44* there
are scores of long monologues on his views on religion.

It might have been a better world if he had become Abbot of Linz.[61]

Joseph Goebbels (1897-1945).

'Those Big Blue Eyes'

Joseph Goebbels noted in his diary of 6 November 1925 on his first meeting with Hitler, 'We drive to Hitler. He is having his meal. He jumps to his feet, there he is. Shakes my hand like an old friend. And those big blue eyes like stars. He is glad to see me. I am in heaven. That man has got everything to be a king. A born tribune. The coming dictator.' And on 23 November, 'Hitler is there. Great joy. He greets me like an old friend. And looks after me. How I love him! What a fellow. Then he speaks. How small I am! He gives me his photograph ... Heil Hitler! I want Hitler to be my friend.' In mid-February 1926 the diary records, 'Adolf Hitler, I love you.' Hitler had this extraordinary effect. He seduced his camp followers. All this seven years before Hitler became Chancellor and about 20 years before he and Goebbels both committed suicide side by side in the Berlin bunker.

Goebbels on Hitler – Disillusionment

Joseph Goebbels was among the first to join the new Nazi party when the ban was lifted on it in February 1925. When he was fired from his job on the

Volkische Freiheit he moved to Eberfeld. From October 1924 he made 189 political speeches in the next year. Initially he and Hitler were at loggerheads. At one meeting he leapt to his feet screaming 'I demand that the petty bourgeois Adolf Hitler be expelled from the Nazi Party', and in his diary he wrote, 'I feel battered. What sort of Hitler is this? A reactionary? Extremely awkward and uncertain. Russian question completely wrong. Italy and England our natural allies. Terrible! Our task is the annihilation of Bolshevism. Bolshevism is a Jewish creation! We must be Russia's heir! 180 millions!' At the next public meeting he confessed, 'I no longer have complete faith in Hitler. That's the terrible thing. My props have been taken away from under me.'[74]

Joseph Goebbels' Damascus

Goebbels was invited to join Hitler for a holiday in Berchtesgaden in July 1926 along with Hitler's secretary Rudolf Hess, his chauffeur Emil Maurice, his photographer Heinrich Hoffman and Gregor Strasser (1892-1934), a radical Nazi leader. Hitler was working on the second volume of *Mein Kampf*. In this intimate magic circle the 28-year-old Goebbels soon had what Strasser and his lieutenant, Karl Kaufmann, described as 'Joseph Goebbels' Damascus'. Goebbels became infatuated, 'He [Hitler] is a genius. The natural creative instrument of a fate determined by God. I stand shaken before him. This is how he is: like a child, dear, good, compassionate, like a cat, cunning, clever and agile, like a lion, magnificently roaring and huge. A fine fellow, a real man.' Goebbels went on, 'Hitler's talk has the ring of prophecy. Above us in the sky a white cloud forms a swastika ...' For the rest of his life – another twenty years – Goebbels adored Hitler. It was as simple as that.[74]

Hitler's Sweet Tooth

Angela Raubal, Hitler's widowed half-sister, suggested to him that Haus Wachenfeld in the Obersalzberg, which he rented in October 1928, needed a resident housekeeper and that she should be his cook/housekeeper. He remembered with pleasure the rich, sugary cakes she used to make and Hitler's photographer's daughter, Henriette Hoffmann recalled that 'she was a kindly, sympathetic woman, an expert in cooking Austrian specialities. She could make feather-light puff pastry, plum cakes with cinnamon, spongy poppyseed strudel and fragrant vanilla pancakes – all the irresistible things her brother loved eating.' Angela also had two nubile daughters, Angela (Geli) and Elfriede.[45]

'Onkel Alf'

There is no doubt that Hitler was deeply in love with his niece. Geli Raubal, younger daughter of his half-sister Angela. Geli (1908-1931) accompanied her mother to keep house for Hitler on the Obersaltzberg in 1925. The pretty blonde girl of seventeen had her own room in the rented villa, Haus Wachenfeld, and also a few years later in No.16 Prinzregentenstrasse, a smart nine-roomed flat in Munich. For six years their romance prospered; possibly it was not consummated. Geli called Hitler 'Onkel Alf'. She loved the theatre and opera and took singing and acting lessons. This period in Munich Hitler later described as the happiest in his life. He idolized the girl, who was flattered and impressed by her famous uncle. In early summer of 1928 Emil Maurice, his chauffeur, by chance surprised Hitler in Geli's room. Hitler always carried a riding whip with him and he tried to thrash Maurice, who escaped by jumping out of a window! Hitler was insanely jealous of Geli. He refused to let her have any life of her own and did not allow her to go to Vienna to have her voice trained. When he discovered that she had allowed Maurice to make love to her he was furious. On 17 September 1931 Hitler left Munich with Hoffmann, his photographer and close friend, for Hamburg. On the way in Nuremberg, Hess telephoned to say that Geli had shot herself dead with Hitler's 6.35 mm Walther pistol in Hitler's flat. For days Hitler was inconsolable and his friends feared for his life. He refused to eat meat thereafter! According to many witnesses Geli was the only woman he ever loved. Her room at the Berghof was kept exactly as she had left it with her carnival costume, books and white furniture. Her photograph hung in his room in Munich and in Berlin and flowers were always placed before it on the anniversary of her birth and death. A bust of Geli was set up in her room and every year he visited her grave. Needless to say there was a great amount of discreditable rumour and he lamented that 'terrible filth' was killing him.

Hitler the Vegetarian

In 1923, after Hitler had laid flowers at his niece, Geli's grave in Vienna, he attended a conference of Nazi party leaders. At an inn he was offered ham for breakfast, at which he recoiled in horror, refused to eat it and told his friend Hermann Goering that it was like eating a dead body. From that day onwards he became a vegetarian .

He often talked to his coterie about the benefits to his health of not eating meat. In July 1942 he noted, 'When I gave up eating meat, I immediately began to perspire much less ... My thirst too decreased considerably ... Vegetarian diet therefore has some obvious advantages.'[21]

Haute Cuisine – 'Say Cheese'

After Geli's death in 1931 Hitler, for various reasons, did not touch meat, chicken, fish or eggs. He was obsessed by what he ate or did not eat and was a dedicated vegetarian; he had a separate kitchen at the Berghof to provide his vegetarian meals. He lived mainly on pasta, mashed potatoes and green vegetables and ended each meal with stewed fruit and mineral water. One of his favourite dishes was mashed potato laced with linseed oil and topped with grilled cheese and he also liked corn-on the-cob and Kai serchmarren, a pudding with raisins soaked in sweet sauce. He drank no alcohol apart from occasionally a glass of watered, sweet white wine, apple or caraway tea, or freshly squeezed juice of fruit and vegetables from the Obersalzberg greenhouses. Two dieticians were employed by him to produce dishes for his irregular appetite and fads, but his favourite cook was Fraulein Constanze Manziarly from Innsbrück who cooked Viennese and Bavarian dishes with skill.

When Hitler was looking for a property to buy, his choice was between the Berghof and one in Steingaden, a region famous for its cheeses. Of the latter he commented, 'If I had taken the place I should have been compelled to become a producer of the famous Steingaden cheese in order to keep the place up. Suppose the price of cheese went up? Everybody would immediately say "The Führer is himself personally interested in the price of cheese!"'[45/61]

The Hitler Diet

Dr Karl Brandt was the Führer's favourite doctor. Others included Professors Werner Haase and von Hasselbach. Dr Theodor Morell was always on hand to give him shots of dextrose hormones or vitamins. Stomach cramps induced by nerves were the most frequent ailment. In May 1943 Brandt, on the advice of Marshal Antonescu, the national leader of Romania, recommended a Viennese dietician, Frau Marlene von Exner who was attractive, young and goodnatured. Hitler adored her, and they recalled their happy memories of life in Vienna. For Antonescu she produced caviar, oysters, mayonnaise and other delicacies, but Hitler's strict diet was a problem. A typical menu prepared for him by her was orange juice with linseed gruel, rice pudding with herb sauce and crispbread with nut and butter paste!

Hermann Goering with Hitler.

The Dishevelled Rabble

Hermann Goering and his wife Carin bought a villa with elegant furnishings in Obermenzing, a fashionable suburb of Munich, mainly with her money. Hitler became a frequent guest, arriving late at night and listening to Goering singing ballads, operatic arias and folk songs in a reasonable baritone. Hitler recalled, 'I liked him. I made him the head of my SA. He's the only one of its heads who ran the SA properly. I gave him a dishevelled rabble. In a very short time he had organized a division of eleven thousand men.' Hitler's group in 1923 reserved a large table, their *stammtisch,* in the Bratwurstglöckel Tavern in the heart of old Munich. At the Easter rally for the SA Hitler used Goering's beautiful 25-horsepower Mercedes-Benz 16 as a saluting base and at the same rally Goering was reportedly seen giving Hitler pocket money! However their relationship was never intimate – always *Sie,* never *du.*

At that time the SA was an ill-organized club of ex-Freikorps, street brawlers and roughs, using brass knuckledusters, rubber truncheons, chair legs, beer steins, occasionally pistols and home-made bombs as weapons. Germany was in a terrible state. There were about fifty organizations, almost parties, of World War veterans often fighting each other. At the beginning of 1923 the mark was valued at 7,000 to the US dollar. By the end of the year it had reached a million, then billions and finally trillions of marks to the dollar. The government refused to stop the printing presses and balance the national budget. It was an ideal time for Hitler and his first Reich Party rally took place with 6,000 stormtroopers in Munich in January 1923.[53]

Hitler and Party colleagues meet in the *Hofbräuhaus* on 24 February 1929 to mark the anniversary of the famous speech. From left to right: Gregor Strasser, Karl Fiehler (back to camera), Christian Weber, Hitler, Julius Schaub (back to camera), Franz Schwarz and Max Amann. Standing in the background, holding the *blutfahne*, is Jakob Grimminger.

Du

In Germany close friends are addressed as *du* (the equivalent of the French *tu*). Albert Speer was a dedicated Hitler-watcher. He and Rudolf Hess, a friend of Hitler's, agreed that there were only five people who could call Hitler *du*.

Dietrich Eckhart, a nationalist poet (1868-1923), an early friend of Hitler's, introduced him to Erich Ludendorff, who was later imprisoned with Hitler in Landsberg. Eckhart's 'Storm Song' ('Germany awake! Break your chains') was a favourite marching song. He was an alcoholic and when he died aged 55, Hitler recalled 'He shone in our eyes like the polar star'.

Hermann Esser, State Secretary for Tourism (1900-1981), a co-founder of the German Workers Party, a young ex-soldier, was an orator and a gutter journalist who wrote for the *Volkisher Beobachter*. He was also a Jew-baiter and a lecherous, crude, noisy thug. An early worshipper, he was the first to call Hitler 'Führer' in public, but in 1933 Esser was demoted to the formal *Sie*.

Christian Weber, a former horse-dealer, who brandished a dog whip and brawled with communists, was foolhardy enough to mock *Mein Kampf* to its author. Thereafter Hitler avoided him!

Julius Streicher and Ernst Roehm (*see below*) were the remaining 'close friends', but in fact Hitler treated Streicher impersonally and later demoted him to *Sie*, and Roehm was killed on Hitler's orders.

Salonfähig

Two wealthy Munich hostesses competed to teach the naïve, gauche, relatively young Adolf Hitler the art of *salonfähig*, to be fit for polite society. They replaced his cheap blue serge suit with tailored suits, well-cut dinner jackets, smarter hats and handmade leather shoes at their expense. Frau Elsa

Right: Hitler's car traverses a road covered with flowers following his successful 1929 Nuremberg rally.

Below: The same occasion from a different viewpoint.

Bruckmann and Frau Helene Bechstein taught him the various grades of hand-kissing (five, apparently, in the 1920s in Munich), how to bone a trout, eat an artichoke and deal with a lobster. Of course Hitler wanted their patronage and financial contributions to party funds and also to persuade them to join the NSDAP.[45]

Hitler's 'Business Dwarf'

Kurt Ludecke knew Max Amann well and described him in 1932 as 'the same little man, strong and active looking with a heavy head on a short neck, almost lost between his shoulders ... his prominent nose and small peculiarly brilliant blue eyes ...' Amann was born in Munich on 24 November 1891 and died

The SA salute Hitler, *c.* 1929.

there in extreme poverty twelve years after the Second World War. From 1915 to 1918 he was Hitler's company sergeant, and joined the SA in 1921. His business training meant that he became party treasurer and manager of the party newspaper the *Völkischer Beobachter*. From 1925 onwards he became essential to Hitler, arranged publication of *Mein Kampf* and skilfully banked or invested the considerable royalties, some in the Munich bank but also in Switzerland and the Netherlands. Amann had several illegitimate children and his wife tried unsuccessfully to drown herself. On the evening of 22 February 1942 Hitler told Himmler, 'Amann is one of the oldest of my companions. He was infinitely valuable to me for I had no notion of what double entry book-keeping was.' And 'I can say positively that he's a genius. He's the greatest newspaper proprietor in the world. Amann controls more than half of the German press. Rothermere and Beaverbrook are mere dwarfs compared to him.' Very intelligently Amann created on the side the Hoheneichen Publishing Co. whose name covered certain publications. He behaved as if the editorial staff and the editors were nothing but a necessary evil. But he earned his Führer a small fortune.

Hitler with Franz
Xaver Schwarz and
colleagues at the
Braunen Haus, 1930.

Alte Kämpfer – The 'Old Fighters'

During the *kampfzeit*, the 'years of struggle', Hitler had shared comradeship and occasionally danger with the 'old fighters', some of them street thugs. His familiars of the Nazi old guard were Goebbels, Ley, Hess, Martin Bormann, Julius Streicher, Christian Weber, Max Amann (the Party treasurer), Heinrich Hoffman (the court photographer and jester), his two adjutants Julius Schaub and Wilhelm Brueckner and his trusted chauffeur, Julius Schreck. It was in this intimate circle talking over the old days that Hitler was most at ease. From time to time Sepp Dietrich, the brutal commander of his SS guard, Otto Dietrich, Reich press chief, Gauleiter Adolf Wagner, Hermann Esser, State Secretary for Tourism, and later on Albert Speer would be invited to join the Hitler coterie. Sometimes too, Hans Bauer, Hitler's pilot was invited. They talked together in the café-restaurants Osteria Bavaria, Café Heck, Carlton's Tearooms, or in Hitler's Munich flat or away in the Obersalzberg or Berghof. It was rare to see Himmler or Goering, but occasionally Goebbels or Hess would be invited. Ladies were not asked, apart from the two rather outrageous Mitford girls. It was important for one's prestige to attend these meals and keep abreast of the daily opinions.

The Brown House and the Colour Brown

Since 1925 the NSDAP – National Socialist German Workers' Party HQ had been in Schellingstrasse in Munich, but on New Year's Day 1926 it moved to the Brown House in Briennerstrasse. Funded by donations, particularly from Emil Kirdorf, a rich coalmine owner, and Fritz Tyssen, a steel millionaire, the palatial private house was rebuilt by Hitler's favourite architect, Paul Ludwig

Troost. In the basement was a restaurant with Hitler's own corner beneath a painting by Dietrich. On the second floor were the offices of the Führer overlooking the Konigsplatz, with a painting of Frederick the Great, a bust of Mussolini and a battle scene from Flanders in the Great War. In the early days the police made determined raids. Hitler recalled: 'I was present when the police took the Brown House by storm. There were gloating faces of fat ecclesiastics from the windows of the Nuncio's Palace opposite ... What a struggle there was before we could obtain the right to to hoist our flag over the Brown House.'

Brown was an important colour for Hitler. The early stormtroopers (*sturmabteilung*) wore brown uniforms and were known as 'brownshirts'. Hitler wore brown satin pyjamas, had a brown silk dressing gown and slept under a brown quilt embroidered with a swastika.

And he married Eva Braun.

Hitler's Occult Adviser

In the late 1920s Hitler discovered an occult adviser, Erik Jan Hanussen, a Jewish 'clairvoyant', who earned a great deal of money in theatres. His real name was Herschel Steinschneider and he genuinely did have extraordinary predictive abilities. When he first met Hitler at a society reception in Berlin he suggested to the Nazi leader that his elocution and speech could be improved. Surprisingly Hitler – politely – asked Hanussen for his recommendations. He was told that although his timing and delivery were impressive, he should improve his body language and gestures and that this would have a greater impact on his audience. And it did! For the next few years the Jewish clairvoyant was Hitler's 'special' guru and moreover was asked to advise Hitler on his choice of colleagues based on his clairvoyant and astrological gifts. On 24 February 1933 Hanussen held a séance in Berlin for a number of important people. He predicted that a large Berlin building would be engulfed in flames, and the Reichstag was set on fire and more or less demolished three days later. In April 1933 by order of Count Wolf Helldorf, chief of police of Potsdam, Hanussen was kidnapped from just outside a theatre and murdered in a wood near Berlin.

Hitler and the Wagner Family

Richard Wagner had always been Hitler's favourite composer, and Winifred Wagner who was married to the composer's son, Siegfried, became one of

Three photographs taken by Heinrich Hoffmann during the period when Hitler was studying gesticulation and presentation.

the closest women to Hitler. Born Winifred Williams in South Wales, she was widowed in 1930 but continued to run the Wagner festival at Bayreuth almost single-handedly. Attending the festival each year was a high point in Hitler's life, and he nearly always stayed with Frau Wagner in Haus Wahnfried, a grandiose house built by Wagner. Hitler was introduced by the Bechsteins, the famous piano makers, to Siegfried and Winifred in the 1920s. He thought young Hitler was a fraud. She thought he was 'destined to be the saviour of Germany' and always in private called him 'Wolf', his secret name when they first met.[14]

The Second Book

Adolf Hitler's *Second Book* was written in 1928 and, for a variety of reasons, was not published in his lifetime. In 1961 the Institute for Contemporary History in Munich published it as *Hitler's zweites buch: ein dokument aus dem jahr 1928*. The English edition was published in 2003 by Enigma Books of New York, edited and annotated by Gerhard Weinberg. It has sixteen chapters and 240 pages and covers much of the same ground as *Mein Kampf*, first published in 1925. It covers potential foreign policy (it was written five years before he became Chancellor) and relationships with England and the British Empire, Italy, France (the inexorable enemy) and Russia (no alliance). Key individuals mentioned are Woodrow Wilson, Gustav Stresemann, co-founder of the German People's Party of 1918, Benito Mussolini, and Andreas Hofer, who founded a South Tyrol radical league. Hitler's heroes were mentioned many times – Otto von Bismarck, Frederick the Great, Napoleon I. His wilder flights of fancy include, 'The greatest danger to England will no longer be in Europe at all but in North America'; but also, 'important English population centres appear virtually defenceless against French air attacks ... and a French

Horst Wessel (left) at the head of a parade of SA stormtroopers, or 'brownshirts', in Nuremberg, Germany, 1929.

submarine war against England ...' Predictably there is his usual vilification of the Jews and Marxism.

Mein Kampf made Hitler a wealthy man. His *Second Book* did not earn him a single Reichsmark![61]

Horst Wessel Song – Hitler's Flags

Goebbels, nicknamed cruelly by the Berliners '*der krüppel*' (the cripple), was a brilliant publicist. In July 1927 he started his own newspaper *Der Angriff* (The Attack), first as a weekly, then a daily. It rapidly became a gutter press suitable for publicizing the Nazi party. Every SA thug involved in a street brawl made headlines and Hitler read it from cover to cover every day. Early in 1930 a young agitator named Horst Wessel was shot by a communist pimp and took six weeks to die. In Goebbels' paper Wessel was called 'a socialist Christ'. At the spectacular funeral the communists got into a pitched battle with the SA. Horst Wessel's own lyric sent to *Der Angriff* read (translated):

'The flags held high! The ranks stand firm together

The SA marches with steady, resolute tread

Soon Hitler's flags will fly over every street!'

It rapidly became the party anthem, sung to a melody adapted from a Salvation Army hymn and took second place only to 'Deutschland, Deutschland über Alles'.[54]

Above left: Horst Wessel's Party membership card.

Above right: Party members and sympathisers outside the Communist Party headquarters in Buelow Platz, Berlin, during a ceremony in remembrance of the Nazi Horst Wessel who was murdered by communists, with the SA *Schalmeienkapelle* band playing.

'Sepp' – 'Cunning, Energetic and Brutal'

Josef 'Sepp' Dietrich (1892-1966) was Hitler's favourite soldier. A sergeant-major in the Great War, he was a typical early Nazi street-brawler, bully-boy who joined the Freikorps. In 1928 he became a full-time commander of Hitler's SS bodyguard. Hitler, on 3 January 1942, described Sepp: 'The role of Dietrich is unique. I've always given him opportunity to intervene at sore spots. He's a man who's simultaneously cunning, energetic and brutal. Under his swashbuckling appearance, Dietrich is a serious, conscientious, scrupulous character. And what care he takes of his troops! He's a phenomenon in the class of people like Frundsberg, Ziethen and Seydlitz. He's a Bavarian Wrangel, someone irreplaceable. For the German people, Sepp Dietrich is a national institution! For me personally there's also the fact that he is one of my oldest companions in the struggle.'

Dietrich later became an SS Major-General in charge of the elite 'Leibstandarte Adolf Hitler' which did special execution work in the Roehm purge of 1934. He fought in France, Greece, Russia and commanded the 1st SS Panzer Corps in Normandy in 1944 and the 6th SS Panzer Army in the Ardennes Battle of the Bulge in mid-winter 1944-45. His much reduced army was sent to defend Vienna in Spring 1945 and when it was overwhelmed by the Russian juggernaut, Hitler dismissed him in a rage. He was fortunate to survive and despite prison sentences, to live to April 1966.

Hitler – Short of Cash

When the Berghof, his Obersalzberg house, was being built, Hitler's architect, Albert Speer, costed the estimates and Hitler told him, 'I've completely used up the income from my book, although Amann's given me a further advance of several hundred thousand. Even so there's not enough money so [Martin] Bormann has told me today. The publishers are after me to release my second book, the 1928 one for publication [out in 1961, sixteen years after death of the author] ... Perhaps later ... Now it's impossible'.[58]

Adolf Hitler with his companions. From left to right) Ulrich Graf, Rudolf Hess, Schant, Hitler, Sleinbinder and Christian Weber, c. 1929.

Hitler at a rally
c. 1931, the strain
visible on his face and
hanging on hard to
the *blutfahne*.

Blood

Hitler pioneered a rather sinister technique – an image of blood to evoke deep-rooted elemental feelings in his Teutonic audiences. For instance, the Röhm putsch was often referred to as the 'blood purge'. Racial intermarriage between German Aryans and Jews was described as *blutschande* or 'blood shame'. In the SS mythology promoted by Himmler, the phrase *'blut und boden'*, 'blood and soil' was used to express the primitive relationship between the peasantry and the earth. Hitler was very keen on pageantry, and flags and standards were particularly important to him. *Blutfahne*, 'blood banner' was a flag made sacrosanct by the very few martyrs of the abortive 1923 putsch. He also had devised many decorations, orders and medals for his Nazi party; *blutorden*, 'blood order' was a prestigious decoration for the faithful few.

Hitler's Court Jester

Artur 'Willy' Kannenberg in the early 1930s ran a small restaurant near Berlin's Anhalter train station. Called Uncle Tom's Cabin, it was frequented by Goebbels, Goering and also Hitler, who admired the vegetarian cuisine. Kannenberg had a most ingratiating manner and a quick wit, but more importantly he was a superb organizer and his attention to detail was legendary. His beautiful dark-haired wife ran a flower shop in Berlin's fashionable Hotel Adlon. They quickly gained Hitler's confidence and he installed Kannenberg as Hausintendant of the Reich Chancellery. Surprisingly he could interrupt Hitler with a comment or joke or with his songs. The audience would laugh and laugh at his quips. Hitler's secretary, Christa Schroeder noted: 'He charmed his

Left: The flower of German youth, *c.* 1929.

Below: Goebbels, Hess and Hitler at a Hitler Youth (*Hitlerjugend*) ceremony.

audience through his rounds of folk song and clowning, which he accompanied on the accordion. He was not only an excellent cook but also an excellent one-man show literally blessed with that Berlin wit and humour.' The words she used, *narren freiheit*, in Hitler's presence were translated as 'freedom of the fool'. He was Hitler's court jester.

Happy Hitler Youth

For young boys aged 10 to 14 the Nazi party set up the Jungvolk, and for girls the Jungmädel. To enter the Jungvolk a boy, known as a *pimpf*, had to pass an initiation test. He had to learn key points of Nazi dogma, recite the Horst Wessel song, learn arms drill (with a broomstick instead of a rifle), practise semaphore, join in strenuous two-day cross-country walks and sprint fifty metres in twelve seconds. All this was in preparation to join the Hitler Jugend (Hitler Youth) for the age group fourteen to eighteen. The Hitler Youth was founded in 1926 as a branch of the SA and by 1934 had a membership of 3.5 million. They had immense pride in their uniform, their military training and discipline. Their special dagger was inscribed 'Blut und Ehre', Blood and Honour. The Hitler Youth fought and died bravely in Normandy in 1944 and during the defence of Berlin in 1945. Hitler told them, 'You are destined to be warriors for Greater Germany'. One important song (translated) was:

Hitlerjugend.

73

Healthy exercise for *Hitlerjugend*.

Hitlerjugend prepare for an expedition.

Hitler at a *Hitlerjugend* rally, being driven by Julius Schreck.

'We are the Happy Hitler Youth
We do not need the virtues of the church
for it is our Führer Adolf Hitler
who stands at our side.'

'Like Ivy Around the Oak'

Martin Bormann (1900-1945) became one of the most powerful men in Hitler's Third Reich. In 1930 he funded the Nazi party's fortunes by an ingenious scheme whereby millions of SA [Sturm Abteilung] members paid 30 pfennigs monthly and stuck stamps onto a yellow card which gave them, or their family, life insurance in case of injury in street fighting and brawling with communists and other opponents. He became Party treasurer and ran the Adolf Hitler Fund into which extorted funds and bribes, many from Jewish businessmen, were paid. Hitler relied on Bormann to deal with his money and property affairs. As Rudolf Hess's Chef de Cabinet Bormann controlled access to the

Hitler being driven by his friend Julius Schreck *c*. 1932. Shreck was chauffeur from 1929 to 1936.

Führer, sometimes blocking Goebbels, Goering, Speer and Himmler. Hitler's every whim or passing comment became a Führer command, elaborated, then circulated to the Party officials. Bormann remained in the background, and in spite of being a pathetic orator, became indispensable, even though Hitler disapproved of his dealing with the Jews and the Church. Robert Ley, a powerful, brutal Gauleiter and head of the DAF (Deutsche Arbeitsfront) said, 'Borman clung to him [Hitler] like ivy around the oak, using him to get to the light and to the very summit.'

Hitler's Buffalo

Julius Streicher (1885-1946) was one of only four men who addressed Hitler as *du*, the German form for close friends. Streicher was Germany's foremost anti-Semite, was editor of *Der Stürmer*, and became Gauleiter of Franconia. He was the No. 2 member of the Nazi Party (Hitler was No. 7), initiated the Nuremberg Rallies and promoted severe decrees against the Jews. He was notorious for his corruption, greed, sexual activities and sadism; he published a violent magazine called *Flamme*, in Coburg. But in 1940 he was dismissed as Gauleiter. Hitler said of him: 'Streicher is irreplaceable. There's no question of him coming back. His name is engraved in the memory of the people of Nuremberg but I must do him justice. If one day I write my memoirs I shall have to recognise that this man fought like a buffalo in our cause. The conquest of Franconia was his work.'

Put on trial at Nuremberg with the other major criminals, he was sentenced to death. At the gallows he shouted 'Heil Hitler' and to the jury, 'The Bolsheviks will get you.'

Bird in a Gilded Cage

Eva Braun (1912-45) was one of Heinrich Hoffmann's more decorative assistants. Hoffmann, a friend and Hitler's personal photographer, had a studio in Amalien Strasse, Munich. Hitler first saw her up a ladder in the studio in 1929 when Eva was 19. This comely young girl, the convent-educated daughter of a schoolteacher, was probably Hoffman's mistress and he often introduced her as '<u>my</u> niece', a cynical joke aimed at 'Onkel Alf' and his genuine niece.

Naughty little Eva set her cap at Hitler and slipped billets-doux into his pockets from time to time. On one occasion Geli discovered a message from Eva, and her continuing jealousy probably led to her suicide. Eva faked a diary in 1935, four years after meeting Hitler, in which she threatened suicide for love. She made sure that Hitler found the diary, then swallowed some sleeping tablets (not too many) and was rushed to hospital followed by Hitler who was scared of being implicated in a second suicide.

Eva attended the Nuremberg Rally in 1936, discreetly in the background. Hitler's Berghof villa became her gilded cage. The staff referred to her as 'EB', addressed her as 'Madame' and kissed her hand. She referred to Hitler as

Eva Braun.

'Chief' and he called her 'Patscherl'. Over the years they exchanged hundreds of letters and Hitler paid her monthly wages to the Hoffmann studios until the end of their lives.

Unhappiest Woman in Germany

Eva was born in Bavaria, at Simbach on the river Inn beside the Austrian border. Although of limited education, she was pretty with a 'pudding face' and had a talent for dancing and amateur photography. She became an assistant in Heinrich Hoffmann's photographic studio where Hitler met her a year after Geli's death. Quite soon she became Hitler's mistress, installed in a Munich flat, but later she moved into the Berghof in Berchtesgaden. Hitler's chauffeur, Maurice, said that she was the unhappiest woman in Germany and spent most of her life waiting for Hitler. For company she often invited her sisters Ilse and Gretl to visit her. After two years with Hitler Eva shot herself – it was the mirror image of Geli. Hitler was desperate and brought her flowers as she slowly recovered. After discussions with the doctor he told Hoffman 'The girl did it for love of me. Obviously I must now look after her [for life].'

Eva's brother-in-law, Hermann Fegelein, eventually was promoted to be an SS Major-General. However, during the last days of the war Hitler had him shot for desertion.

Later, in her diary Eva wrote, 'I am so endlessly happy that he loves me so much and pray that it will always be so.' Nevertheless she tried to commit suicide a second time with an overdose of sleeping pills. Found by her sister, she was saved by a Jewish doctor who tactfully told Hitler that it was an accidental overdose brought on by tiredness![30/25]

Eva's Treasures

Hitler was, by his standards, very generous to Eva Braun. Initially he bought her medium-priced jewellery and in 1932, three years after meeting her in the photographer Hoffman's studio, an apartment on Munich's Wiedenmayer Strasse. For her twenty-first birthday he gave her a matching set of ring, earrings and bracelet of tourmalines. It remained her favourite jewellery. Then he bought a house for Eva and her sister Gretl at 12 Wasserburgstrasse and in March 1936 a Mercedes car and driver! Soon Eva was buying handmade Italian shoes, dresses by Fraülein Helse, a Berlin couturier, silk underwear from Paris and sports outfits from Vienna. Hitler was also generous to Gretl and he gave Fritz, Eva's father, a gold watch and a dog on his sixty-fifth birthday.

An original Hoffmann photograph of Hitler being driven in a car with some very early SA uniformed troops.

In her will dated 24 October 1944, Eva listed fifty pieces of jewellery, many containing emeralds, diamonds, rubies, beryl, sapphires and gold, and a dozen fur coats, including one of sable, another of mink.[25]

Staying at the Kaiserhof

In September 1930 Hitler achieved almost world-wide publicity. Tall, lumbering, half-American Putzi Hanfstaengl placed three articles by Hitler in the US-based Hearst press. The high fee of $1,000 for each article was divided, with Hitler keeping 70%. The author was delighted. Now he could stay at the Berlin Kaiserhof Hotel – elegant and expensive. Moreover he was interviewed by the London *Times* and sold an article to Britain's *Sunday Express*. At the dinner table on 6 July 1942 Hitler recalled, 'When I visited Berlin before we came to power [i.e. 1931-32] I used to stay at the Kaiserhof, accompanied by the complete General Staff. I booked a whole floor and our bill for food and lodging usually came to about ten thousand marks a week [actually 1,300 marks]. I earned enough to defray these costs mostly by means of interviews and articles for the foreign press. Towards the end of the 'Struggle Period' [*Kampzeit*] I was being paid as much as two or three thousand dollars a time for such work.' Rags to riches indeed![63]

The Churchill Visit

In 1932 Randolph Churchill, Winston's son, was a correspondent for the *Sunday Graphic* and visited Germany. On Hitler's achievement of power in January 1933 the brash young journalist sent a telegram to the Führer congratulating him on his success. Randolph persuaded his father, who was visiting the Blenheim battlefield, that he should meet Hitler. So Winston Churchill spent nearly a week at the Regina Hotel in Munich, where he met 'Putzi', Ernst Franz Hanfstangl, Hitler's wealthy companion of the early 1920s. Indeed, Putzi had sheltered the wounded Adolf after the 1923 'putsch' had failed. Now in 1923 he was foreign press adviser to the Nazi party. Putzi was rich with an American mother and American wife and charmed the Churchills with his piano playing and familiar English songs. Winston recalled, 'He said I ought to meet him [Hitler] who came every day to the hotel about 5 o'clock and would be very glad indeed to see me. I had no national prejudices against Hitler at the time. I knew little of his doctrine or record and nothing of his character. I admire men who stand up for their country in defeat, even though I was on the other side.'

For a variety of not very convincing reasons, Hitler avoided a meeting and Putzi later took him to task. 'You should have been there. Among other things Churchill sketched out the idea of an alliance with a request that you should think about it.' Hitler repled that Churchill was in (political) opposition and 'no one pays any attention to him'. 'People say that same thing about you', Putzi retorted.[14]

Hitler's Funding

The royalties from *Mein Kampf* made Hitler wealthy but crafty, devoted Martin Bormann devised other sources of income. In 1932 a *compulsory* accident insurance plan for Nazi party members produced considerable profits. With Hitler's approval Hoffman, his photographer, his friend Ohnesorge, Minister of Posts, and Bormann also ensured that Hitler earned a minute royalty on the tens of millions of postage stamps sold with his head on them. The Adolf Hitler Endowment Fund of German Industry was set up in the economic boom of the mid-1930s. Business leaders, particularly Jewish ones, were bluntly told to show their appreciation by *voluntary* contributions to the Führer. Dr Hjalmar Schacht, a brilliant Nazi financial wizard paid for the Reich's expansion with special 'mefo' bills to pay armaments manufacturers.

Hitler's head on the 42 Pfennig stamp. Hitler earned a royalty from every stamp used; a scheme devised by post minister Ohnesorge with encouragement from photographer Heinrich Hoffmann and Martin Bormann.

Supreme Pied Piper

Group Captain Malcolm Christie, born in Germany, was the Air Attaché in the British Embassy in Berlin and was a friend of Hermann Goering. In spring of 1932 Christie was sure that Hitler would go down in history as 'the consummate drummer or the supreme pied-piper but never as a great statesman'. Christie's report to the Foreign Office portrayed Hitler as unstable, unreliable, with the temperament of an artist, more of a loud-mouth than a statesman, whose outbursts of rage could be attributed to an inferiority complex deriving from his lack of education. Christie thought that he should be treated as a dangerous politician and that in 1931-32 there were close parallels between Nazism and Italian Fascism.

The Consul-General in Munich, D. St Clair Gainer, wrote on 10 July 1934 to Sir Eric Phipps, the British Ambassador in Berlin, who was detested by Hitler, that the feeling amongst the Reichswehr officers was Hitler had given the army back its self-respect and therefore they were prepared to co-operate with him provided he would modify his Socialist programme somewhat and keep his followers in proper subjection.[41]

Hitler's Third and Fourth Books

Timothy Ryback's book *Hitler's Private Library* charts Hitler's work in 1926-27 on a volume about his Great War experiences, using a style based on Ernest Jünger's *Fire and Blood*. The manuscript was probably destroyed deliberately by fire in front of his adjutant Julius Schaub and secretary Christa Schröder in late April 1945.

The fourth book composed of a 324-page typewritten manuscript (Target No. 589) was discovered in a strongbox in the publisher Franz Eher Verlag's offices in Munich. In May 1928 it was intended to be the third work in a trilogy based on *Mein Kampf*. The manuscript was discovered by Captain Paul Leake of the US Army Signal Corps and identified as Target No 589. Ryback produces evidence that Hitler's 'money man' had returned from

A Hoffmann portrait photograph of Hitler, *c.* 1932.

Heligoland to Munich in mid-July with a carbon copy of the Hitler manuscript and locked it up in the safe at 11 Thierschstrasse, Munich and then it was moved by Joseph Berg, the technical manager of Verlag, to 35 Scheubner Richterstrasse.

In 1928 after reading Mussolini's own memoir, Hitler told Gauleiter Frank: 'What beautiful Italian Mussolini speaks and writes. I am not capable of doing that in German. I just cannot keep my thoughts together when I am writing ... *Ich bin kein schriftsteller'* (I am not a writer).'

Stateless

Hitler was born in the old Austrian Empire and was therefore legally an Austrian citizen. He formally renounced Austrian citizenship in April 1925. In 1932 he stood for election to the Presidency of the German Republic and urgently needed to become a legal German citizen. He was made Counsellor to the State of Brunswick legation in Berlin and swore loyalty to the Weimar Republic.

So for seven years Hitler was stateless!

Hitler with his 'signature' salute.

The Chameleon – 'Multiplicity'

Hitler arrived at the Berlin-Staaken airport on 27 July 1932 for a meeting, one of three, scheduled for that day in the Brandenberg and Berlin stadiums. It was a very tight schedule. Albert Speer witnessed the arrival of the three motored planes and Hitler, associates and adjutants got out. Hitler reproved his companions because the cars had not yet arrived. He paced up and down slashing at the tops of his high boots with a dog whip, giving the impression of an angry, uncontrolled man who treated his associates with contempt. He was 'very different from the man of calm and civilised manner which had so impressed me ... I was seeing an example of Hitler's remarkable duplicity – indeed "multiplicity" would be a better word. With enormous histrionic intuition he could shape his behaviour to changing situations in public while letting himself go with his intimates, servants or adjutants.'[58]

Hitler and Suicide

Henriette von Schirach née Hoffman, a noted beauty whose name was once linked to Hitler, was married to the head of the Hitler Youth movement. She wrote in 1932, 'I believe there are certain people who attract death and Hitler was definitely one of them'. Certainly he was in suicidal mode after the Beer

Max Amann with Robert and Inge Ley.

Hall Putsch of 1923 and the Strasser crisis of 1932 and probably after he ordered the execution of his friend Ernst Roehm during the Night of the Long Knives. Geli, his niece and mistress committed suicide in 1931, Renate Mueller, another friend, in 1937. Other suicides were Inge Ley, wife of Dr Robert Ley, Unity Mitford in 1939 (she lingered until 1948) and Eva Braun. Before he married her in the Berlin bunker in April 1945, Eva had tried to commit suicide in November 1932, again in 1935 and finally she swallowed cyanide a few hours after her marriage in a suicide pact with Hitler.

Moscow's Views on Hitler

The membership of the British Communist Party in the early 1930s was about 3,000 and in the General Election about 50,000 voters supported them. Their paper *The Daily Worker* was ill-prepared when Hitler acceded to the Chancellorship on 30 January 1933. Moscow laid down the line that Hitler represented 'the dictatorship of the big capitalist exploiters' and the 'extreme intensification of class contradictions in Germany'. A reading of *Main Kampf* would have clarified Hitler's extreme views on Bolshevism to the British comrades.

Joseph Goebbels making a speech.

Hitler's Oratory – The Demagogues

Albert Speer had fifteen years of service with Hitler and Goebbels, the two main Nazi speech-makers, and wrote of them that they both understood how to unleash mass instincts at their meetings, how to play on the passions that underlay the veneer of ordinary respectable life. Practised demagogues, they succeeded in fusing the assembled worker, petits bourgeois and students into a

Left: A woman overcome with emotion and reduced to tears.

Below: Mass support.

homogenous mob whose opinions they could mould as they pleased. That was his opinion in 1930, but when Hitler came to power in 1933 things altered. Now the two politicians were in fact moulded by the mob itself, guided by its yearnings and daydreams. Of course Goebbels and Hitler knew how to penetrate through to the instincts of their audiences, but in a deeper sense they derived their whole existence from these audiences. Certainly the crowds roared to the beat dictated by the batons of Hitler and Goebbels. Yet they were not the true conductors. The mob determined the theme. 'To compensate for misery, insecurity, unemployment and hopelessness, this anonymous assemblage wallowed for hours at a time in obsessions, savagery, licence. This was no ardent nationalism ... Frenzy demanded victims. And Hitler and Goebbels threw them the victims.'[58]

Café Society – The Ostaria Bavaria

'But come for lunch in the Osteria' was a familiar invitation by Hitler in the 1930s to his coterie. Around half past two this small artists' restaurant would be crammed full. Herr Deutelmoser was the owner of the Osteria Bavaria in Munich, which was to become famous. As a frustrated artist Hitler liked the atmosphere. But the early guests had to wait for Hitler to arrive in his black Mercedes. The group would probably consist of his adjutant, SS GruppenFührer Julius Schaub, Adolf Wagner, Gauleiter of Bavaria, a rather drunken thug, Heinrich Hoffman, a boon companion, often tipsy, Dr Otto Dietrich, Hitler's press secretary, invariably Martin Bormann, Rudolf Hess's inconspicuous secretary, and quite often, Albert Speer, Hitler's architect. Speer describes a typical late lunch at the Osteria, 'On the street several hundred people would be waiting, for our presence was indication enough that *he* would be coming. Shouts of rejoicing outside. Hitler headed toward our regular corner which was shielded on one side by a low partition. In good weather we sat in the small courtyard where there was a hint of an arbour. Hitler gave the owner and the two waitresses a jovial greeting, "What's good today?"' The only ladies ever to be seen at Hitler's table were Unity and Diana Mitford.[58]

Diana Mitford
with Ernst 'Putzi'
Hanfstaengl.

The Matinée Idol

The Labour Party newspaper was the *Daily Herald*, with a circulation of over two million daily – the biggest in Britain. On 31 January 1933 the paper published an article entitled 'Hitler the Clown who wants to play Statesman'. The Führer was described as a 'stubby little Austrian with a flabby handshake, shifty brown eyes, and a Charlie Chaplin moustache. Nothing in the public career of little Adolf Hitler, highly strung as a girl and vain as a matinée idol indicates that he can escape the fate of his immediate predecessors whose terms of office as Chancellors of Germany had lasted only a matter of weeks.'

Gemütlichkeit

Hitler was besieged by women after he became Chancellor. Hundreds of letters were sent to him every week. Ladies of all ages pursued him. He did not particularly want beauty, wit or class and he certainly would never have married a foreigner. What he wanted was *gemütlichkeit,* a domestic, non-threatening cosiness. 'A woman must be a cute, cuddly, naïve little thing – tender, sweet and dim.'[49]

Cartoons – Tat Gegen Tinte

The Führer had a strange hobby – he collected cartoons of himself which appeared frequently in the German press, certainly up until 1933, but much more cautiously after that. With Hitler's permission Putzi Hanfstaengl decided to use the cartoons for propaganda purposes, with a careful commentary explaining the myth behind the cartoonists' 'lies'. So a 174-page book appeared entitled *Hitler in der Karikatur des Welt: Tat gegen Tinte* (Hitler in the caricature of the world: Fact versus ink), a picture compilation by Ernst Hanfstaengl. Putzi of course had access to all cartoons published in the USA. Three editions appeared in 1933, 1934 and 1938 and all the profits went to 'Putzi'. Where are the original cartoons now?

The Reichstag Fire (1)

The Reichstag building, a square stone structure with a dome and Corinthian columns, built in 1894, housed the parliament in Berlin. A month after Hitler became Reich Chancellor, the building was burnt to the ground on 27 February

President Paul von Hindenburg and Chancellor Hitler, 1933.

1933. Hitler was dining that evening with Joseph and Magda Goebbels. Looking out of the window he could see flames in the sky above the Tiergarten and immediately cried, 'It's the communists'. He and Goebbels set off at once to the blazing Reichstag where they found Hermann Goering busy saving the valuable Gobelin tapestries (which were his own private property). Since August 1932 Goering had been President of the Reichstag and was then living in the old Prussian presidential palace nearby. Goering, as if on cue, shouted 'This is the start of a communist uprising. Not a moment must be lost.' Hitler went into overdrive, 'Now we'll show them. Anyone who stands in our way will be mown down. The German people have been soft too long. All communist deputies must be hanged this very night. All friends of the communists must be locked up, social democrats and the Reichsbanner as well.' Immediately the SA arrested four thousand leading communists, plus many social democrats and liberals, including Reichstag members immune from arrest. An arsonist, a simple-minded young Dutch communist, Marinus van der Lubbe, was charged and after imprisonment and trial was beheaded. Forensic evidence showed that the fire had been so professionally started in various parts of the building that one man alone could not have done it; he had clearly been given expert help. The show trial in Leipzig in September acquitted the leading communists – Torgeler, Dimitrov and many others. Goering, '*Der Dicke*' as the Berliners called him, stormed and ranted at the trial and was ridiculed in the world's press. It seemed almost as though the Nazis were on trial.[54]

After the Reichstag fire, 28 February 1933.

The Reichstag Fire (2) – The Plot and Aftermath

The probability remains that Hitler wanted to wipe out the hundred or so communist seats out of the 600 deputies in the Reichstag. Hitler controlled 250 seats, which was not quite overall control of the house. So Hitler had a word with Hermann Goering, his deputy and Prussian Minister of the Interior, who had a word with Reinhard Heydrich's SS intelligence department (*sicherheitsdienst*) and on the night of 27 February the SD agents secretly entered the Reichstag through an underground tunnel that connected Goering's official residence to a cellar in the parliament. After the fire Hitler persuaded President Hindenburg to sign a decree for 'The Protection of the People and State', an order suspending civil liberties and freedom of expression. In the March elections after a media frenzy by Goebbels, and the imprisonment of the communist deputies, Hitler's Nazi party gained five million votes with 44 per cent of the vote. With yet another 'Law for the Removal of Distress of People and Reich' Hitler gained control of parliament.[3]

Right: Marinus van der Lubbe in custody.

Presiding Judge Dr Wilhelm Bürger of the Fourth Criminal Court of the Fourth Penal Chamber of the Supreme Court at Leipzig conducted the trial of Marinus van der Lubbe between 21 September and 23 December 1933. In this photograph Count Helldorf confronts Van der Lubbe. He was guillotined on 10 January 1934.

The Reichstag and the Lickspittle

In 1928 Hitler's Nazis had 12 seats in the Reichstag, in 1930 the number had increased dramatically to 107 and by 1932 more than doubled to 230 seats. By the time it was burned to the ground on 27 February 1933, a month after Hitler became Reich Chancellor, the Nazis had 288 seats out of 635. The next day President Hindenburg decreed that all civil liberties were suspended in the 'Emergency Decree for the Defence of Nation and State'. So in March Hitler became, in effect, a dictator, and Germany a police state.

Earlier, in November 1931, Hitler had confided his plans to the aged Marshal Hindenberg, who was totally unimpressed. He said to Franz von Papen, who was Chancellor in 1932, and Hitler's deputy in 1933-4, '<u>That</u> man for Chancellor? I'll make him a postmaster and he can lick stamps with my head on them.'

Four Nazis sing outside a Woolworth store thinking the founder was Jewish; March 1933.

The night of book burning, 10 May 1933.

Gleichschaltung

1933 was a wonderful year for Hitler. 1933 was a terrible year for Germany. It was the year of 'the co-ordination of the political will'. In January there were Nazi parades in Berlin and in February no fewer than thirty-three decrees were published banning rival political meetings or publications and dissolving the Prussian parliament. Communist party offices were raided. On 27 February the Reichstag fire (qv) took place and Hitler was given emergency powers by presidential decree. In March Goering, on Hitler's orders rounded up and imprisoned thousands of communists and other opposition elements and Dachau, the first concentration camp was opened, to be followed by no fewer than fifty by the end of the year. The last free elections were held in March with the Nazis getting 44 per cent of the vote. The SA (qv) Sturmabteilung, the Brownshirts, forced German state government resignations. Prussia had gone, now Bavaria was suppressed. Henrich Himmler was made Bavarian Police President. Amnesties were granted to all Nazis who had committed

Above: A *Hitlerjugend* parade, 27 August 1933.

Right: The Nuremberg Rally, *Reichsparteitag des Sieges* (Reich Party Congress of Victory), 30 August – 3 September 1933. The *Reichsparteitage* were held at the Nazi party rally grounds in Nuremberg from 1933 to 1938.

crimes during the *Kampf* years of struggle. *Ermächtigungsgetz* or Enabling Law was passed, giving Hitler extraordinary powers for the next four years. Goebbels was made Minister for Propaganda. The First Co-ordinations Law of States and Reich was passed giving total control to the Chancellor. In April Jewish shops and professional men were boycotted. May saw all non-Nazi publications and all labour unions banned. Goebbels organized the 'Burning of the Books', an outrageous act. In July the Nazis became the *only* legal party. In October Hitler took Germany out of the League of Nations. In November the Kraft durch Freude (Strength through Joy) movement was founded (qv). The National Referendum in November showed that 95 per cent of the population approved Nazi policy.

It is unlikely that any sophisticated, civilized country in the world had surrendered their freedoms so quickly – and apparently so willingly – as in the year of *Gleichschaltung*.

The cruise ship *Robert Ley*.

Sea Cruises for All

In April 1933 Hitler had been Chancellor for two months of a bankcrupt economy and huge unemployment. He banned the Communist Party – all six million of them – and introduced strict price and wage controls. He closed down all Trade Unions and in 1934 merged them into the DAF (German Labour Front) with thirty million members – the largest Trades Union in the world. The DAF funded the Volkswagen factory (people's cars), food factories, a German Labour Bank, housing schemes, hotels for workers' holidays and convalescence homes for sick workers. Holiday cruise liners were provided so that workers could see the outside world (Europe only). The DAF regularly received 95% of subscriptions due which showed how popular Hitler's plans were for the workers. The armed forces quickly doubled, then tripled in size, thus diminishing the unemployment problem. The DAF was an astonishing success. Hitler wrote, 'In future every worker will have his holidays – a few days in each year which he can arrange as he likes. And everybody will be able to go on a sea cruise once or twice in his life.'

The 'Brown Pages'

The Ferschungsamt (FA) wire taps were important security measures introduced by Hitler to control his police state. The so-called 'Research Office' was set up in April 1933 and controlled by Hermann Goering. The wire taps printed on unusual brown paper were sent in locked despatch boxes or by pneumatic post direct to carefully chosen ministers. Some of those known to be spied on included Hitler's adjutant, Fritz Wiedemann, Gauleiter Julius Streicher, Goebbels' several mistresses, Princess Stephanie Hohenloe and Unity Mitford. Polish, Czech, French, British, Italian, Japanese and Belgian diplomats were routinely tapped as were the British and US Embassies in Berlin. The London *Times* correspondent and the church leader, Pastor Martin Niemoller were 'bugged'.

A rally in Nuremberg, 9 November 1933. Parliamentary elections in Germany took place on 12 November 1933. They were the first under Nazi Party rule. All opposition parties had been banned by this time, and voters were presented with a single list containing Nazis and 22 non-party 'guests' of the Nazi Party. Such delegates, who included the likes of Alfred Hugenberg, still fully supported the Nazi regime.

So Churchill had the daily German Enigma reports intercepted by ULTRA. Hitler had his FA wire taps daily recording telephone calls between key 'targets' in Germany who were communicating externally to London, New York, Paris and Moscow.

Hitler's SS Bodyguard

The ReichsFührer SS, Heinrich Himmler 'discovered' two secret plots against Hitler's life in 1933 just after the success of the Reichstag fire. One by Count Arco-Valley, the other by three Soviet agents who had perhaps hidden grenades for Hitler's car to drive over! Himmler put up another smokescreen of 'French attempts on the life of the Chancellor of the Reich'. Hitler lived in constant fear of being assassinated, so he asked Himmler to set up a special guard of SS for his personal security. Thus was formed the Führer's personal bodyguard, Leibstandarte – SS Adolf Hitler, under Joseph 'Sepp' Dietrich. Sepp, who later was promoted to SS General and became Hitler's favourite soldier.[3]

Obergruppenführer Sepp Dietrich.

The Führer's Paladin

Hermann Goering, named as Hitler's successor and Reichsmarshall, was terrified of Hitler and confessed to the banker Hjalmar Schacht, 'Every time I stand before the Führer, my heart falls into my trousers'. But when the Nazi party took power in 1933 he declared, 'No title and no distinction can make me as happy as the designation bestowed on me by the German people, "The most faithful paladin of the Führer".'

The Mitford Girls: 'Sitting Beside the Sun'

At the Bayreuth Wagner Festival in July 1933, the two good-looking daughters of Lord Redesdale, Unity Valkyrie Mitford and her sister Diana met Hitler, who warned them of 'the Jewish and Bolshevik dangers'. They both fell under his spell and Unity said that sitting next to Hitler was 'like sitting beside the sun'. Diana was in the throes of divorcing Bryan Guinness, by whom she had two sons, and marrying the leader of the British Union of Fascists, Sir Oswald Mosley, an admirer of Mussolini and a notorious womanizer. At her second wedding, guests included Hitler and Goebbels (who found the Mitfords 'boring as ever'), which

Left: Hermann Goering.

Above: Carin Goering's re-burial, 21 June 1934. She suffered from tuberculosis and a heart condition and died unexpectedly on 17 October 1931. She was initially interred in her homeland of Sweden. Her death came as a great blow to Goering. He named the baronial hunting lodge he built from 1933 Carinhall, in her honour. It was there that he had her body re-interred.

horrified the Mitford family and scandalized British society. Unity Mitford became a member of the Hitler social group, with Albert Speer, the photographer Heinrich Hoffmann and Martin Bormann. One tacit agreement which prevailed at the tipsy lunches (the Osteria Bavaria, Munich was a favourite) was that no one must mention politics, except for Unity who pleaded with Hitler to make a deal with England. In September 1939 when the two countries declared war on each other, Unity shot herself with a small pistol, appropriately in Munich's Englischer Garten. Hitler had the best specialist care for her and sent her back to England through Switzerland in a special railroad car.

Hitler recalled in August 1942: 'Churchill and his friends decided on war against us some years before 1939. I had this information from Lady Mitford. She and her sisters were very much in the know, thanks to their relationship with influential people.' The Mosleys were arrested in England and detained for three and a half years.

The English Court

Leopold von Hoesch, the German Ambassador in London, sent a despatch No. A2705 headed 'Subject: German-English relations' on 16 August 1933 back to the Foreign Minister in Berlin, Baron Konstantin von Neurath and thence to Hitler. Part of it read, 'We must mention the English Court where true sympathy

Oswald Mosley with other British Black Shirts and Diana Mitford, at Nuremberg, September 1933.

Leopold von Hoesch, German Ambassador to the Court of St James.

for Germany is still to be found. To be sure King George [V] has become more and more critical in his attitude towards the German revolution and various statements which I know him to have made recently are in fact anything but friendly. On the other hand the Queen [Mary, who was German by birth] and various princes and princesses who are connected by family ties with Germany still entertain a warm feeling for our people and country and also a certain sympathy, or at any rate a lively interest in the most recent German developments. Most pronounced are the sympathies and the interest in the case of the successor to the throne [the Prince of Wales, who beecame King Edward VIII Jan–Dec. 1936], for whom I have often had opportunities for a frank and detailed discussion.'

Edward VIII was bilingual in German, spoke German with his mother and earlier with Kaiser Wilhelm II 'Uncle Willi', his favourite uncle. As the Duke of Windsor he continued his friendship with the Nazi regime.[72]

Secret Memory Box

In 1933 Christa Schroeder, a well-trained secretary with shorthand and typing experience, aged 25 volunteered to join NSDP (the Nazi Party) liaison staff

Gerda Christian and Christa
Schroeder, two of Hitler's secretaries.

in Berlin. In the Staircase Room (*treppenzimmer*) in Berlin's Radziwill Palace
she became one of Hitler's devoted secretaries. They were permanently on
standby regardless of the hour should he need to give a dictation. Hitler had
his breakfast in the Winter Garden dining hall and in the afternoon talked to
his visitors whilst strolling along the garden path. She later wrote: 'One day
Hitler happened to pass the Staircase room at tea time, saw us sitting there and
asked if he might join us. This hour of easy chatter was so much to his liking
that he later came to tea almost daily. It was a place where he felt unburdened. I
always had the impression that what he said there came from a secret memory
box which at all other times he kept locked shut.'

Christa stayed with Hitler until his end despite the fact that he vetoed her
engagement to a Yugoslav diplomat in 1941.

Hitler's Appearance – A Masculine Viewpoint

William Shirer, the American CBS journalist in Berlin, expected on arrival to
see a 'mad, brutish dictator'. Instead he found a man 'with a rather common
face. It was coarse. It was not particularly strong. Sometimes when he was
obviously fatigued from the long speeches, the hours spent in reviewing his
troops, it appeared flabby... He was about five feet nine inches tall and weighed
around 150 pounds. His legs were short and his knees turned in slightly so
that he seemed to be a bit knock-kneed. He had well formed hands with long
graceful fingers reminiscent of a concert pianist. He used them effectively in
gestures during a speech or when talking informally with a small group.' But
he had a straight, large nose broadened at the base with thick nostrils, which
all betrayed the brutal side of him. Shirer thought that the famous Charlie
Chaplin moustache was grown to soften the coarsest features. His mouth was
expressive and could reflect his many moods.[57]

A Hoffmann portrait
photograph of Hitler,
c. 1934.

Arisierung *or Aryanization*

Many of the 525,000 Jews in pre-war Germany owned businesses, factories, shops and art and were targeted by Nazi 'hooliganism'. The first Nazi boycott of all Jewish shops and businesses was personally planned by Hitler for 1 April 1933. This pogrom was supervized by the SA General Julius Streicher. Shop windows were covered with anti-semitic slogans and clients who tried to enter were physically bullied. The historian Saul Friedlander pointed out that it became increasingly clear to Hitler himself that Jewish economic life was not to be openly interfered with, at least as long as the German economy was still in a precarious position. Indeed as late as 1938 the powerful Dresdener Bank still had five Jewish directors and there were three Jews out of eight directors with the German Central Bank.

The second phase of persecution was that all 5,000 Jewish civil servants were fired, and 30 per cent of the 4,585 Jewish lawyers were ejected from the National Association of lawyers. Jewish musicians, actors, film producers, boxers and doctors and physicians were soon disbarred, threatened or dismissed.

Travellers in Söhren, a popular tourist attraction and resort in Schleswig-Holstein, 28 June 1935. The Nazi recreation programme for organised sports, cultural activities, travel, outings, etc., was met with enthusiasm after its introduction in 1933.

Strength Through Joy – The Master Race

Kraft durch freude (KdF) or 'strength through joy' was first proposed to Hitler by Dr Robert Ley, leader of the German Labour Front (DAF) in 1933. Based on the funds confiscated from the original trade unions, an immense business was created to finance the *kraft durch freude*. It was an imitation of Mussolini's *dopo lavoro* or *nach der arbeit* ('after work'). But Hitler had already adopted some of the philosophies of Nietzsche, who praised strength and denounced weakness in trenchant prose. From 1880 to 1914 the Arbeiterturnerbund (Workers' Gymnastic Association) had encouraged millions of Germans to engage in physical education. With the upmarket Deutsche Turnerschaft they had together reached two and a half million members. Sports and games were introduced from Britain: football, tennis, swimming, water polo, boxing, wrestling, athletics, rowing and mountaineering (but not cricket). Hitler even approved of women boxing and wrestling! His SA organized its own Sports Badge and Reich Sports contests. From 1933 subsidized holidays, sports facilities, cruises, dancing, concerts, films, exhibitions, theatre and concerts were all designed by Hitler to raise the physical fitness of the nation – not necessarily for peaceful purposes. But he himself said, 'People sometimes ask me why I play no games. The answer is simple. I'm no good at games, and I refuse to make a fool of myself!'[61/20]

'Frightfully Stiff and Bombastic'

Stephanie von Hohenlohe, née Richter (1891-1972) became a princess by marrying Prince von Hohenlohe in Westminster in May 1914. She was a citizen of the Austro-Hungarian Empire and most of her lovers were archdukes. By 1932 she had persuaded her friend, Lord Rothermere, the newspaper proprietor, to give her a three-year contract as his agent, which remained in force until 1938 and earned her over £1 million in today's money. She travelled to Hungary, the Netherlands and Germany, where she soon became the mistress of Hitler's adjutant, Friedrich Wiedemann. In December 1933 she met Hitler and handed over a letter from Lord Rothermere suggesting a meeting. His *Daily Mail*, a mass-circulation newspaper, often carried articles about the virtues of Nazi Germany. The Führer wore his usual fawn military-style jacket, a white shirt, brown tie fastened with a swastika tie-pin and black uniform trousers, plus black socks and black patent leather gloves. Princess Stephanie thought he looked like a minor clerk, albeit very neat and tidy. Hitler kissed her on the hand and gave her tea, but Stephanie, a Viennese and a dedicated social snob, thought that his Austrian accent was 'of the lowest class like someone who is trying to express himself in a language that he is not born to. Frightfully stiff and bombastic.' Returning to London with Hitler's letter, Rothermere's agent was paid a bonus of £2,000 and a strong pro-Hitler campaign appeared in Rothermere's newspapers.[56]

Pecking Order

Between 1 and 10 January 1934 Hitler published a series of 'thank-you notes' in 'his' paper, the *Volkischer Beobachter*. The pecking order at that time was Hess, Schwarz (Nazi party Treasurer), Max Amann, Himmler, Roehm, Goebbels and Rosenberg. Then followed Goering, Robert Ley, Baldur von Schirach (head of the Hitler Youth Movement), Walter Buch (Chairman of the USCHLA, Nazi disciplinary court), Franz Seldte (leader of the Stahlhelm, the militant ex-servicemen's association) and finally Richard Walter Darré (organizer of the NS-Bauernschaft Nazi farmworkers, who became Minister of Food and Agriculture). It is interesting that Goering, listed No. 8, became Hitler's successor-designate.

Unity – Stalking Hitler

Unity Valkyrie Mitford, known as 'Bobo' to her family, may have been Hitler's lover. She was certainly a very close friend in the four-year period 1935-39, when they met on no fewer than 180 occasions. She was born in 1919, tried to commit suicide twice, suffered and died in 1948. Aged 15, Unity owned a copy of *Jew Süss* by Leon Feuchtwanger. She was a tall, strapping blonde girl nearly six foot tall with large, pale blue eyes and was a great show-off who had peculiar pets – a rat and a snake. A great giggler, she attracted the young Randolph Churchill. With her sister Diana they visited the Nuremberg Parteig in 1933 and admired the Nazi party and its leader on display. On her return to

Unity Mitford.

England Unity attended Mosley's British United Front rallies, proudly wearing a black shirt, and sold copies of the *Blackshirt* magazine from the BUF office in Oxford. She persuaded her parents to let her spend a year in Germany at finishing school in Munich to learn the language and thus stayed with Baroness Laroche at 121 Königinstrasse. She worked hard on her German language studies and wore a black shirt and BUF badge to classes. Having made up her mind that she wanted to meet Hitler, she discovered from a Frau Baum that he often lunched at the restaurant Osteria Bavaria and had tea at the Carlton tearooms. In June 1934 she saw Hitler in the tearooms, but did not meet him on that occasion. Her sister, Nancy Mitford caricatured Unity in her novel *Wigs on the Green*, as 'Eugenia', a Fascist activist![46]

A Pipeline to Buckingham Palace

Leopold von Hoesch, the German Ambassador in London in the early 1930s, was entertained at Windsor Castle on 25 April 1934 by King George V, Queen Mary, the Duke of Kent (Prince George) and other members of the royal family. Hoesch reported back to Berlin: 'The King engaged me in a long political conversation, and did not hesitate to express some adverse criticism of the dictated peace of Versailles. In this connection he made the war itself [the Great War] as a human madness, responsible for such deplorable consequences.' King George went on to say that 'as long as he was living, England would not again

Diana and Unity Mitford.

become involved in war. Accordingly, out of his firm conviction that a new war would mean the ruin of everybody, he would do everything in his power to forestall every possibility of war.'

The cousins of the royal family in St Petersburg had been swept away in the Russian Revolution so there was no love of Bolsheviks in Windsor Castle. And it was clear that Hitler's main object was to defeat Bolshevism.

No wonder Rosenberg reported to his master, Adolf Hitler, that there was 'a pipeline to Buckingham Palace'.[73]

More Hitler Cartoons

In September 1934 Putzi Hanfstaengl had his second book published, which contained refutations of the adverse Hitler cartoons emanating from the world's press. It was called *Tat gegen Tinte* and was a mixture of satire and humour with themes such as 'Hitler der Friedensstorer' (Hitler the Troublemaker) and 'Hitler der Terrorist' (Hitler the Terrorist) and the rather convoluted (translated) 'Hitler as Cultural Reactionary Suppressor of Culture and Racist Politician'! A postscript to the book carried the friendly assurance that it had been read and approved by the Führer.[14]

The Turkish Whore

Putzi Hanfstaengl had an important PR meeting at dinner on 27 April 1933 with Louis Lochner (Associated Press), his aristocratic wife, Hilde, a General Wilhelm Groener, George Messersmith, the US Consul General and other

German film star and Goebbel's mistress, Lida Baarova in a still from the film *Patrioten*.

bigwigs. Putzi refused to wear a Nazi party uniform and ordered a chocolate brown gaberdine cloth from a London tailor to be made up into a uniform with delicate little gold epaulettes. Putzi thought he looked terrific. Hitler, however, was appalled, 'You look like a Turkish whore' he said.[14]

Rival Factions

After 1933 – the watershed – the main players developed their own cliques, but not a power base. Goebbels surrounded himself with literary and cinema stars, producers and, particularly, actresses. Hess had interesting acquaintances, enjoyed chamber music and delved into homeopathic medicines. Himmler became almost a deity with his tough, brutal SS hierarchy. His missionary zeal (he initially recruited sons of princes and counts) made him feel superior to the others. 'Der Grosse' Hermann Goering entertained his large family and Luftwaffe friends lavishly at Carinhall, One way and another he became very rich and looted the art treasures of Europe. Hitler held these four divergent groups together politically as the only thing they had in common was the success of the Third Reich and their fear of the Führer's power.

Hitler meets Mussolini at Venice on his first trip to Italy, 14 June 1934.

The Garrulous Monk

The first time that the two European dictators, Benito Mussolini and Adolf Hitler, met was on 14 June 1934 in the Royal Villa at Stra, near Padua. The Führer was surrounded by a cohort of fully armed SS men led by the tough, brutal 'Sepp' Dietrich. Mussolini was profoundly unimpressed. He noted Hitler's lank, ill-brushed hair and watery eyes, and his yellow mackintosh, striped trousers and patent leather shoes. Mussolini, of course – *bella figura* – as a proper Duce was wearing a splendid Fascist uniform with ceremonial dagger and black boots with silver spurs. They conversed in German (Mussolini spoke several languages) and agreed that they both disliked Russia and France. Austria was a problem where the Nazis were using 'terrorist' tactics. The conference transferred to Venice where Hitler spouted much of his *Mein Kampf* from memory to the bored Duce, who after the meeting expressed his contempt for the 'silly little clown' and 'the garrulous monk'.[31]

The Ranting Demagogue

William Shirer, the American journalist, observed the Führer closely during a week spent at the Nuremberg Rally: 'All of us in the West, our political leaders and our newspapers above all, had underestimated Adolf Hitler and his domination of this land and its people. His ideas might seem half-baked and often evil – to me they did. But the unpleasant fact was not only that he believed in them, fanatically, but also that he was persuading the German people to believe in them. He might seem like a demagogue – he often was during those days in Nuremberg. But his oratory, his drive, his zeal, his iron will and the power of his personality were having an immense impact on the

Hitler with Mussolini at Venice.

citizens of this country. He was convincing them that the new Germany, Nazi Germany, under his leadership, was great, was strong, and had a manifest destiny. He was demanding sacrifices and promising them glory. They were willing to make the first to achieve the second.'

The Swastika 'Blood Flag' and the Thousand Year Reich

The Nuremberg Rally starting on 4 September 1934 was beautifully and frighteningly organized. In the huge Luitpold hall there were almost 30,000 Nazi party supporters. Hitler had brought pageantry back to Germany. A large symphony orchestra played the Brandenweiler March, which was played only when the Führer was involved in a special occasion. Hitler appeared in the back of the auditorium followed by Hermann Goering, Joseph Goebbels, Rudolf Hess and Heinrich Himmler – the five individuals who controlled the Third Reich. All were dressed in brown uniforms except Himmler, in the black garb of the SS. As soon as the Nazi chiefs were seated on the huge platform backed by the swastika 'blood flag' of the 1923 beer hall putsch, and five hundred SA flag-standards, the orchestra played Beethoven's *Egmont Overture*. Great klieg lights played on the stage as Rudolf Hess, the tall, strong, brutal deputy to Hitler read out slowly the names of the Nazi so-called 'martyrs' – brownshirts – who had been killed during the putsch. Hitler was saving his voice as he was

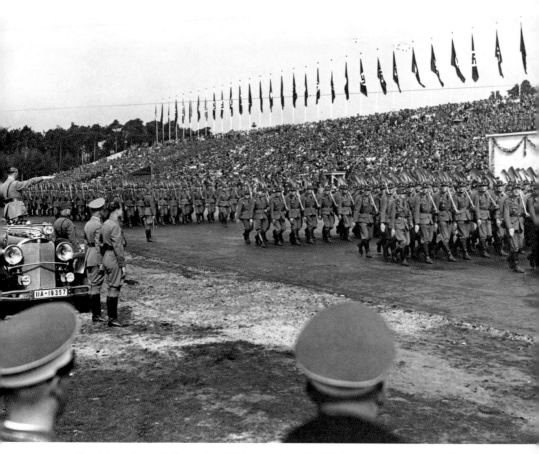

The Nuremberg Rally – the *Reichsparteitag der Einheit und Stärke* (Reich Party Congress of Unity and Strength); 5-10 September 1934.

scheduled to give seven speeches during the rally so Gauleiter Adolf Wagner of Bavaria read out the Führer's speech to the 30,000 faithful. 'The German form of life is definitely determined for the next thousand years. For us, the nervous nineteenth century has finally ended. There will be no revolution in Germany for the next one thousand years.'[57]

Blood and Soil

Richard Walther Darré (1895-1953) was a friend of Hitler's in the early days who had interesting views on agriculture and selective breeding. Born in Argentina and educated partly in England, he preached the agrarian philosophy of *Blut und Boden* (Blood and Soil). Hitler had been heavily influenced by Darré, who was also an early party member and friend who had written a

Hitler at a rally, probably *c.* 1934.

book on the German peasantry, *Life source of the Nordic race*. Darré was
appointed the party's agricultural adviser and his peasant programme was
published over Hitler's name on 6 March 1930. Besides economic aid for
German farmers there were state-credits, reduction and remission of taxes,
higher protective tariffs, cheaper artificial manures, cheaper electricity and
revision of inheritance laws. The tenor of the proposals was to emphasize the
value of the peasantry and farming activities to the population as a whole.
Darré organized Nazi farmworkers as the 'NS-Bauernschaft' in 1933. Hitler
later said, 'Darré has done two good things: the law of agrarian inheritance
and the regulation of markets.' Unfortunately Darré became corrupted on a
huge scale, made himself rich and in 1942 was dismissed ignominiously.

Um Blut und Boden – The 'Green' Führer

Although Hitler all his life was an urban creature, he was a passionate
advocate of 'blood and soil' policies. Abbreviated to *Blubo* the word endorsed
the primitive relationship of the German peasant (his blood) with the earth
(*boden*). He set up a National Peasants Assembly with a Harvest Festival,
promotion of local and peasant art, the wearing of regional costumes and
encouraged 'Germanic' dances. The Kreisbauernschaft was a governmental
agency authorized by Hitler to collect rural folklore, rituals, songs and dances.

Arbeitsdienst – Labour, 6 September 1934. '*It is a great undertaking to educate an entire Volk in this new concept of work and this new opinion of work. We have taken up the challenge, and we will succeed, and you will be the first to bear witness to the fact that this work cannot fail! The entire nation will learn the lessons of your lives! A time will come when not a single German can grow into the community of this Volk who has not first made his way through your community.*' Adolf Hitler.

Arbeitsdienst – a celebration of work.

The Perfect Goose-Step

Hitler's Labour Service Corps, his *Arbeitsdienst*, was launched to the German public at Nuremberg on 6 September 1934. Fifty thousand highly trained, semi-military young men –fanatical Nazi youths – were on parade in the early morning sunlight. Instead of guns they bore shiny spades. The first thousand were bared to the waist and without warning they broke into a perfect goose-step, strutting proudly. This struck an inner chord in the strange soul of the German people and the tens of thousands of spectators jumped up spontaneously and shouted their applause. The Labour Service boys then formed an immense *sprechchor* – a chanting, shouting chorus intoning, 'We want one Leader! Nothing for us! Everything for Germany! Heil Hitler!' A few years later these proud young goose-steppers marched their way through Poland, the Low Countries and France.[57]

Hitler's Architectural Sketches

According to Speer Hitler perpetually drew sketches, which were tossed off casually but accurate in perspective. He drew outlines, cross-sections and renderings to scale which could not have been done better by an architect. Sometimes he would show Speer a well-executed sketch he had prepared overnight, but more often his drawings were done in a few hasty strokes during their discussions. Speer kept 125 of Hitler's 'quick' sketches, a quarter of which related to the 'Linz project' which was always close to Hitler's heart, and many of them were sketches for theatres.

The Nuremberg Rally.

The Blood Purge (1)

On 30 June 1934 a 'second revolution' was plotted by Hitler's old friend Ernst Roehm, chief of the brown-shirted SA (Sturmabteilung, the storm troopers). That day came to be known as the 'blood purge' or the 'night of the long knives'. The SA had 4½ million members, mainly rough, unemployed ex-soldiers, who frequented Munich beer halls. Their uniform, raised army salute and swastika derived from the recently disbanded Freikorps. Frequently the SA clashed with Himmler's elite 100,000-strong SS (Schutzstaffel, defence unit). Hitler's close supporters, Goering, Werner von Blomberg (Minister of Defence), Himmler, Reinhard Heydrich, Werner Best and Victor Lutze (a SA leader who wanted to oust Roehm) all urged him to act against the SA. Hitler flew to Munich with Goebbels at dawn on 30 June in Operation Colibri, drove to Bad Weisee and arrested Roehm and other SA leaders. The Stadelheim prison was crammed with SA prisoners. Operation Hummingbird was the signal for Goering in Berlin to take the local SA leaders to Lichterfelde army cadet school, where they were all shot. Hitler had his good friend Roehm shot in his prison cell on 1 July. In the massacre General von Schleicher, former Reich Chancellor and his wife, Gregor Strasser, a key radical Nazi and another of Hitler's friends, Edmund Heines, Nazi boss of Silesia, Dr Erich Klausner and Gustav von Kahr were all slaughtered. In his speech in the Reichstag on Friday 13 July, Hitler screamed 'The supreme court of the German people during those twenty-four hours consisted of myself'. He claimed that 'only' 19 senior and 42 other SA men had been shot, plus 13 'resisting arrest' and three had committed suicide. In the 'Roehm purge', probably more than 1,000 were killed, mostly SA but also others for the sake of vengeance.

However, Hitler said to his loyal secretary Christa Schroeder, 'So! Now I have taken a bath and feel clean as a newborn babe again.'

Edelweiss – Hitler's Favourite Flower

Around 1934 a delegation of Berlin's women's organizations was planning to welcome Hitler at Anhalter station and hand him flowers. So a telephone call was made to Karl Hanke, State Secretary in the Reich Ministry of Propaganda. 'What was Hitler's favourite flower?' Hanke asked Hitler's adjutants and the answer was that despite Hitler's walks and rambles in the lovely countryside around the Berghof, he had no favourite flowers. Hanke asked Speer, 'What do you think? Should we say edelweiss? I think edelweiss sounds right. It's rare and comes from the Bavarian mountains. Let's simply say that officially the edelweiss is "The Führer's flower."'

Himmler and his SS strike against Roehm's SA.

The Times *of London and Hitler*

Geoffrey Dawson, Editor of *The Times,* in 1931 met Alfred Rosenberg, who had joined Hitler's movement in 1920 and become editor of the Nazi party's own newspaper, the *Volkischer.* Rosenberg impressed Hitler with his views on racialism, Communism and his similar philosophy. He wrote 'The Future Course of German Foreign Policy' and played host in Germany to a number of eminent British people including Thomas Jones, several peers, two generals, an admiral and a number of journalists. In 1933 whilst Goering and his stormtroopers bullied the electorate and Goebbels' persuasive propaganda was in full flow, *The Times* carefully wrote, 'No one doubts Herr Hitler's sincerity. That nearly 12 million Germans follow him blindly, says much for his personal magnetism.'

Even after the infamous 'Night of the Long Knives' on 30 June 1934, *The Times* drew the conclusion that 'during the next few years there is more reason to be afraid for Germany, than to be afraid of Germany'.

When Hitler withdrew Germany from the Disarmament Conference in Geneva and from the League of Nations in October 1933, Geoffrey Dawson in *The Times* pleaded, 'The German Case', that their impatience had been understandable, and 'Hitler should be given the chance of showing that he is something more than an orator and an agitator'.

Hitler's Overwhelming Eyes

Professor William E. Dodd, the American Ambassador in Berlin in the mid 1930s had a vivacious young daughter. After the 'night of the long knives' Putzi Hanfstaengl tried to find someone suitable for Hitler who could charm him into a pro-Western and pro-American attitude. Putzi, a Harvard graduate with an America mother, introduced Martha Dodd to Hitler and suggested that she should try to persuade him to marry her! Hitler's shyness and occasional charm captivated Martha but her father, the ambassador, thought that Hitler was a dangerous madman and kept them apart.

Martha told William Shirer, the American journalist to 'watch out for Hitler's eyes, they are unforgettable. They overwhelm you.'[17]

Hitler's Hypnotic Eyes

Hitler's eyes dominated his otherwise common face. They were hypnotic, piercing, penetrating. They appeared to be light blue, but the colour was not the most noticeable thing about them – it was their power. They stared at and through the person on whom they were directed and seemed to immobilize them, frightening some and fascinating others, especially women whom they dominated. He was like the Medusa, whose stare was reputed to turn men to stone or make them impotent. During the days at Nuremberg hardened old party leaders, even though they had spent years with Hitler, would freeze when he spoke to them, hypnotized by his penetrating glare. And not only Germans reacted in this way: foreign diplomats also appeared to succumb to the famous eyes.[57]

Hitler's Films

Goebbels often presented selections of films to his Führer. These were shown in the music salon in the Reich Chancellery or in the Berghof. Every evening a crude movie projector was set up to show a newsreel and one or two films. Usually Hitler wanted two films every evening and made running comments, often vetoing a film half way through and walking out in disgust. He preferred light entertainment, love and society films but no comedies (Chaplin and Buster Keaton were out). Two of his favourites were 'Mutiny on the Bounty' and 'The Hound of the Baskervilles'. Films with Emil Jannings, Heinz Ruehmann, Henny Porten, Lil Dagover and Jenny Jugo were popular, as were Mickey Mouse cartoons and revues with lots of leg on display were often shown. Hitler was

Ribbentrop, Bormann and others
watch a film with Hitler.

a self-confessed fan of Shirley Temple and Jeanette MacDonald and 'Donkey
Serenade' was his favourite Hollywood movie tune.

On Wings Before Bismarck

Hitler was short-sighted but would never be seen wearing spectacles in public.
He refused to have his speeches taken down in shorthand so the Silenta brand
of typewriter that his two favourite secretaries, Schroeder and Daranowski
used had to be adapted with special 12mm characters so that he could read
the script in public without glasses. Schroeder described a typical dictation:
'As a rule Hitler would be standing at or bent over his desk working on the
punchlines for his speech. Often he would appear not to notice my presence,
when I was at my typist's desk. A while would pass in silence. Then he would
begin to dictate calmly and with expansive gestures. Gradually getting into his
stride he would speak faster. Without pause one sentence would then follow
another while he strolled around the room. Occasionally he would halt, lost
in thought before Lenbach's portrait of Bismarck gathering himself ... His
face would become florid and the anger would shine in his eyes. He would
stand rooted to the spot as though confronting the particular enemy he was
imagining. Apparently he felt himself as if on wings ... From the beginning of
the war Hitler would never deliver a speech without a manuscript. "Now we
are at war I must weigh carefully every word for the world is watching and
listening."'

Goering's Assurance – 'No Enemy Planes'

The key showpiece in the grandiose Hitlerian plan for the future, Adolf Hitler
Platz in Berlin, was to be the great domed hall – an assembly chamber for
twelve hundred deputies, representing a future Germanic population of 140

Joseph Goebbels with
Hermann Goering.

millions. It would hold up to 180,000 standing people, have a diameter of 825 feet and rise to a height of 726 feet. The interior would contain sixteen times the volume of St Peters in Rome. The final turret would be crowned by an eagle with a swastika. The Reich Air Ministry was told of the plans for a building which would act as an ideal navigational guide to enemy bombers, but Hitler answered their fears, 'Goering has assured me that no enemy plane will enter Germany. We will not let that sort of thing stand in the way of our plans.'

Rassenkunde – Racial Science Brainwashing

Hitler had a withering contempt for schoolteachers and never forgave those who had refused him entry to the Vienna Academy of Fine Arts. Hitler made Dr Bernhard Rust the Minister for Education and Gauleiter of Hanover; his boast was that he was 'liquidating the school as an institution of intellectual acrobats'. His job was to 'Nazify' the educational system. For a long time Germany had had a magnificent reputation for its fine universities and schools. In the first five years of Hitler's rule very nearly 3,000 professors and instructors at universities had been dismissed – a quarter of the total. University enrolment reduced in six years from 127,920 to 58,325. At the institutes of technology the number of scientists and engineers fell from 20,474 to 9,554. The University of Berlin under the new rector soon had five new courses in *rassenkinde* (racial science).[57]

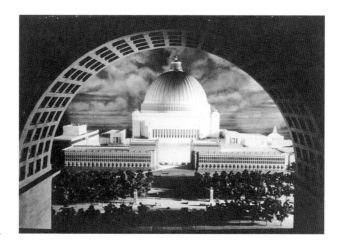

Speer's model for
Adolf Hitler Platz.

Hitler's Tax Returns

Hitler's annual tax returns from 1924 to 1935 can be seen either in the Bavarian
State Archives or the Alderman Library of the University of Virginia, USA.
They comprise some 200 items. A full analysis is contained in O. J. Hale's *Adolf
Hitler Taxpayer*, American Historical Review of 1955. Hitler described himself
to the tax authorities as 'writer' and was liable for income tax, turnover tax
(*umsatzsteuer*) on sales of *Main Kampf* and for property tax (*vermögenssteur*).
Julius Schaub negotiated on behalf of Hitler, usually with Fritz Reinhardt, a
long-term Nazi, who was Secretary of State to the Reich Ministry of Finance.

Duke of Linz Perhaps?

Hitler thought all kings were monumentally stupid. To his dinner companions
on 5 July 1942, he recounted, 'About a year after the victory of our Party,
one of our former potentates, Rupprecht of Bavaria, sent an emissary to
me to say that he was sure I would recognise the necessity of restoring the
monarchy [in Germany]. The emissary, following his instructions went on to
say quite frankly that I could not, of course, remain as Reich Chancellor in the
restored monarchy because my continued presence would be an obstacle to
the unification of the German people. I should however, be most generously
treated and should be rewarded – with a dukedom!' Duke of Linz perhaps? He
went on 'The idiot imagined that some confounded nincompoop could tempt
me to give up the leadership of this great people – by making me a Duke.'[61]

Himmler and Roehm together some time before 30 June 1934.

Hitler – Mickey Mouse Fan

In the mid and late 1930s Goebbels controlled the film and theatre production in Germany. He censored and rated every film for tax purposes, and read film scripts nearly every evening. Hitler and he were passionate fans of cinematic art. In one year Goebbels gave Hitler thirty serious films and eighteen Mickey Mouse films as Christmas presents.[52]

The Blood Purge (2)

Hitler was extremely excited in the days following the SA massacres. He told his young architect friend, Speer, how he had forced his way into the Hotel Hansel Mayer in Wiesee. 'We were unarmed, imagine, and didn't know whether or not those swine might have armed guards to use against us ... in one room we found two naked boys in bed [Heines and friend who were both shot]. I alone was able to solve this problem [quelling the so-called putsch]. No one else!' The newspapers reported that President von Hindenburg had officially praised Chancellor Hitler and Prussian Prime Minister Hermann Goering for their prompt action. Hitler was overjoyed, 'When circumstances require it, one must not shrink from the most extreme action. One must be able to spill blood also.'

Edmund Heines (1897-1934).

One interesting theory is that Stalin in the Kremlin, where the 'Roehm purge' was greeted with approval, had instigated rumours through the Soviet intelligence service about Roehm's intentions. Roehm favoured an alliance with France rather than with the USSR, which was not what Stalin wanted.[37]

Game, Set and Match

After a year as Reich Chancellor and Führer, Hitler, who was delinquent with his annual tax returns put fairly discreet pressure on the Ministry of Finance. As a result, on 19 December 1934, confirmed on 25 February 1935, a memorandum from Dr Lizius, chief of the Finance Office, Munich-East, noted, 'The order to declare the Führer tax-exempt was therefore final. Thereupon I withdrew all the Führer's records, including the tax cards from official circulation and place them under lock and key.' Game, set and match to the tax-exempt Führer!

Paula Hitler (1896-1960)

Hitler's younger sister, Paula lived mainly in Vienna where she ran an arts and crafts shop. When her brother Adolf became notorious or famous she changed her name to Wolf. She never married and from 1935 she occasionally acted as housekeeper at the Berghof. Hitler made her an allowance of 250 marks

Heinrich Himmler
and his SS, 1934.

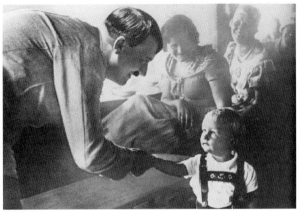

The fatherly Adolf.

per month and in 1938 increased it to 500 marks. At Christmas he gave her a present of 3,000 marks and helped her buy a villa. He also left her money in his will.

Hitler on Motherhood

Hitler wanted to increase the Aryan population of Germany. Whilst one way or another he drove out the Jews and Romanies, he led a big drive for motherhood. He outlawed abortion, forbade campaigns to promote contraception, instituted a system of marriage-loans (a certificate of a thousand Reichmarks for a couple to buy furniture) and made it compulsory for husbands to leave their property to their wife and children. Since motherhood was the highest calling for German women they must also be physically strong like the Valkyries of legend. The Bund Deutscher Mädl was formed for all girls from the age of 14 (those under

Hitler relaxing at home.

that age joined the Jungmädel). A new ideal of 'Aryan maidenhood' was drawn up which included physical prowess, an outdoor 'natural' life which would include a year of farm or domestic service. So the fit young girls became fit young brides and fit young mothers.

The Führer Niche

In the 1930s the popular admiration for Hitler was at its zenith. The vast majority of Germans now venerated him thanks to his powerful rhetoric on the radio and at Nazi rallies. Little Goebbels kept up a never-ending barrage of media adulation. All the attributes of a superman were attributed to Hitler. His physical unapproachability enhanced his prestige. The cult of the Führer found expression in the letters and presents daily arriving. In the eyes of many Germans, particularly the women, Hitler as a substitute for God stood above basic earthly concerns. If there were any perceived evils, shocks or horrors it must have been because the Führer knew nothing about them. Many households set up in their living room, in place of a religious shrine, a 'Führer niche' with his picture and flowers.[52]

Hitler's Oratory

Albert Speer described Hitler's gift for oratory: how in a low voice, hesitantly and somewhat shyly he began a kind of historical lecture rather than a speech. There was something engaging about it – all the more so since it ran counter to everything his opponents' propaganda had led one to expect: a hysterical

Hitler speaking to the Nation.

demagogue, a shrieking, gesticulating fanatic in uniform. He did not allow the applause to tempt him from his sober tone. It seemed as if he were candidly presenting his anxieties about the future. His irony was softened by a somewhat self-conscious humour. His South German charm reminded Speer agreeably of his native region. Hitler's initial shyness soon disappeared; at times his pitch rose and he spoke urgently and with hypnotic persuasiveness. Speer was carried away on the wave of enthusiasm which almost physically bore the speaker along from sentence to sentence. It swept away any scepticism, any reservations. Opponents were given no chance to speak. The citizens of the Third Reich listened spellbound and at the end the applause was shattering – frightening even.

Speer – Almost Hitler's Friend

Albert Speer (1905-51) from May 1933 until the end was the 'court favourite'. From a middle-class Mannheim family, happily married with six children, Speer first attracted Hitler's attention by making the 1934 Nuremberg Rally a brilliant spectacle. His undoubted architectural skill meant that Hitler made him the court architect, and he proposed grand schemes for Berlin, Linz and all

Another Hoffmann photographic
portrait *c.*1934.

of Hitler's fancies, which included twenty-five 'reconstruction cities'. Intelligent
and amiable he was not seen as a threat by Hitler's 'mafia' court. Hitler liked
Speer: 'He is a building person like me, intelligent, modest and not an obstinate
military head.' He was the nearest Hitler came to having a friend and Speer
certainly befriended – platonically – Eva Braun. Speer wrote of her: 'When
we became more familiar [at the Berghof] with one another I realised that
her reserved manner, seen perhaps as haughty, was merely embarrassment. She
was well aware of her dubious position in Hitler's court.'

On Honour

In a letter to Lord Rothermere on 3 May 1935 Hitler wrote 'Since the [Great]
War as an active politician, I have preached unswervingly the necessity of both
nations [England and Germany] burying the hatchet for ever. I am convinced
that such an understanding can only take place between honourable nations.
I hold that there is no possibility of concluding agreements with a people
without honour, and I regard such agreements as entirely worthless.' Hitler
ruthlessly disregarded all the political agreements with most of the European
countries and Russia.[56]

Hitler with
Albert Speer.

Hitler watching a
rocket engine test
at Kummersdorf,
21 September 1933.

Nuclear Research, Stage One

The great German universities in the 1930s taught *German* physics, *German* chemistry and *German* mathematics. Hitler had a great respect for Professor Philipp Lenard of Heidelberg University, a Nobel Prize laureate in physics (1920). Lenard joined the Nazi party in its early days and told Hitler that 'science, like every other human product, is racial and conditioned by blood'. He attacked Einstein and the Theory of Relativity, and persuaded Hitler that

Hitler with Grand Admiral Raeder on the gun deck of a battleship, probably the *Scharnhorst*.

'the Jew conspicuously lacks understanding for the truth ... in contrast to the Aryan research scientist with his careful and serious will to truth. Jewish physics is thus a phantom and a phenomenon of degeneration of fundamental German physics.' Professor Wilhelm Mueller of Aachen Technical College and Professor Ludwig Biererback of Berlin University were unanimous: modern physics, and this included nuclear physics, was in reality a bid for 'Jewish world rule'. So to Hitler nuclear physics were 'Jewish physics', therefore Alfred Rosenberg, later Minister of Education, took his cue from his master and totally failed to support nuclear research.[57]

'Happiest Day of My Life'

The Anglo-German Naval Agreement was finally concluded by an exchange of notes on 18 June 1935. After the First World War the victorious Allies signed a series of treaties fixing the relative sizes of the British, American, Japanese, French and Italian navies in the ratio 5:5:3:1:1. Hitler had publicly declared his intentions that the nascent German Navy should be built up to be at a strength of 35 per cent of the British Navy. Von Ribbentrop, Erich Kordt, assistant to Konstantin von Neurath, and Hitler's interpreter Paul Otto Schmidt plus three German experts took on the British Foreign Office and the British Admiralty. For two weeks the negotiations rumbled on. The German

The Nuremberg rally – the *Reichsparteitag der Freiheit* (Reich Party Congress of Freedom), 10-16 September 1935.

team won hands down. The American journalist, William Shirer wrote, 'The Wilhelmstrasse were elated. Germany gets a U-boat tonnage equal to that of Britain. German submarines almost beat them in the last war and may in the next.' It was undeniably a great victory for Hitler's foreign policy. Ribbentrop flew to join Hitler and Admiral Raeder in Hamburg. The Führer declared that the conclusion of the Agreement marked the happiest day of his life.[57]

Hitler's Appearance – A Feminine Viewpoint

Princess Stephanie von Hohenlohe left a vivid description of her meetings with Hitler in the mid-1930s: 'his light brown hair, not black at all, his oft-caricatured forelock, combed diagonally across his forehead'. She did not like his nose, moustache or coarse feet! Nor did she like his small mouth. His front teeth were edged with a thin gold strip, but his pale blue eyes were pleasant and could even be called beautiful except that they protruded slightly. His skin was very fine, almost translucent, always very pale with little pink spots on his cheeks. The Princess thought he was probably not healthy. She admired his artistic hands but noticed that he constantly scratched nervously with his thumbnail on the skin of his index finger so that it was always sore.

A relaxed Hitler in a civilian suit
c. 1935.

Tschapperl

Eva Braun was in charge of Hitler's private life and was his personal guest at the magnificent Berghof in Berchtesgaden, but Martin Bormann paid her allowance from Hitler, and all other household expenses. In front of the staff Hitler addressed her as 'Fraulein Braun', but in private he called her '*Tschapperl*', which translates roughly as 'bumpkin', 'little idiot' or 'wench'. The jealous Nazi wives called her (not to her face) 'EB' or '*die blöde kuh*' (silly cow). By the beginning of 1936, however, her role was more clearly defined and Hitler instructed his staff and servants at the Berghof to call her '*Chefin*', or '*gnädiges fraulein*', respectable forms of address, or '*kindl*', '*patscherl*' or '*schnacks*', which are pet names for 'child'. After a number of years together Eva was allowed to call her lover '*du*', Adolf or Adi. To everyone else after he became Chancellor he was addressed by the formal '*Sie*' and known as Der Führer, even by old 'friends' such as Goering.

Hitler's Sense of Humour

Being a dictator is a serious business – foes in front and foes behind – and his courtiers maintained that Hitler had no sense of humour and never laughed. At a Nuremberg rally William Shirer saw him laugh heartily at least a dozen

The re-occupation
of the Rhineland,
7 March 1936.

times. 'He would rear back his head as he did so, the forelock of his dark brown hair, parted on the right side, would fall over his left temple to the eye until, still laughing, he would shake it back by a jerk of the head or the swish of his hand.'[57]

Operation Schulung and the King's Promise

Under Hitler's orders in May 1935 General von Blomberg, the Minister of Defence and Commander in Chief of the Wehrmacht, produced the highly secret Operation Schulung to seize and reoccupy the demilitarized Rhineland – 'The surprise blow at lightning speed'. On 16 June Colonel Alfred Jodl, soon to become Hitler's Chief of Operations, reported on the forthcoming offensive. On 7 March 1936 the Wehrmacht, with only three battalions and horsedrawn transport 'recovered' the frontier cities of Aachen, Trier and Saarbrücken. Baron Konstantin von Neurath, Hitler's Foreign Minister, summoned the ambassadors of Britain, France, Belgium and Italy, the Locarno signatories, to his office in the Wilhelmstrasse, Berlin. He denounced the Locarno pact – Hitler's first treaty broken. But the Führer immediately proposed to a hysterical audience of brown-shirted deputies of the Reichstag, his latest 'peace' plans, with five different proposals and pacts. Facing across the new frontier was the mighty blue-clad French army, who, of course, did nothing martial at all. Weak in morale and equipment, they were just a paper tiger. On the night of 7 March Albert Speer, Hitler's architect and friend, was part of Hitler's entourage travelling by train to Munich. At one station a message was handed to Hitler, who sighed with relief, 'At last! The King of England will not intervene. He is keeping his promise. That means it can all go well.'[5]

The speech to the Reichstag, 7 March 1936.

The Rhineland 'Coup'

In February 1936 Hitler summoned Ribbentrop, von Neurath and Field Marshal Werner von Blomberg to a conference to discuss three options for the French-occupied Rhineland. Hitler preferred unilateral remilitarization by force – the third option. At once Ribbentrop blurted out, 'The third, *mein* Führer, the third' before the other two could give a view. Blomberg felt the Wehrmacht was not ready. Neurath thought that negotiation to re-occupy would succeed.

On Ribbentrop's advice Hitler chose a weekend – 7 March – to launch his coup, and also issued a lengthy diplomatic memorandum with various points to confuse England and France. Better still it caused a serious split between the two countries. France, whose security was based on the Versailles and Locarno agreements, wanted to put strong pressure on Hitler to withdraw. The British Foreign Office vacillated and did not support France. Anthony Eden asked Hoesch, the German Ambassador in London, for some German concessions to appease the French! Hitler stood firm and the pacifism of the English and French public opinion was paramount. A plebiscite at the end of March showed that 98 per cent of Germans approved of Hitler's coup in the Rhineland. The Führer took Ribbentrop and his wife on a special cruise on the Rhine to celebrate, and on 20 June Ribbentrop had a *private* audience with King Edward VIII!

Karl Eduard, Duke of Saxe-Coburg and Gotha, Queen Victoria's grandson, speaking as an SA officer at a rally in 1936.

Hitler's Emissaries to the Royal Family

Hitler kept up a dialogue with the British Royal family. Baron William de Ropp, from an aristocratic Baltic family, married an English woman, was naturalized British and joined the Royal Flying Corps in World War I, where he met Frederick Winterbotham. In the late 1920s he moved to Berlin, became a political journalist and wrote for the London *Times*. He could pass as a German, a Russian, a Balt or an Englishman! De Ropp met Rosenberg, established himself in Nazi society and developed a personal relationship with Hitler. He became Hitler's chief agent of rapprochement between Germany and England's influential 'players' and was also a double agent. He brought peers, generals, an admiral and many journalists to Germany to meet Hitler, Hess and Rosenberg. In January 1935 De Ropp met the Duke of Kent (Prince George) who told him that Britain was reconciled to the re-armament plans of Hitler. He visited the Duke again in January 1936 supposedly 'at the request of King Edward VIII'. Rosenberg recorded in his diary, 'R. gave the Duke the benefit of his personal experience of many years'. But in 1936 Hitler deployed Karl Eduard, Duke of Saxe-Coburg-Gotha, a cousin to the British Royal family and a senior officer in the SA, Hitler's stormtroopers. On his visits to London he stayed at Kensington Palace, called on the new King Edward VIII at Fort Belvedere and had tea with Queen Mary and attended a State dinner at Buckingham Palace. Saxe-Coburg asked the king whether a meeting between Hitler and the PM, Stanley Baldwin, might be considered and reported to Hitler that the answer was, 'Who is king here, Baldwin or I. I myself wish to talk to Hitler and will do so here or in Germany. Tell him that, please.'

The Olympic Torch, 1 August 1936.

Approach to Churchill

When Ribbentrop arrived in London in October 1936 he hoped to win useful friends in England by large-scale bribery. Hjalmar Schacht, the President of the Reichsbank, had produced a grant of one million Reichsmarks for this purpose. Ribbentrop's reports to Hitler of 29 October and 12 November 1935 (preparing for his mission of 1936) contained references to making a financial approach to Winston Churchill! Ribbentrop did have a meeting with Churchill – a rather stormy one. At one stage Ribbentrop said, 'war is inevitable' and Churchill replied, 'If you plunge us all into another Great War, we will bring the whole world against you, like last time.'[5]

The Olympic Games of 1936

For the first two weeks of August 1936, the XIth modern Olympiad – 'Hitler's Olympics' – took place in Berlin. It was held in the biggest stadium in the world, designed by Albert Speer, Hitler's favourite architect, in an imposing classical style. The crowd numbered 110,000 and overhead the massive airship *Hindenburg* trailed the Olympic flag. Swastika banners wreathed the city

Above: The XIth modern Olympiad.

Left: Jesse Owens won the gold for the 100 metres and the 200 metres during the games of August 1936. Hitler had originally forbidden Blacks and Jews to participate, but when threatened with a boycott of the Games by other nations, he was forced to relent.

of Berlin and Richard Strauss conducted a choir of a thousand singing the national anthem 'Deutschland, Deutschland über alles', then the Nazi party anthem 'Horst-Wessel Lied' and the new 'Olympic Hymn'. Extravaganzas were organized by Hermann Goering and Joseph Goebbels. Although the German athletes won the most medals, the world remembers that Olympiad for the magnificent Jesse Owens, the American negro who won *four* gold medals. Hitler attended every day and it was a huge propaganda success for the Nazi regime with four million spectators attending, and over 3,000 radio programmes in 50 languages were broadcast round the world. Hitler was delighted because 'the young sportsmen of the Reich took thirty-three gold medals and the British notwithstanding the advantages of their college system of education, were only able to win eight!'

Ulrich Friedrich Wilhelm Joachim
von Ribbentrop (1893-1946).

Hitler's Lickspittle

Ribbentrop had set up two 'friendship societies' in Berlin: the Deutsch-Englische Gesellschaft, linked to the Anglo-German Fellowship in England; and the Deutsch-Französische Gesellschaft linked to the Comité France-Allemagne in Paris. The Dienststelle Ribbentrop was the key player in organizing fairly discreet Nazi propaganda. Personalities and delegations from both England and France visited Germany and often had the doubtful pleasure of an audience with Hitler. Banquets were given, periodicals were published, letters were written to newspapers. Ribbentrop also organized pressure groups to lobby for the return of the German colonies sequestrated in 1919, and also for a 'friendship' alliance with the Japanese Military Attaché in Berlin, Lieutenant-Colonel Oshima Hiroshi. Erich Kordt, who served Ribbentrop from 1934 to 1940 wrote, 'he endeavoured to anticipate Hitler's opinions and if anything to be in advance of Hitler along the path he might follow ... when he had gained from Hitler's hangers-on what the Führer's course might be, he strongly came out in favour of that policy as his own. If Ribbentrop found that Hitler had taken a stand different from what he had expected, he would immediately change his attitude.' And Himmler noted, 'Ribbentrop was irreplaceable ... For Hitler trusted no one so much as him. No one could explain foreign policies to him so well. Ribbentrop's art of exposition was unique and entirely suited to Hitler's way of thought.'[5]

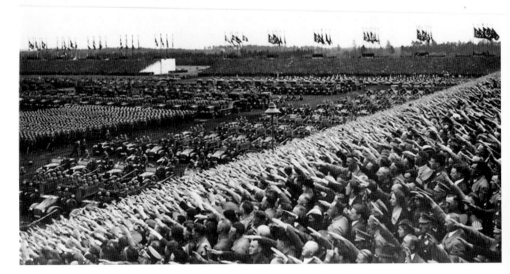

The Nuremberg rally – *Reichsparteitag der Ehre* (Reich Party Congress of Honour),
8-14 September 1936.

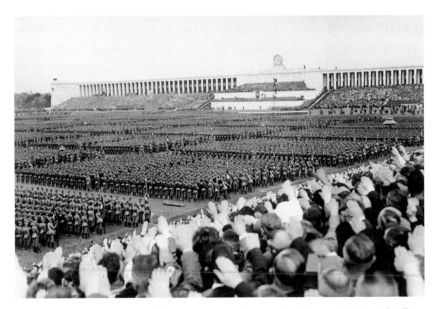

Each year the *Reichsparteitag* became more sophisticated and more lavish, with Albert
Speer behind some of the design and spectacular sets.

Hitler's Train

In mid-1936 Hitler's own special train, rather strangely called 'Amerika' was completed. It consisted of a steam engine and fifteen Pullman carriages, protected at front and rear by banks of 2-cm, quick-firing anti-aircraft guns mounted on flat cars, manned by a crew of twenty-six. Hitler's own Pullman, No. 10206, was in the centre, along with that of the press chief (Goebbels, who used it occasionally), a communications centre with a 700-watt shortwave radio transmitter, a kitchen and an ablutions carriage.[54]

'My Dear Princess'

Princess Stephanie von Hohenlohe was for six years an influential go-between bearing Lord Rothermere's expensive gifts to the Führer and meeting all the Hitler coterie. Ribbentrop detested her and told Hitler that she was a 'full Jewess'; Goebbel's diary commented that 'the Princess is very pushy'; and Putzi Hanfstaengl warned Hitler to be very careful of her. The Gestapo had investigated her family tree and found it to be unexceptionable. Hitler wrote letters to her and made her a present of a signed photograph in a silver frame bearing the dedication 'In memory of a visit to Berchtesgaden'. Hitler's letters to Stephanie always started off 'My dear Princess'. On *tête à tête* Hitler stroked her hair and once gave her an intimate pinch on the cheek. He also gave her a dog – which she never collected. In 1937 Hitler approved a presentation to her of a medal, the Honorary Cross of the German Red Cross by its president, the Duke of Saxe-Coburg-Gotha. The next year, on 10 June, in the Reich Chancellery, she became a 'Bride of the National Socialist Workers' Party' and the Führer pinned the Gold Medal of Honour to her bosom. His signature was engraved on its reverse. She was now a *de facto* party member and an 'honorary Aryan'.

It all ended in tears. Hitler fired his adjutant Wiedemann for his liaison with the Princess and Lord Rothermere's contract ended in January 1938. She rashly sued him, lost, and fled to the USA with her German lover.[56]

Hitler's Unshakeable Squire

On 30 October 1936 the Propaganda Minister, Joseph Goebbels celebrated his ten-year anniversary as Gauleiter of Berlin-Brandenburg Gau. There were exhibitions and presents including a simple log cabin, and a midnight rally at which Hitler praised him as 'a faithful unshakeable squire of the party ... had

Hitler with *Hitlerjugend* at Obersalzberg near to Berchtesgaden, 1936.

marched on ahead of this Berlin, a fanatic filled with faith. Your name stands inscribed over this ten-year struggle of the National Socialist movement in Berlin!' Then, most unusual for Hitler who disliked being touched, apart from handshakes, he thumped Goebbels awkwardly on the shoulders. No wonder Goebbels wrote in his diary, 'Hitler has honoured me as never before ... How happy I am.'[52]

Hitler's Best Horse

In 1936 the Nazi party radicals, Goebbels, Rosenberg, Himmler and Ley, plus Goering doubted whether it was worth trying to secure the friendship of the English. The October Protocols signed on 23 October were hailed by Mussolini as the foundation of a new Rome-Berlin Axis. The Nazi radicals in the aftermath of the Rhineland 'coup' and the huge, fairly secret re-armament plan felt that England and France were on the sidelines. Hitler, however, sent Ribbentrop with a retinue of 44 to London on 25 October. Hitler's parting words to Ribbentrop were 'Bring England into the Anti-Comintern Pact: that would fulfill my dearest wish. I have sent you to England as the best horse in my stable. See what you can do.'[5]

Hitler and Goebbels watch a projectionist display a propaganda film.

The Abdication – the Führerprinzip

The Führer was baffled and disappointed when King Edward VIII put his personal happiness before his royal duties and abdicated on 12 December 1936. Ambassador von Ribbentrop explained to Hitler that Stanley Baldwin's real motive had been to defeat those 'plotters' who had been working through Mrs Simpson and the King with the object of reversing present British policy and bringing about an Anglo-German entente. Hitler looked on 'the King as a man after his own heart and one who understood the *Führerprinzip* and was ready to introduce it into his country'. He thought Edward was the most intelligent prince he had ever met. Speer was told, 'I am certain that through him [Edward] permanent friendly relations with England could have been achieved. If he had stayed everything would have been different. His abdication was a severe loss to us.'

Germany's Regained Honour

In 1936 admiration for the Führer was widespread throughout Germany. Unemployment had been practically wiped out, living standards were undoubtedly improving and more consumer goods were available. The dance-halls and cinemas were full, the German Labour Front organized 'Strength through Joy' camps and cruise ship voyages abroad. The Volksemfanger people's radio was in three-quarters of German homes and by 1939 almost

Hitler with children.

four million sets had been sold. In a mere three years Hitler had apparently rescued his country from the shame and misery of the Weimar 'democracy'. The loss of civil rights, repression of the Left, discrimination against the Jews and other unfortunates appeared to be a price worth paying. 'In those three years (1933-6), Germany has regained its honour, found belief again, overcome its greatest economic distress.' Hitler also stated 'we have no territorial claims to make in Europe'. In the 29 March 1936 election the Nazi party (the only one standing) had a vote of 98.9 per cent backing Hitler.

Hitler – Baby Snatcher and Brainwasher

On May Day 1937 in Berlin Hitler made a speech which included a rare joke, about the deliberate brainwashing of the German youth. 'We have begun, above all, with the youth. There are old idiots out of whom nothing can be made any more' – pause for laughter – 'We take their children away from them. We bring them up to be a new kind of German. When a child is seven it does not yet have any feeling about its birth and origin. One child is like another. At that age we take them and form them into a community until they are eighteen. But we don't let them go then. They enter the party, the SA and SS and other formations, or they march directly into the factories, the Labour Front, the

Hitler and Baldur von Schirach inspecting *Hitlerjugend*.

Labour Service and they go into the army for two years.' From 1933 onwards the whole of Germany, or anyway about 95 per cent, marched dutifully behind the Führer and his Third Reich.

The Messiah

Hitler, Goering and Himmler, prominent members of the Nazi party, were deeply steeped in magical and occult practices as well as having rather strange religious views. Hess too, Bormann, Goebbels and Rosenberg had more than a sprinkling of occultism. Hitler had been presented to the country by himself of course, but vehemently by Goebbels, as the German 'Messiah'. The Nazi rallies were carefully staged in a quasi-religious atmosphere, with no reproaches from the Christian churches. The mayor of Hamburg stated, 'we can communicate directly to God through Adolf Hitler' and in 1937 a group of German Christians claimed, 'Hitler's word is God's law'. The head of the Hitler Youth, Baldur von Schirach, said at the Nuremberg Trials, 'The service of Germany appears to us to be genuine and sincere service of God: the banner of the Third Reich appears to us to be His banner and the Führer of the people is the saviour whom he sent to rescue us.' Hitler had given the nation back its pride, reduced massive unemployment to full employment. He had smashed the feudal class system of the Weimar republic. Hitler was their Messiah![20]

The Duke of Windsor at the Berghof; Robert Ley at the left of the photograph. During the visit the Duke gave a Nazi salute, and much publicity was given in the German press.

The Windsor Visit

The Duke of Windsor and his new wife made a two-week visit to Germany in October 1937, ostensibly to study housing and working conditions. They were entertained by the Goerings, visited Essen where Krupps were very busy producing armaments, Leipzig, and Dresden, where the Duke of Coburg gave a dinner party for them and the Duchess was addressed as 'Your Royal Highness' and the Duke gave numerous Nazi salutes. They also visited Nuremberg and Stuttgart and on 22 October took tea with the Führer at Berchtesgaden. Hitler said to Schmidt, his interpreter, 'She would have made a good queen'. The Duchess wrote later, 'I could not take my eyes off Hitler ... admired his long, slim hands and felt the impact of a great inner force. His eyes were truly extraordinary – intense, unblinking, magnetic, burning with peculiar fire.' In August 1939 the Duke and Hitler exchanged telegrams.

Hitler recalled later, in 1942 'The real reason for the destruction of the Duke of Windsor was, I am sure, his speech at the old veteran's rally in Berlin, at which he declared that it would be the task of his life to effect a reconcilation between Britain and Germany, That rally in Berlin bore the stamp of sincere and mutual esteem and the subsequent treatment of the Duke of Windsor was an evil omen: to topple over so fine a pillar of strength was both wicked and foolish.'

In 1940 Walter Schellenberg, head of SD and Abwehr intelligence, set up a cloak and dagger scheme to kidnap the Duke of Windsor, then in Portugal, and to hold him as a very valuable hostage. The scheme failed!

The Reluctant Butcher's Dogs

Colonel Friedrich Hossbach, Hitler's Wehrmacht adjutant, took the minutes of a top-level meeting chaired by Hitler in the Chancellery on 6 November 1937. Werner von Blomberg, Minister of Defence, Admiral Raeder, commander of the navy, Hermann Goering, commander of the Luftwaffe, Werner von Fritsch, commander in chief of the army and von Neurath, the Foreign

Above left: Walther Friedrich Schellenberg (1910-1952).

Above right: Colonel Friedrich Hossbach seated behind Hitler and Mussolini on their way to the *Reichsparteitag der Arbeit* (Reich Party Congress of Work), September 1937.

Minister, attended. The meeting was called to discuss and agree a rearmament programme (yet another) and the allocation of materials and arms between the three services. Hitler instead delivered a four-hour monologue on the need for *lebensraum* and how this was to be won. 'Germany's problem could only be solved by means of force ... the extra space would have to be in Europe but there were two hate-inspired antagonists, Britain and France, to whom a German colossus in the centre of Europe was a thorn in the flesh.' Germany's military might would reach its peak by 1943-44, after which the other powers would catch up. The first moves would be the annexation of Austria and Czechoslovakia, which would secure the eastern and southern flanks. He thought that Britain and France had already tacitly written off Czechoslovakia and would not interfere. His broad plan was in *Mein Kampf* but nevertheless the generals were 'shaken to the core'. 'Generals should be like a butcher's dog who has to be held fast by the collar because otherwise he threatens to attack anyone in sight.' Hitler was contemptuous of Blomberg and Fritsch and the next year the SS framed both of them for sexual misdemeanours – probably with help from Goering. Both were forced to resign and Hitler put his own choices in their places.

In the history books the meeting was called the 'Hossbach memorandum'.[19]

Hitler, Wie ihn Keiner Kennt

Heinrich Hoffmann was a talented photographer and an album of his 'court' photographs is housed in the Imperial War Museum in London. In 1937 his

Goebbels and Blomberg at a festival in Bayreuth, July 1937.

book *Hitler, ihn keiner kennt* (The Hitler nobody knows) had to be reissued. Photographs of Hitler being friendly with Ernst Roehm, whom Hitler had just had killed, were not *comme il faut*. So Hitler chose the new photographs for Hoffmann's opus. Now he would be shown as a good-natured, casual, private individual in leather shorts, or rowing a boat, picnics in the meadows, walking in the Bavarian woods, surrounded by children or youngsters, in artists' studios. But always friendly, relaxed, accessible – and harmless. The book proved to be Hoffmann's greatest success!

'Simplicity Makes a Striking Effect'

On 13 March 1938 German troops marched into Austria. Hitler sent for a map of central Europe and showed his entourage how 'Czechoslovakia was now caught in pincers'. He also said he would 'remain eternally grateful to the Duce' who had given his consent to the invasion of Austria! His Italian journey in May 1938 was made in order to show Mussolini and King Victor Emmanuele his gratitude and also to view the art treasures of Rome and Florence. Resplendent uniforms were designed for the German entourage

Heinrich Hoffmann, Hitler's photographer, at the Berghof.

Von Rundstedt, Hewel and Ribbentrop with Hitler; the two officers facing Hitler are unidentified.

to match the pomp and ceremony of the Italian courtiers. Hitler loved this pomp but his own dress was always modest – a matter of careful strategy. 'My surroundings must look magnificent. Then my simplicity makes a striking effect.'[58]

Hjalmar Horace Greeley Schacht
(1877-1970).

Case Otto – Austria

In July 1936 Hitler's German General Staff had drawn up plans for the occupation of Austria, codenamed Case Otto. On 24 June 1937 the plans were updated, and on 5 November Hitler told his dubious chiefs of the armed forces his plan for *Lebensraum*, starting with Austria. On 11-12 March 1938 a very muddled invasion took place. The majority of the panzer tanks broke down; defects appeared in the motorised SP guns; the road from Linz to Vienna was just one immense traffic jam. General von Reichenau, Hitler's special favourite, Commander of Army Group IV was responsible for the military debacle. Hitler was absolutely furious – it certainly wasn't a *blitzkrieg*.

Hitler's Spring Clean

On Saturday 5 February 1938 Hitler, in another astonishing 'coup', smashed the German army High Command whom he suspected might not carry out his orders for the campaigns he had secretly planned ahead. Having cashiered the two men who had built up the German army from scratch: Field Marshal Werner von Blomberg, Minister of War and commander in chief of the armed forces; and General von Fritsch, commander in chief of the Wehrmacht, he then made himself Supreme Commander of the Armed Forces, relieved sixteen

Work in progress.
Speer with Ernst Gall
and Hitler in Munich.

Right and overleaf:
Reichsparteitag
Großdeutschland
(Reich Party Congress
of Greater Germany),
5-12 September 1938.

senior generals of their commands and transferred forty-four others. Three
key diplomats were fired or replaced: the ambassadors in Rome, Tokyo and
Vienna, plus the old financial wizard Dr Schacht, who had kept Nazi Germany
solvent. It was Hitler's terrible 'spring clean'.

'Napoleon After Austerlitz and Jena'

When, on 5 February 1938, Hitler dismissed General von M. Fritsch and had General Werner von Blomberg cashiered for marrying a prostitute, he assumed control of the German war machine. Winston Churchill described it: 'Hitler had the power of Napoleon after Austerlitz and Jena without of course the glory of winning great battles by his personal direction on horseback, but with triumphs in the political and diplomatic field which all his circle and followers knew were due <u>alone to him</u> and to his judgement and daring.'

The Game of Danger

'You cannot understand what it is to live in a dictatorship: you can't understand the game of danger but above all you cannot understand the fear on which the whole thing is based. Nor I suppose have you any concept of the charisma of a man such as Hitler.' For twelve years, from the age of 29 Albert Speer, with his keen intelligence, was Hitler's personal architect and worked closely with him. Speer's friend and colleague, Karl Hettlage told Speer in the summer of 1938, 'You are Hitler's unhappy love', to which Speer answered, 'And you know what I felt? Happy, joyful'.

Neville Chamberlain, British ambassador Neville Henderson, German foreign minister Ribbentrop and Hitler at Munich, 15 September 1938.

A Nervous Breakdown

The shrewd American journalist, William Shirer, on 22 September 1938 saw Hitler in the garden of the Dreesen Hotel, Godesberg and described him as walking in a ladylike way with dainty little steps. He cocked his right shoulder nervously after every few steps and his left leg snapped up at the same time in a nervous tic. He had ugly black patches under his eyes and it was obvious he was on the edge of a nervous breakdown. Hitler was preparing to have a top-level meeting with Neville Chamberlain, the British Prime Minister and was rehearsing to himself what his demands were going to be.[57]

'Hitler's Terrific Victory'

In Munich on 30 September 1938 it was game, set and match to Hitler and his team – Goering, Ribbentrop, Goebbels, Hess and Keitel. They swaggered out of the Führerhaus at 2 a.m. after Hitler and Mussolini had beaten a submissive Neville Chamberlain and a totally broken Daladier. The latter was reputed to be afraid to return to Paris in case he was attacked by a hostile mob. He had sacrificed France's position and lost her main prop in eastern Europe. A disastrous day for France. Chamberlain and Daladier had told Dr Mastny, the Czech Minister in Berlin, and Dr Masaryk of the Prague Foreign Office at 1.30 a.m. that Czechoslovakia would have to accept defeat and surrender the Sudentenland. Chamberlain saw Hitler the following morning and cobbled together a 'spin' so that he could boast from No. 10 Downing Street, 'Peace with honour, I believe it is, peace in our time.' The gullible British public sang 'For he's a jolly good fellow', presumably meaning Chamberlain and not Hitler!

The British are invited to an evening discussion with Adolf and Benito, 29 September 1938.

Only Winston Churchill got it right, 'We have sustained a total, unmitigated defeat ... all the countries of Mittel Europa and the Danube valley, one after the other will be drawn into the vast system of Nazi politics ...' All the German papers said the same thing, 'Hitler's terrific victory over Britain and France'.

Teppichfresser

The journalists covering the negotiations between Germany and the Sudentenland, Czechoslovakia and Austria in the 1930s kept talking amongst themselves about Hitler the '*teppichfresser*'. When the Führer was suffering his worst nervous crises in private it would take a bizarre form. Whenever he threw a tantrum and screamed in fury or frustration about Benes, the Czech president, or anybody else who had crossed him, he would fling himself onto the floor and chew the edge of the carpet. Hence *teppichfresser*, the 'carpet chewer'.[57]

The Scrap of Paper

Case Green was Hitler's plan for the invasion and conquest of Czechoslovakia planned for 1 October 1938. The British government learned of this in August, so the Cabinet met on the 30th and agreed to put pressure on the Czechs to give in to Hitler. Border incidents were staged and in conference on 2 September Hitler declared in ringing tones '*Es lebe der krieg*', 'long live war – even if it lasts from two to eight years'. President Benes accepted London's view and conceded most of Hitler's demands. The French, who had a treaty with Czechoslovakia had a collective collapse of nerve. Neville Chamberlain, the English prime minister, went to Godesberg to visit Hitler, who, like Oliver

'Peace with honour, I believe it is, peace in our time.'

Twist made more demands. Eventually the Munich Agreement was signed on 24 September and Hitler had the Czechoslovak Sudenten territory ceded to the Third Reich. Chamberlain, having sold out the Czechs, flew back to London in triumph declaring he had obtained 'peace in our time'. Hitler and von Ribbentrop were cheated of the war they desired and Hitler assured the latter, 'Don't take it all so seriously. That scrap of paper is of no significance whatever.' In March 1939 – the next spring – Hitler's troops marched unopposed into the remainder of Czechoslovakia.[5]

The Kristallnacht Pogrom

This single terrifying action on the night of 9-10 November 1938 opened the eyes of the world to the realities of the Nazi regime. A German Jewish refugee in Paris, 17-year-old Herschel Grynszpan, murdered a German Legation secretary, Ernst vom Rath. The intended victim was the German Ambassador, although von Rath was totally opposed to Nazism. With Hitler's express approval, Reinhard Heydrich, Chief of the Reich Security head office, organized the pogrom after Goebbels had advised that 'spontaneous' anti-Jewish riots would not be discouraged. Heydrich sent urgent orders to all police HQ for 'spontaneous' riots across Germany. As a result 191 synagogues were set on

Herschel Grynszpan (1921-1944?).

fire, 815 Jewish shops and 171 Jewish homes were destroyed, 74 Jews were killed and no less than 20,000 arrested. Damage costing 25 million marks was caused including five million for broken glass windows – hence the name of the pogrom. Germany's 600,000 Jews were collectively fined one billion marks and many Jewish businesses and property were confiscated, which was known as Aryanization. The US Ambassador to Germany was recalled and Roosevelt made a speech condemning Kristallnacht on 14 November. Jewish emigration swelled to a torrent. Public opinion in Britain was horrified, although the appeasers continued their pathetic efforts.

Churchill on Hitler's Prime

Churchill observed: 'Hitler's genius taught him that victory would not be achieved by processes of certainty. Risks had to be run. The leap had to be made. He was flushed with successes, first in rearmament, second in conscription, third in the Rhineland, fourth by the accession of Mussolini's Italy. There are no certainties in human life ... Hitler was resolved to hurry, and have the war while he was in his prime.' Czechoslovakia, Poland, the Low Countries and France were soon to follow.

Kristallnacht, 9-10 November 1938.

Rousseau, Mirabeau, Robespierre and Napoleon

Hugh Trevor-Roper, the brilliant 'Hitler watcher' wrote of Adolf Hitler, 'he was the Rousseau, the Mirabeau, the Robespierre and the Napoleon of his revolution [the creation of the Third Reich]; he was its Marx, its Lenin, its Trotsky and its Stalin. By character and nature he [Hitler] may have been far inferior to most of these but he nevertheless managed to achieve what all of them could not: he dominated his revolution in every phase, even in the moment of defeat. That argues a considerable understanding of the forces he evoked!'

Attempts on Hitler's Life

On 9 November 1938 Maurice Bavaud, a 22-year-old Swiss waiter, stalked Hitler with a gun in the Bürgerbräukeller, Munich and on the Obersaltz mountain. After a secret trial by the People's Court, he was tried, sentenced and after initial imprisonment he was eventually guillotined in May 1941.

Another attempt was made by Johann Georg Elser, a 36-year-old Swabian watchmaker who, in November 1939 constructed a time bomb and placed it in

The *Bürgerbräukeller*
in Munich, 1923.

The *Bürgerbräukeller*
in Munich,
9 November 1939
after the failed
assassination attempt.

a pillar in the huge Burgerbrau beer cellar in Munich. It exploded eight minutes after Hitler had left for Berlin by train, killing and wounding many of Hitler's faithful supporters. Elser was caught, imprisoned in secrecy at Dachau, and shot under Hitler's orders on 9 April 1945, just four weeks before the end of the War.

Count von Stauffenberg placed a bomb under a table at an important conference at Obersaltzberg on 20 July 1944. He was part of a substantial conspiracy to kill Hitler – a military putsch, (*see p.* 225-6).

Hitler Mutti

Many women, including middle-aged ladies fell under Hitler's spell. In 1938 the women attending his meetings responded even more enthusiastically and generously than the men. Some of these devoted females were of the hysterical

Above: The Berghof. Hitler initially rented a property on this site at Obersalzburg in 1925, then bought it in 1927. It was rebuilt, much expanded and renamed in 1935. It was destroyed at the end of the war and finally bulldozed in 1952.

Right: At the Berghof with Goering *c.* 1938.

type, who 'found an emotional ecstasy in surrender to the man on the platform. He could twitch their very nerves with his forcefulness.' Most of these women, however, were as intelligently interested as the men and without their financial aid the early years of the Party would have been much more difficult.

Many of them looked upon Hitler as a favourite son and they became known as 'Hitler mutti', Hitler mothers. Frau Helene Bechstein, a very wealthy patroness, and Frau Elizabeth Buechner, a towering Brünhilde type, both gave the 40-year-old orator rhinoceros-hide dog whips! That shows devotion![63]

'Fraulein Braun and My Dog'

Before the Second World War Hitler talked to his closest friends of the time when his political goals accomplished, he would withdraw from the affairs of state and retire to live in Linz. He would not interfere and people would turn to his successor quickly enough. Then he himself would be quickly forgotten. 'Perhaps one of my former associates will visit me occasionally. But I don't

Inside the Berghof.

count on it. Aside from Fraulein Braun, I'll take no one with me. Fraulein Braun and my dog. I'll be lonely. Nobody will take any notice of me any more. They'll all go running after my successor. Perhaps once a year they'll show up for my birthday.'[58]

Hitler's Secret Bank Account

In the file FO371/23083 in the Public Record Office, Kew, UK is a letter received at the Foreign Office on 25 March 1939, index number C3982. It was written by Nevil Bland of the British Legation in the Hague to Sir William Strang at the FO. 'My dear William, You may be interested to know that the father of the Commercial Secretary's Dutch clerk who is employed in the local Tax Collector's Office has informed Laming that there is an account with the Netherland Postal Cheque and Clearance Service in the name of Eber Nachfolger GmbH, Thierstrasse 11, 22 Munich Giro number 211846 and that according to an Inspector of Taxes, who in the course of his investigations discovered the fact this account belongs to Herr Hitler. Apart from Eher being spelt Eber all the details are correct.'

Almost certainly Max Amann was squirrelling away Hitler's substantial profits from the publishing house into Holland. Probably *Mein Kampf* royalties too.[63]

Above and below: Hitler at the Reichstag session, Kroll Opera House 1938 with Rudolf Hess, and on the left, Joachim von Ribbentrop 'the Nazi almost all the other leading Nazis hated'.

Hitler, the orator. 'It cannot be said that brevity is Hitler's most noticeable characteristic.'

Hitler's Terrible Stew

On 31 March 1939 Neville Chamberlain 'looking gaunt and ill' (according to Harold Nicolson's Diary) read out a statement to the House of Commons guaranteeing support for Poland's independence. When the news broke in Hitler's Reich Chancellery in Berlin, the Führer fell into a hideous rage: 'With features distorted by fury, he stormed up and down his room, pounded his fists on the marble table-top and spewed forth a series of savage imprecations. His eyes flashed with an uncanny light' according to Admiral Wilhelm Canaris, head of the German military intelligence serve. 'He then growled this threat, "I'll cook them a stew that they'll choke on."' In 1934 Hitler had signed a ten-year non-aggression pact with Poland. In September 1939 on the pretext of annexing Danzig, Hitler's armies invaded Poland, which despite heroic defence was swiftly overwhelmed.[22]

Count Ciano's Diary and the 'Pact of Steel'

Count Galeazzo Ciano, the Italian Foreign Minister, who was married to Benito Mussolini's daughter, Edda, wrote in his diary on 28 April 1939, 'The Führer has delivered his speech in Berlin. It lasted exactly two hours and twenty minutes; it cannot be said that brevity is Hitler's most noticeable characteristic.

Count Galeazzo Ciano (1903-1944) to the left of the photograph.

Generally speaking the speech is less bellicose than one might have supposed on the information coming to us. The first reactions to the speech in the different capitals are also rather mild. Every word which leaves any hope of peaceful intention is received by the whole humanity with immeasurable joy. No nation wants war today: the most that one can say is that they know war is inevitable ...'

Hitler's speech demanded that Poland hand the city of Danzig over to Germany. He also revoked the German Non-agression Pact with Poland and rejected President Franklin D. Roosevelt's offer of mediation.

On 21 May Ciano arrived in Berlin for the formal signature of the 'Pact of Steel', which linked Mussolini's Fascist Italy with Hitler's Nazi Germany. Their 'united forces will act side by side for the securing of their living space and the maintenance of peace'. Of course neither dictator had the faintest intention of keeping the peace.[1/7]

'We Must Burn Our Boats'

Hitler's Wehrmacht adjutant Lieutenant Colonel Rudolf Schmundt took notes of a confidential meeting held on 23 May 1939 in the Chancellery. Hitler forbade any minutes but Schmundt's notes were found after the war was over. To his top military leaders, Goering, Generals Beck, Keitel and Brauchitsch, Admiral Raeder, plus Ribbentrop and Neurath, he made it clear that there should be an 'attack on Poland at the first suitable moment ... then the fight must be primarily against England and France ... Therefore England is our enemy and the showdown with England is a matter of life and death.' Holland and Belgium would have to be over-run. Declaration of neutrality would be ignored. He was confident of defeating France and the bases on the west coast would enable the Luftwaffe and U-boats to effect the blockade that would bring Britain to its knees. 'We must then burn our boats', and a war of ten to fifteen years might be necessary.[40]

Above left: Ribbentrop in Moscow; Vyacheslav Mikhailovich Molotov, Minister of Foreign Affairs signing the Pact, 23 August 1939.

Above right: Ribbentrop, Stalin and Molotov, 23 August 1939.

Left: General Friedrich Fromm (right) with General Maxim Purkajew of the Soviet Union photographed in 1939 after the signing of the Ribbentrop-Molotov Pact.

Death Knell of the British Empire

On the night of 21 August 1939 at supper a note was handed to Hitler who flushed deeply, then banged on the table so hard that the glasses rattled, and exclaimed in an excited voice, 'I have them. I have them.' Speer recalled that no one dared to ask any questions and the meal continued. At the end of it Hitler told his entourage, 'We are going to conclude a non-aggression pact with Russia. Here, read this. A telegram from Stalin.' A secret protocol, not for publication, was appended to the Non-Aggression Treaty whereby Stalin and Hitler agreed to divide Eastern Europe into spheres of influence: Finland, Estonia and Latvia to Russia, Lithuania and Vilna to Germany, and poor Poland would be partitioned along the rivers Narew, Vistula and San. Goebbels held an evening press conference two days later and Hitler wanted to know how the foreign correspondents had reacted. Goebbels answered, 'The sensation was fantastic.

A jubilant Hitler congratulates his foreign minister.

And when the church bells simultaneously began ringing outside, a British correspondent fatalistically remarked, "That is the death knell of the British Empire."' Hitler's euphoria knew no bounds. He was out of reach of fate.[58/7]

'Hero of Ancient Myth'

After the German-Russian pact was signed in Moscow the Hitler coterie was divided into two camps. Goebbels spoke openly and anxiously about the danger of war; the Propaganda Minister considered the risks excessively high. Rather surprisingly, Hermann Goering, the most martial of the Hitler clique, recommended a peaceful line. The war-mongers were Field Marshal Wilhelm Keitel, Chief of Staff of the Armed Forces (OKW) and von Ribbentrop. Speer commented, 'In those days he [Hitler] seemed to me like a hero of ancient myth, conscious of his strength [who] could masterfully meet the test of the wildest undertakings.'

Hitler's view was that because of Germany's rapid rearmament it held a four to one advantage in strength ... 'we have new weapons in all fields, the other side obsolete types'. The 'other side' Hitler had in mind of course, was Poland. Not even Mussolini's inability to keep its alliance obligations could put off Hitler's launch of Operation White.[58]

'The World in My Pocket'

Hitler had prepared very carefully for the invasion and conquest of Poland. Case White was the code for the total Wehrmacht, panzer and Luftwaffe Stuka

Warsaw in ruins, a child in quiet despair.

dive-bomber attacks. Operation Himmler was the code for the SD under Reinhard Heydrich, Himmler's SS deputy, who would stimulate fake Polish incidents on the Danzig corridor in Operation Himmler by seizing the Gleiwitz radio station. Operation Canned Goods was a revolting plan using condemned men from concentration camps dressed in Polish uniforms who were killed beforehand by lethal injections and placed for the Nazi photographers as evidence of Polish "aggression". Hitler and Ribbentrop desperately wanted a non-agression pact with Stalin via Molotov, his Foreign Minister. The surly Russians were worried about Japanese military activities on their eastern borders and were relatively happy to sign a vast trade agreement *and* a non-aggression pact with Germany. Hitler's *der tag* for Case White was 4.30 a.m. on 26 August 1939. As the countdown for total war approached both Ribbentrop and Hitler were hysterical and close to nervous breakdowns. Moreover, England and France who had detected many signs of the impending invasion, had to be kept reassured about Hitler's peaceful intentions. Finally, Hitler could bear the suspense no longer and sent a personal telegram to Stalin. Ribbentrop flew to Moscow and eventually on 24 August the non-agression pact between Russia and Germany was signed. Hitler was ecstatic, sipped champagne although he was teetotal and exclaimed, 'Now Europe is mine – the others can have Asia. The world is in my pocket.' Hitler's armies launched their Blitzkrieg on 1 September.[5]

11.15 a.m. Sunday 3 September 1939: *'I am speaking to you from the Cabinet Room at 10 Downing Street. This morning the British Ambassador in Berlin handed the German Government a final Note stating that, unless we heard from them by 11 o'clock that they were prepared at once to withdraw their troops from Poland, a state of war would exist between us. I have to tell you now that no such undertaking has been received, and that consequently this country is at war with Germany.'*

Chamberlain – The 'Schweinehund'

The day after the Non-Aggression Treaty was signed with Russia, Hitler briefed all his top military chiefs before the assault on Poland. General Halder and Admiral Bohm recounted Hitler's speech: 'Essentially all depend on me, on my existence, because of my political talents ... no one will ever again have the confidence of the whole German people as I have ... No one knows how long I shall live. Therefore a showdown had better take place now ... A life and death struggle. The destruction of Poland has priority. A quick decision, in view of the season ... Close your hearts to pity! Act brutally! Eighty million people must obtain what is their right. Be steeled against all signs of compassion.' The only thing that worried Hitler was that Neville Chamberlain might pull another Munich on him. 'I am only afraid that some *schweinehund* will make a proposal for mediation.'[26/65]

'Destruction and Barbarism the Real Victors'

President Daladier of France exchanged letters with Hitler in the last desperate days of August 1939. Hitler had already warned the people that the political situation was very grave. A week earlier, on 21 August, the incredible volte-

The Wehrmacht marches into Warsaw.

face of the Russian-German pact was announced almost simultaneously with Hitler's arrogant demands to Poland. Daladier wrote a noble letter to the German leader asking Hitler to hold back from war, saying that there is no question which cannot be solved peacefully and reminding him that Poland was a sovereign nation. Daladier claimed that France would honour its obligations to Poland. Hitler regretted that France intended to fight to 'maintain a wrong' and said that Danzig and the Polish Corridor must be returned to Germany and that he realized full well the consequences of war. In Daladier's final letter, he said, 'If French and German blood is now to be spilled, as it was 25 years ago ... then each of the two peoples will fight confident of its own victory. But surely Destruction and Barbarism will be the real victors'.

The Chicago Gangsters

In the Danzig Guild Hall, a gothic building of great beauty, on 19 September 1939 Hitler made a conqueror's speech and ranted and roared, with carefully orchestrated effect and 'hysterical rage', mainly against Britain. A group of international journalists had been invited to the Guild Hall to hear the Führer, amongst whom was William Shirer. When Hitler, Himmler, Brueckner, Keitel and others passed him, all in dusty field grey, he noted that they were unshaven and looked like a pack of Chicago gangsters.[57]

Victorious Wehrmacht soldiers take a cigarette break and smile for the camera.

Unity Mitford's Near-Suicide Expenses

After Unity Mitford's near-suicide, Hitler personally guaranteed to pay for her treatment. Account No. 4415 at the Bayerische Gemeindebank in the name of Unity Mitford received on 1 November 1939 various payments from Hitler. Professor Magnus of the Chirurgische Universitatsklinik received over 3,000 marks. A further 1,300 marks were needed for hospital treatment and X-rays from Dr Albert Kohler. Unity had a private room in the Klinik with a nurse in constant attendance. Hitler also paid for her repatriation to England. It was a sad ending to their strange relationship.

Stalin's Amusement

A few days after the double event of the 8 November 1939 bomb attack in the Munich Bürgerbräukeller and the entrapment of British agents in the Venlo Incident, Hitler, Himmler, Heydrich and Colonel Walter Schellenberg were dining together. The latter was asked for his views and replied, 'Great Britain will fight this war with all the fury and tenacity of which she has given proof in all wars in which she was thoroughly engaged.' Even if Germany occupied England the government would conduct the war from Canada. 'It will be a life and death struggle between countries of the same stock – and Stalin will look on with interest and amusement.'[3]

'Bloodless Victories Demoralising'

After Poland was over-run in late 1939 Hitler frequently expressed this view:

'Do you think it would have been good fortune for our troops if we had taken Poland without a fight after obtaining Austria and Czechoslovakia without fighting? Believe me, not even the best army can stand that sort of thing. Victories without loss of blood are demoralising. Therefore it was not only fortunate there was no compromise: at the time we would have had to regard it as harmful and I therefore would have struck in any case.'[61]

Messrs HHHH

Churchill believed that Hitler's almost feverish efforts to secure some kind of peace treaty with England meant that his overall war strategy was 'ripe for exploitation'. One of Churchill's oldest friends was Rex Leeper, head of Special Operations 1 (SO1) part of the new Special Operations Executive (SOE). Leeper's unit was based in Woburn Abbey and specialized in political warfare. Leeper, Leonard Ingrams and Richard Crossman devised a 'Black Propaganda' scheme to fool Hitler, coded 'Messrs HHHH' which stood for Hitler, Hess, and Karl and Albrecht Haushofer, two of Hitler's geopolitical advisers. It would be a 'sting' to upset, disturb and possibly wreck Hitler's strategic plans. The plan was to encourage the Germans to attack Russia by misleading Hitler, hinting that many politicians in Britain and the USA preferred to see the overthrow of Russian communism rather than the German regime. A compromise peace between Britain and Germany would combine to destroy the *common* enemy, communism. Churchill knew that, as part of their peace treaty, Stalin was supplying Hitler with oil, petrol, food, munitions and machine parts – all the sinews of war – to end in England's destruction. Stalin's Russia in 1940 was a staunch German ally and Messrs HHHH probably helped persuade Hitler to act in Barbarossa.[3/70]

Anti-Semitism in the Inner Circle

For all his life Hitler was tormented by the thought of his Jewish blood. But most of his repulsive henchmen were in the same boat! Himmler had Jewish relatives, Rosenberg had a Jewish mistress and almost certainly Jewish ancestors. Reinhard Heydrich, chairman of the Wannsee ('the Final Solution') committee in January 1942, almost certainly had a Jewish father whose real

Clearing the streets of a village in Denmark.

name was Suss and a mother called Sarah. Goebbels was once engaged to a Jewish girl and was nicknamed 'the Rabbi' by his staff. Adolf Eichmann (1900-1962) was set up by Himmler as head of the Central Office for Jewish Emigration in Vienna. As a boy he was frequently taunted for his semitic looks and semitic family background. Karl Haushofer had a Jewish wife; Hitler's occult adviser Erik Jan Hanussen was Jewish; Luftwaffe General Milch was Jewish. Only Goering, Hess and Speer were prototype Aryans in the Hitler court. Himmler, Heydrich and Goebbels were the most rabid persecutors of the Jewish race in the Third Reich and seemed to vie with each other in their frenzied attacks.

Happy Christmas 'Cemented By Blood'

Hitler and Ribbentrop wired their Christmas greetings to Comrade Joseph Stalin in Moscow on 21 December 1939. 'Best wishes for your personal well-being as well as for the prosperous future of the peoples of the friendly Soviet Union.' To which Stalin replied, 'The friendship of the peoples of Germany and the Soviet Union, *cemented by blood*, has every reason to be lasting and firm.' Eighteen months later in Operation Barbarossa the temporary alliance certainly was 'cemented by blood' as millions of soldiers and Russian civilians were slaughtered. As Poland was being devastated by Germany and Russia at the end of 1939, Shirer, the American journalist wrote, 'And now darkness. A new world. Black-out, bombs, slaughter, Nazism. Now the night and the shrieks of barbarism.'[57]

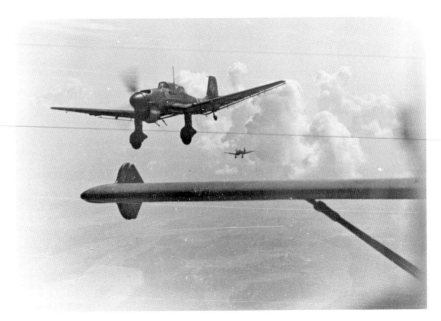

A JU 87 'Stuka' dive bomber in flight.

Hitler's Avalanche

In 1940 Hitler said to Himmler, Heydrich and Schellenberg, 'At the beginning I wanted to collaborate with Great Britain. But she rejected my advances ... our real enemies to the east wait tranquilly for Europe to be exhausted ... Churchill must understand that Germany also has the right to live. And I shall fight England till she gets off her pedestal ... The day will come when she will show herself disposed to envisage an accord between us.' The young, tough SS Colonel Schellenberg questioned his Führer, 'But a war like this is comparable to an avalanche. And who would venture to plot the course of an avalanche?' 'My dear boy,' replied Hitler, 'those are my worries. Leave them to me.'[3]

Weser Exercise

Hitler's skilful operation to seize Denmark and Norway, code name Weser Exercise, depended on the German navy seizing possession of the harbours, particularly in Norway, to give German naval forces direct access to the Atlantic and assure the flow of iron ore from neutral Sweden. On 8 April 1940 in the garden of the Chancellery, Hitler told Goebbels about the Weser Exercise, involving 250,000 men. Curiously the Führer mentioned that the Norway operation was the *only* assignment he would give the navy, implying that a

The invasion of France and the Low Countries began on 10 May 1940.

successful landing in England was hardly possible! Therefore Goebbels was told to maintain the public hatred of England at the previous level and not create expectations of an invasion of that country. On 16 July Hitler had *half-heartedly* given instructions for Operation Sealion, a landing operation on the English coast. In his diary, Goebbels noted in Hitler a certain 'fear of the water'.[52]

The British Toehold

The Norwegian campaign had been brilliantly planned by Hitler's commanders Keitel, Jodl and Raeder, although Hitler described it as 'the cheekiest operation in modern history'. Troop transports were disguised as coal steamers, with heavy equipment, artillery, ammunition and provisions concealed below the coal. Fast German warships under cover of British flags would land troops at Trondheim, Stavanger and Narvick. Two battleships and ten destroyers guarded more troop ships and the treacherous Major Quisling was waiting to form a German-controlled government. Paratroops landed and Oslo soon surrendered. But the Royal Navy sank half the German navy and two British troop landings at Namsos and Harstad brought Hitler to the verge of a nervous breakdown. In a panic he ordered the Luftwaffe to destroy Namsos and Aandalsnes and told his adjutants, 'I know the British. I came up against them in the Great War. Where they once get a toehold there is no throwing them out again.'

A clean and efficient-looking German tank with a British prisoner of war.

Annihilating England

Hitler, Goebbels and Speer were sitting in Hitler's Berlin salon in autumn 1939 watching the Luftwaffe Stuka bombers destroying Warsaw. Hitler was fascinated. The film ended with a montage of a plane diving towards the outlines of the British Isles. A burst of flame followed and the island flew into the air in tatters. Hitler's enthusiasm was unbounded. 'That is what will happen to them. That is how we will annihilate them.'[58]

De Gaulle's Help

In 1925, when Hitler was writing *Mein Kampf*, he detailed his plan to invade France through the Low Countries. This was confirmed in the secret Hossbach Memorandum of 1937. By 1940 the war was having an effect and severe rationing was unpopular, although supplies from Russia, Austria and Denmark were helping. Germany badly needed the prosperous treasure troves of the Low Countries and France. Hitler planned *Fall Gelb* ('Operation Yellow') brilliantly. On 10 May 1940 the *Blitzkrieg* started under Luftwaffe bombing of cities, Stukas dive-bombing resistance points and paratroopers dropping on fortresses and strong points. Panzer tanks thrust through Dutch, Belgian and French defences and the Fifth Column of saboteurs was in action. It was horrible but savagely effective. 'The hour of the decisive battle for the future of the German nation has come. The battle for the future of the German nation has come. The battle beginning today will decide the future of the German nation for the next thousand years,' Hitler promised on radio. Rotterdam was pulverized and Hitler threatened to do the same to Utrecht, Amsterdam and Paris. The French Maginot Line defences were bypassed and the *poilus* surrendered in their thousands. The German Rundfunk military communiqué called it 'a French rout'. Hitler refused to allow publication of casualty lists

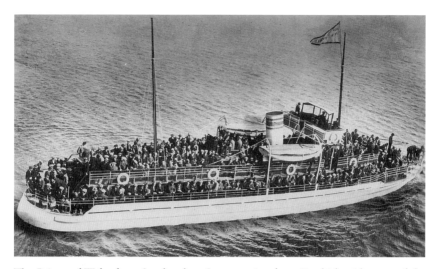

The *Prince of Wales* from Southend-on-Sea returning from Dunkirk with some of the evacuated army.

and every victory broadcast ended with the marching song, 'We march against England, Today we own Germany, Tomorrow the whole world.' Hitler claimed total credit for the success of *Fall Gelb*, 'I have again and again read Colonel de Gaulle's book on methods of modern warfare employing fully motorised units. I have learned a great deal from it.'

Dunkirk Evacuation: 'Hitler Rages and Screams'

The Wehrmacht, Luftwaffe, parachute and glider troops preceded by ten Panzer divisions had in Operation Yellow swept through the Low Countries and northern France, starting on 10 May 1940. Hitler had personally conceived the brilliant airborne drops that had captured vital bridges and the Eben Emael fortress. Over the river Meuse by 13 May the German High Command became alarmed at the success of General von Kleist's Panzer army. On the night of 16 May Hitler personally halted the Panzer advance. His chief of staff, General Franz Halder, kept a diary. '18 May. Every hour is precious, Führer's HQ sees it quite differently. Führer keeps worrying about south flank. He rages and screams that we are on the way to ruin the whole campaign. He won't have any part in continuing the operation in a westward direction [towards Dunkirk].' On 21 May a British tank counter attack near Arras caused alarm in the German Fourth Army. Hitler visited Field Marshal von Runstedt's HQ at Charleville on 24 May. General Blumentritt, a key officer at the meeting told Liddell Hart, the British military historian 'Hitler was in a very good humour.

Oil tanks burn at Dunkirk.

He admitted that the course of the campaign had been "a decided miracle" and the war would be finished in six weeks. He then astonished us by speaking with admiration of the British Empire, of the necessity for its existence and of the civilisation that Britain had brought into the world ... He concluded by saying that his aim was to make peace with Britain on a basis that she would regard as compatible with her honour to accept.' Between 27 May and 4 June 338,000 British and French troops were got away by sea – the 'miracle of Dunkirk'. On 2 June again at Charleville Hitler addressed von Rundstedt and his generals and again praised Britain and her mission for the white race!

Hitler's Revenge and Triumph

On 21 June 1940, in a little clearing in the forest of Compiègne, Hitler taking his revenge for the German capitulation in the same place in 1918, humiliated the French politicians and generals. In the middle of the clearing was the original old railway Wagon-Lit of Maréchal Foch, hauled out to its original

Right: General Charles Huntziger of France signs the armistice in the railway carriage (the *Wagon de l'Armistice*) in Compiègne, on 21 June 1940.

Below: Field Marshal Wilhelm Keitel at Compiègne.

Rommel with captured British officers at Cherbourg.

location from the museum, whose walls the Germans had just pulled down. It was a lovely summer's day and the sun beat down on the elms, oak, pines and cypress surrounding the glade at Rethondes. At 3.15 p.m. Hitler and his entourage arrived in a caravan of black Mercedes. He wore a double-breasted grey military uniform; Goering wore his sky-blue Luftwaffe uniform; Generals Keitel and von Brauchitsch wore field-grey uniforms; Grand Admiral Raeder wore a dark blue naval uniform. Rudolf Hess and Ribbentrop were there, but not Goebbels. They all read the inscription on the Alsace-Lorraine statue, which read (translated): 'Here on the eleventh of November 1918 succumbed the criminal pride of the German Empire – vanquished by the free peoples which it tried to enslave'. Hitler's face was seen to be 'afire with scorn, anger, hate, revenge, triumph'. Inside the railway carriage with the French delegation, led by General Charles Huntziger, Hitler pointedly sat in the seat Foch had occupied at the signing of the 1918 Armistice; then as a snub to the French, he walked out, leaving Keitel to negotiate – or dictate – the terms of the new armistice.[57]

Hitler's Art Tour

With a small select group Hitler visited Paris early in the morning of 28 June 1940: Speer, his invaluable architect, his adjutant Lieutenant Wilhelm Brueckner, Colonel (later General) Wilhelm Speidel (assigned by the new German Occupation Authority) and Arno Breker, Hitler's sculptor. Three days after the armistice the party flew to Le Bourget airfield and then on Hitler's

Adolf Hitler visits Paris with architect Albert Speer (left) and artist Arno Breker (right), 23 June 1940. Hitler took his favourite photographer, Heinrich Hoffman, with him to record his triumph.

art tour in three large Mercedes cars. 'He seemed fascinated by the Opera, went into ecstasies about its beauty, his eyes glittering, with an excitement that struck me [Speer] as uncanny. Then to the Madeleine, the Champs Elysées, the Trocadero, the Eiffel Tower, Arc de Triomphe, tomb of the unknown soldier, the Invalides (Hitler spent a long time examining Napoleon's tomb) and the Pantheon.' Speer noted rather sadly that Hitler displayed little interest in the most beautiful works in Paris – Place des Vosges, the Louvre, Palais de Justice, Sainte-Chapelle. He did, however, become animated by the elegant houses in the Rue de Rivoli. By 9 a.m. the tour was over. Hitler told his group, 'It was the dream of my life to see Paris. I cannot say how happy I am to have that dream fulfilled today.'[58]

The Madagascar Plan

The German Foreign Office and Central Office for Reich Security (*Reichs sischerheitshauptamt*; or the RHSA) had developed a plan for deporting all European Jews to French-owned Madagascar. On 12 July 1940 after the fall of France, Hitler had given the go-ahead to plans for deportation and declared that France had to renounce the island. He wanted a 'forced ghetto' there, accepting that there would be many casualties involved. Hans Hinkel, head

The incongruity of war; a kitten and a grenade.

of the Jewish section of the Propaganda Ministry, reported on 8 September that provided transportation was available the 72,000 Berlin Jews could be moved out in two months. On 17 September Hinkel reported to Hitler that to 'evacuate' 3.5 million European Jews to Madagascar required the successful ending of the war with Great Britain. Only in 1941 was the Madagascar plan abandoned.[52]

The Thoughtful Duchess: Operation Willi

After 1937, the exiled Duke of Windsor had been serving as a Major-General with the French military mission near Paris. The Duchess liked Paris, which was to become her home later on. After the success in 1940 of *Fall Gelb* (Operation Yellow) to knock France out of the war, the Windsors escaped through Spain to Portugal. The Duke bitterly attacked Churchill's continuation of the war and foresaw that 'protracted heavy bombardment would make Britain ready for peace'. Von Ribbentrop in Operation Willi sent Walter Schellenberg (who became head of the SS foreign intelligence department in 1941) to Lisbon to ensure that no harm came to the Duke who was living in some style in a Portuguese banker's mansion. The Duke told Schellenberg of his loathing of Churchill, of the war with Germany and of his willingness to accept high office

A Messerschmitt 109 flies along the French coast with the White Cliffs of Dover in the background.

in a defeated Britain. The Windsors' passports had been impounded by the British Embassy in Lisbon, but Schellenberg arranged that they could cross into Spain if they wished. On 11 July Ribbentrop cabled the German ambassador in Madrid that Germany would smooth the way for 'the duke and duchess to occupy the British throne'. The Duke replied that the British Constitution forbade an abdicated monarch to return to the throne. The Germany emissary suggested that a conquered Britain would need a new Constitution and 'the duchess in particular became very thoughtful.' On 1 August the Windsors flew to the Bahamas.

A Revolution in Britain?

William Shirer, the famous American journalist for CBS was allowed to visit all the Channel ports where the Wehrmacht and the German navy were making preparations for Hitler's Directive No. 16, *Unternehmen Seelöwe*, ('Operation Sealion'), for the invasion of England. On 21 July 1940 the Führer had told his generals in Berlin, 'England's situation is hopeless. The war has been won by us. A reversal of the prospects of success is impossible.' Shirer was amazed that all the preparations he saw along the coast were defensive, not offensive. When, on Hitler's orders, Goering launched *Unternehmen Adlerangriff* ('Operation

An RAF ground crew and armourers prepare a Spitfire in readiness to fend off a Luftwaffe attack.

Eagle Attack') he saw the daily Luftwaffe attacking planes leaving the French airfields for the huge onslaught of 15 and 16 August. But Berliners were stunned when on the night of 25 August the RAF bombed Berlin – which Goering had assured them was impossible. Hitler kept on deferring a decision to invade England and when on 16 September the RAF smashed a large German training exercise at sea, Hitler did three things. He stepped up plans for Barbarossa, the invasion of Russia; he sanctioned indiscriminate mass bombing of London; and on 12 October he postponed *Seelöwe* until the spring of 1941. According to a senior officer in OKW (Armed Forces High Command), Lieutenant-Colonel Bernhard von Lossberg, Hitler quite seriously expected a revolution to break out in Britain as a result of the devastating bombing of London.[57]

Operation Moonlight Sonata

When the RAF bombed Munich rather lightly in early November 1940, Hitler personally demanded revenge for this insult. 'Operation Moonlight Sonata' was the codename for the Luftwaffe attack of Kampfgeshwader 100 bombers

The twisted wreckage of a double-decker bus in London, 1940.

– 450 of them – which attacked Coventry on the night of 14 November. A 'pathfinder' squadron was equipped with an *X-Gerät* or X-beam computerized system to guide them to their target. A continuous radio beam to the target changed its note if the bomber strayed from its line; near the target a second and third beam cut across the first, indicating 'bombs away'. Churchill called this 'The wizard war'. The problem was partly solved by a brilliant young scientific officer, R. V. Jones, who jammed or diverted the Luftwaffe's X-beam.

Unlimited Power

General Gotthardt Heinrice noted a Hitler speech at the end of 1940: he said that he was the first man since Charlemagne to hold unlimited power in his own hand. He did not hold the power in vain but would know how to use it in a struggle for Germany. If war were not won that would mean Germany had not stood the test of strength; in that case she would deserve to be, and would be, doomed.

Luftwaffe crew in a Heinkel 111, 1940.

Bunkers

When the RAF air raids became heavier after the token efforts of 1940, Hitler issued orders for substantial bunkers to be built for his personal protection. As the calibre and weight of the British (and later American) bombs increased, so did the thickness of the concrete roofs of the bunkers. Eventually the concrete depth reached sixteen-and-a-half feet. There were Hitler bunker systems built in Rastenburg, in Berlin, in Pullach near Munich, in the guest palace near Salzburg, at Obersaltzberg, at the Nauheim HQ, a complex near the river Somme, and, late in the war, in two underground HQs in the Silesian and Thuringian mountains. Biggest of all was the 'Giant' near Bad Charlottenbrunn, which cost 150 millions marks to build with its 328,000 cubic yards of reinforced concrete, six bridges, 36 miles of roads and 62 miles of pipes. Of course, all the Gauleiters – on orders from their Führer – had additional shelters and bunkers built for their safety. Goering built substantial underground installations at Carinhall and Veldenstein near Nuremberg, and the 50-mile road from Carinhall to Berlin had to be provided with concrete shelters at regular intervals.

Another He-111 on its way to bomb England.

London's Burning

Late in 1940 Hitler made a speech in the Chancellery. 'Have you ever looked at a map of London? It is so closely built up that one source of fire alone would suffice to destroy the whole city, as happened once before two hundred years ago. Goering wants to use innumerable incendiary bombs of a new type to create sources of fire in all parts of London. Fires everywhere. Thousands of them. Then they'll unite in one gigantic area conflagration. Goering has the right idea. Explosive bombs don't work, but it can be done with incendiary bombs – total destruction of London.' Operations 'Sealion' and 'Adlertag' (Eagle Day), the proposed invasion of Britain, and the air offensive known as the 'Battle of Britain' had failed. Hitler turned to the planning of Barbarossa, the destruction of Russia, and allowed Goering's Luftwaffe to attempt to destroy London.[58]

The Greatest Conqueror?

William Shirer watched in mounting horror and fascination as Hitler crushed the human spirit and freedom in Germany, persecuted the Jews and then destroyed them and anyone who opposed him, and dragged his nation towards war. Most Germans happily endorsed this 'Nazi barbarism'. Shirer observed the political, social and military scene, mainly in Berlin, from the summer of 1934 until December 1940, fifteen months after Hitler plunged Europe into war. 'When I departed Berlin, German troops after their quick and easy conquests of Poland, Denmark, Norway, Holland, Belgium and France, stood watch from the North Cape to the Pyrenees, from the Atlantic to beyond the Vistula. Britain stood alone. Few doubted that Hitler would emerge from the conflict as the greatest conqueror since Napoleon. Not many believed that Britain would survive.'[57]

Operation Sealion

Hitler's detailed plan for the invasion of England is in a 446-page volume *Militargeographiske Angaben uber England Südküste*. It detailed every attack point between Lands End and Foreness Point in Kent. The main attack would be with six divisions directed on Kent via Ramsgate and Folkestone. Two groups of several divisions would invade Dorset via Lynne Bay, and Hampshire and Sussex via Brighton and the Isle of Wight. Very detailed maps showed contours, rivers, railways, shingle or quicksand and of course towns, villages, streets and roads. Many postcards were available to show landmarks such as Brighton Pier, Penzance and Lands End.

Three factors influenced the Führer's final decision: Hermann Goering's Luftwaffe failed to destroy the RAF fighter squadrons; the Royal Navy was still a major force to thwart Admiral Doenitz's naval assault convoys; and Hitler in his heart of hearts preferred Operation Barbarossa – the invasion of Stalin's Russia. But it was a close-run thing, as the Duke of Wellington would have said.

Hess's Dramatic Exit

On the night of 10 May 1941, a Scots farmer was more than a little surprised to come across a German in Luftwaffe uniform with a broken ankle. The man said to him in careful English, 'I have an important message for the Duke of Hamilton.' He was quickly arrested.

Rudolf Hess had left Augsburg airport earlier that evening – anxious it is thought, to impress his Führer by sealing a peace agreement with Britain – and thus ensuring a German victory – and had secretly flown to Scotland and parachuted in to talk peace terms with the Duke of Hamilton.

Hitler, Goering, Ribbentrop and Bormann were horrified and distinctly panicky, 'If Hess really gets there just imagine: Churchill has Hess in his grasp! What lunacy on Hess's part. They will give Hess some drug or other

Rudolf Hess
(1894-1987).

Goebbels with
a new recruit to
the *Deutsches
Jungvolk*,
c. 1940

to make him stand before a microphone and broadcast whatever Churchill wants' were Hitler's immediate reactions. After ten attempts at an official communiqué Hitler insisted on the inclusion of the phrase, 'it was the action of a madman'. The British had in any case quickly come to the same conclusion – even if he was not mad, he was certainly mentally ill. Hess had been at Hitler's side since the Great War: served in the same regiment, marched with him in the beer hall putsch, was in prison with him at Landsberg, he was a very close friend and colleague and the whole world was astonished. In the event Hess achieved nothing and remained in captivity for the rest of his life, dying in Spandau prison, Berlin, in 1987. Hitler later always emphasized how much 'he had esteemed his friend, upright and honest until he was led astray'.

Some leading Nazis relax; Hewel, Speer and Karl Brandt *c.* 1940.

Himmler presents a painting to Hitler as a birthday gift.

Hitler's Clockwork Precision

John 'Jock' Colville, Churchill's Assistant Private Secretary, was a friend of Herschel Johnson, Minister at the American Embassy in London. Colville had an interesting thesis, that 'Hitler had been so impressed by the skill of his own staff work and by the speed and regularity with which his objects (up to July 1941) had been achieved, that he has ceased to believe anything impossible. Whereas our authorities are apt to take a gloomy view of an operation and in any case to prepare a very slow timetable, German [land] operations have invariably succeeded. German squadrons and divisions are moved from east to west or north to south in as many days as our forces require weeks. Thus I believe that Hitler did not contemplate the possibility of a check in Russia. Everything would work out with the same clockwork precision as before.'[13]

Blondi (1941-1945), given to Hitler as a gift by Martin Bormann. On 30 April 1945 Hitler tested a cyanide tablet on Blondi to ensure it was effective before taking his own life.

The Unknown Painter

'I must say' wrote Hitler in July 1941, 'I always enjoy meeting the Duce. He is a great personality. It's curious to think that, at the same period as myself he was working in the building trade in Germany ... If the Duce were to die it would be a great misfortune for Italy. As I walked with him in the gardens of the Villa Borghese, I could easily compare his profile with that of the Roman busts and I realized he was one of the Caesars. There's no doubt at all that Mussolini is the heir of the great men of that period. Despite their weaknesses, the Italians have so many qualities that make us like them. The Italian people's musical sense ... the beauty of its race ... The magic of Florence and Rome, of Ravenna, Siena, Perugia! Tuscany and Umbria, how lovely they are! ... My dearest wish would be able to wander about in Italy as an unknown painter.'

One of the Jewels of Europe

Field Marshal Guenter von Kluge asked Hitler on the evening of 29 October 1941 for his views on Paris, which he had visited the year before.

'I was very happy to think that there was at least one city in the Reich that was superior to Paris from the point of view of taste – I mean, Vienna. The old part of Paris gives a feeling of complete distinction. The great vistas are imposing ... At present Berlin doesn't exist but one day she'll be more beautiful than Paris. It

Molotov in Berlin, 12 November 1940. Later Molotov continued his talks with the German Foreign Minister, Ribbentrop. Their meeting was interrupted with an air raid on Berlin by the RAF. They moved to Ribbentrop's private air raid shelter to continue the meeting. Allegedly Molotov was treated to a long monologue by Ribbentrop on why the British were 'finished', leading Molotov to comment: *If that is so – then why are we in this shelter – and whose are those bombs that are falling?*

Wehrmacht training camp in Poland, spring 1941.

was a relief to me that we weren't obliged to destroy Paris … Every finished work is of value as an example. The Ring in Vienna would not exist without the Paris boulevards. It's a copy of them.' Hitler approved of the Invalides, the Madeleine, the Paris Opéra and the Eiffel Tower but found the Sacré Coeur appalling and the Panthéon a horrible disappointment (the busts were alright but the sculptures!). 'But on the whole, Paris remains one of the jewels of Europe.'[58]

Blondi – Hitler's Favourite

Since 1921 Hitler had owned dogs, including a sheepdog called Muck and a sheepdog bitch called Blondi. 'I love animals and especially dogs', he recalled. He thought that sheepdogs were 'extraordinary – lovely, loyal, bold, courageous and handsome'. Blondi was unusual in that she was a vegetarian, like her master, and enjoyed eating herbs! Nevertheless Hitler, as he was a dog owner, made a point of washing his hands for hygiene reasons.

Blondi was taken everywhere, to all of Hitler's headquarters, and was only fed by her owner. Speer noted them together, 'The dog probably occupied the most important role in Hitler's private life. He meant more to his master than the Führer's closest associates.' During conferences that lasted for hours Blondi would lie down in a particular corner with a protesting growl and slowly inch herself closer and closer until, after elaborate canine manoeuvres, she placed her snout on Hitler's knee – only to be banished back to her corner.[58]

The initial attack in Operation Barbarossa, 21 July 1941.

Operation Barbarossa, July 1941.

'That Cunning Caucasian'

Three weeks after the successful launch of Operation Barbarossa, Hitler told his dinner companions 'Stalin is one of the most extraordinary figures in world history. He began as a small clerk and he has never stopped being a clerk. Stalin owes nothing to rhetoric [unlike the speaker!]. He governs from his office thanks to a bureaucracy that obeys his every nod and gesture. It's striking that Russian propaganda, in the criticisms it makes of us, always holds itself within certain limits. Stalin, that cunning Caucasian, is apparently quite ready to abandon European Russia if he thinks that a failure to solve her problems would cause him to lose everything. Let nobody think Stalin might reconquer Europe from the Urals ... This is the catastrophe that will cause the loss of the Soviet Empire.' Hitler's armies had made extraordinary progress in Barbarossa and it looked as though Moscow would be taken by Christmas 1941. But when Stalin's son was captured Hitler ordered that he should be given especially good treatment.[61]

Hitler on Jewry

Himmler and the equally evil SS General Reinhard Tristan Heydrich (1904-42) were Hitler's dinner guests on 25 October 1941. Hitler told them, 'From the rostrum of the Reichstag I prophesied to Jewry that in the event of war's proving inevitable, the Jew would disappear from Europe. That race of criminals has on its conscience the two million dead of the first World War

186

Above: 'Digging in' shortly after the advance in Russia.

Right: Reinhard Tristan Heydrich (1904-1942).

and now already hundreds of thousands more. Let nobody tell me that all the same we can't park them in the marshy parts of Russia! Who's worrying about our troops? It's not a bad idea by the way that public rumour attributes to us a plan to exterminate the Jews. Terror is a salutory thing. The attempt to create a Jewish State will be a failure.'

By 1941 there were already many concentration camps including Ravensbrück and Auschwitz. Himmler himself ordered that Birkenau in Poland should become a killing centre for Russian officers and that Chelmno, also in Poland, should be the first extermination camp: both of these in 1941, before the cosy little supper party with the Führer.

Hitler with Generalissimo Francisco Franco (1892-1975), during Hitler's only official meeting with Franco at Hendaye, France, 23 October 1940.

'Let the English Come to their Senses Soon'

Christa Schroeder, Hitler's personal secretary, spent nine weeks in Hitler's 'Wolf's Lair' in the summer of 1941. The Führer showed no political restraint or secrecy and talked freely to Christa (and Daranowski). She wrote frequently to her friend Joanna Nusser. On 20 August Hitler's views were: 'There is nothing I want more deeply than for the English to propose peace once we've taken care of Russia ... I can't understand why the English are being so unreasonable. Once we've spread out to the east we won't need their colonies ... It's all so simple and makes so much sense. Please God, let the English come to their senses soon.'

Operation Unternehmen Feurzauber

In September 1936 Hitler was anxious to support General Francisco Franco's forces in their fight in the Spanish Civil War. So 'Operation Magic Fire' (derived from Siegfried's ring of fire to rescue Brünnhilde) was launched and showered largesse on Franco; the Condor Legion (Luftwaffe) and nearly 7,000 military were despatched. Spain was now the battlefield against the 'Bolshevik wire-pullers' of Russia. But a face-to-face meeting on 23 October 1940 in Hitler's train at the frontier town of Hendaye was distinctly unsatisfactory. The fat little

Caudillo listened to a long harangue. Hitler proposed an alliance with Spain to join in the Axis war in January 1941, to be rewarded by the 'gift' of Gibraltar. However, Franco had a long shopping list for armaments, munitions and food products. The meeting was not fruitful. Franco told his Foreign Minister, 'These people [Hitler and Ribbentrop] are intolerable.' And in Florence a few days later Hitler told Mussolini, 'He would prefer to have 3 or 4 teeth taken out than another nine hours with Franco.'

The Path to War with America

President Roosevelt's naval policy was to keep the sea routes open to Europe and not to be intimidated by Hitler's submarine blockade. The March 1941 Lend Lease agreement made between Roosevelt and Churchill, which meant extensive American and British merchant ships carrying cargo across the North Atlantic, spurred on Hitler's U-boat fleet. Admiral Raeder wanted to attack US merchant shipping, which Hitler flatly refused. In September 1941 the US destroyer *Greer* was attacked and Roosevelt gave a 'shoot on sight' order. In October the USS *Kearney* was attacked and the USS *Reuben James* sunk. On 28 November the Japanese were suggesting a military alliance with Germany for a war against the USA and Great Britain. On 4 December Hitler had already decided to go to war against America, hoping that the Americans would have to fight two naval wars, giving him more time to finalize the Russian campaign. Nevertheless the news on 7 December of the Japanese attack on the American fleet came as a complete surprise to Hitler (as it did to Churchill). Ribbentrop was ordered to tell the American chargé d'affaires, Leland Morris, on 11 December that Germany now declared war on the USA. Hitler then told the Reichstag that war had been declared, blaming Roosevelt for provoking war.

Ribbentrop addresses the audience gathered to witness the signing of the Three Power Pact, establishing the Rome-Berlin-Tokyo Axis, 27 September 1940.

Goebbels was delighted and said 'the USA will need all their military weapons to fight Japan, not supply England'. Hitler then signed the German-Italian-Japanese tripartite agreement with the 'unshakeable decision' not to lay down their arms until the war against the USA and England was won.[52]

Mixed Feelings about the Fall of Singapore

Yosuke Matsuoka, the Japanese Foreign Minister, visited Moscow and Berlin in March 1941. Both von Ribbentrop and Hitler were anxious for Japan to strike and seize Singapore, the key target to start the destruction of the British Empire.

Hitler boasted to Matsuoka: 'Since the war began the many German military triumphs include the elimination of sixty Polish, six Norwegian, eighteen Dutch, twenty-two Belgian and one-hundred-and-thirty-eight French divisions. Also twelve or thirteen British divisions have been driven from the Continent. The real U-boat warfare was just beginning. In the air Germany had complete supremacy. The effectiveness of the German blockade has made rationing more severe in England than in Germany.'

In the next year Singapore was captured and Hitler told von Ribbentrop: 'This is wonderful though perhaps also sad news.' And he said to the Romanian leader, Antonescu: 'We've got to think in centuries. One day the showdown with the yellow race will come.'

General Heinz Guderian (1885-1954).

A Führer Rage

General Heinz Guderian (1885-1954) was Hitler's most famous tank and panzer expert. Rommel will be remembered for his Afrikakorps successes and ultimate failure in Africa and perhaps Normandy, but Guderian's record with command of armour in Poland, the Low Countries, France and Russia was far superior. Blunt and outspoken to Hitler's face in his criticisms of the other's decisions, he describes a Führer rage. 'His fists raised, his cheeks flushed with anger, his whole body trembling, the man stood in front of me beside himself with fury, having lost all self-control. After each outburst Hitler would stride up and down the carpet edge, then suddenly stop immediately in front of me and hurl his next accusation in my face. He was almost screaming, his eyes seemed almost to pop out of his head and the veins stood out on his temples.' On Christmas Day 1941 Hitler fired Guderian for carrying out a sensible withdrawal in contravention of Hitler's specific order. He was reinstated in March 1943, became Army Chief of Staff and was fired again by Hitler on 28 March 1945. It took immense personal bravery to stand up to the Führer and many who tried ended up in concentration camps – or worse.

Syphilis

There is an unpleasant chapter in *Mein Kampf* about syphilis and it is possible that Hitler associated with prostitutes during his time in Vienna. He certainly insisted on taking Gustl Kubizek on a tour of the red-light district.

Hitler's medical condition has been debated extensively; it is thought that he contracted syphilis in Vienna before the First World War and by the 1940s was suffering badly from its effect. His mania in his last years was indicative of the condition and he had an abnormal heartbeat that suggested syphilitic aortitis. The diary kept by Dr Theodor Morell, Hitler's favourite doctor, gives some circumstantial evidence. Hitler was prone to encephalitis, dizziness, flatulence, neck pustules, chest pain, gastric pain and restrictive palsies, which are all symptoms of syphilis.

Morell was dismissed by Hitler in 1944 when his medical rivals gained the upper hand. He buried his diaries near his private bunker at Bad Reichenhall at the end of the war. Captured by the Allies, but not prosecuted, he died in 1948.[42]

Field Marshal Wilhelm Bodewin Johann Gustav Keitel (1882-1946).

Nacht und Nebel

In December 1941 Hitler ordered Wilhelm Keitel, Chief of Staff of the OKW (*Ober Kommando der Wehrmacht*) to issue *Nacht und Nebel* (Night and Fog). This was one of the most terrifying 'laws' of the Third Reich. The Gestapo and SD (*Sicherheitsdienst*), Himmler's and Heydrich's brutal intelligence and security body of the Nazi Party, could seize <u>any</u> person they thought dangerous in Germany or occupied territories and these prisoners would vanish into the Night and Fog, never to be seen or heard of again. No questions would be answered about the prisoner's charge, whereabouts or fate. People arrested were lost to the outside world. Keitel wrote: 'Effective and lasting intimidation can only be achieved by <u>capital</u> punishment or by means which leave the population in the dark about the fate of the culprit.' Keitel was sentenced to death at the Nuremberg Trials and hanged there in 1946.

It was one of the most horrific and macabre of Hitler's orders – the knock on the door at night ...

Hitler's Peace Feelers

In 1941 the British government issued a report to the British Ambassador, Lord Halifax, for confidential information to President Roosevelt, on *sixteen* peace attempts made by the German government between the summers of

Martin Ludwig Bormann (1900-1945).

1939 and 1941. Some came with Hitler's overt blessing, some more deviously through intermediaries in Sweden, Switzerland, Spain or Portugal. Amongst the intermediaries were the Papal Nuncio, King Gustav V of Sweden, the German Ambassador in Washington and General Franco. Lord Halifax had been privy to many of these peace feelers in his previous capacity as Foreign Secretary. Hitler's 'players' included Hitler's personal legal adviser Dr Ludwig Weissauer, Franz von Papen, Josef Goebbels, Reichsbank president Hjalmar Schacht, former German war minister Dr Gessler, Hermann Goering and Heinrich Himmler (four times). But from the moment that Winston Churchill became Prime Minister, the answer was categorically negative.[71]

The Führer's Peasant Shadow – 'Mephistopheles'

A grey, inconspicuous, hardworking, crafty bureaucrat, Reichsleiter Martin Bormann was Hitler's shadow from 1934 onwards. Initially secretary to Hess, he wormed his way into becoming indispensable to Hitler, and by 1942 he had, with Hitler's compliance, succeeded in controlling his Führer's appointments calender. So no civilian members of the government or party, including ministers, Reichsleiters or Gauleiters, could gain access to Hitler without Bormann's approval. Bormann also controlled Hitler's personal finances. Even Eva Braun had to ask him for maintenance funds. The vast building complex of Hitler's Obersalzberg was under his control. The military chieftains could

Three of Bormann's nine children with Hitler at the Berghof *c.* 1941. The three eldest boys were named Adolf, Rudolf and Heinrich respectively after Hitler, Hess and Himmler. Clearly Bormann was not concerned about sycophancy.

gain access easily through Hitler's three or four military adjutants, although their purse-strings were controlled by Bormann. He accompanied his master on every trip and never left his side in the Chancellery until Hitler went to bed early in the morning. On 12 April 1943 Bormann became officially 'Secretary to the Führer' and he was hardworking, reliable and ultimately indispensable. However Speer thought that he was a brutal, coarse, uncultured subordinate who behaved like a peasant. His nickname was 'Mephistopheles'.

Hitler's Simple Swashbucklers

When Hitler came to power he organized a system for Greater Germany of forty-three regions (*gau*) run by a *leite* who was appointed personally by him. In December 1942 all *gau* became Reich defence districts and the Gauleiters became Reich defence commissioners. One rule was that no deputy could succeed his chief as gauleiter. 'In this way, we National Socialists guard ourselves against a stab in the back' Hitler wrote. He was displeased with the Gauleiter of Salzburg and sent him to Syria. Another rule was that no office in *gau* or state or party was hereditary. Moreover under Hitler's policy of 'divide and conquer' all the gauleiters, as party functionaries, reported to Bormann, but if a matter of defence, reported to Himmler, the Minister of the Interior.

Goering, Hitler and Speer, August 1943.

Rudolf Schmundt (left) Karl Friedrich Otto Wolff (centre) and Himmler. General Schmunt (1896-1944) died from wounds following the Operation Valkyrie attempt on Hitler. Wolff (1900-1984) was a General of the Waffen-SS. He became Chief of Personal Staff to Himmler and SS Liaison Officer to Hitler until his replacement in 1943.

Hitler advised Speer: 'never underestimate their [*gauleiters*] power.' He was aware of their shortcomings: 'many were simple-hearted swashbucklers, rather rough, but loyal'.

Hitler's View on Character

'I consider [4 April 1942] that the only men suited to become rulers are those who have valiantly proved themselves in war. In my eyes firmness of character is more precious than any other quality. A well-toughened character can be the characteristic of a man who in other respects is quite ignorant. The men who should be set at the head of the army are the toughest, bravest, boldest and above all the most stubborn and hardest to wear down. The same men are also the best chosen for posts at the head of State – otherwise the pen ends by rotting away what the sword has conquered. In his own sphere the statesman must be ever more courageous than the soldier who leaps from his trench to face the enemy.'

On Women

'At this period [1925] I knew a lot of women. Several of them became attached to me. Why then didn't I marry? To leave a wife behind me? At the slightest imprudence, I ran the risk of going back to prison for six years. So there could be no question of marriage for me. I therefore had to renounce certain opportunities that offered themselves.'

And again later in 1942, looking back Hitler remarked. 'It's lucky I'm not married. For me marriage would have been a disaster. There's a point at which misunderstanding is bound to arise between man and wife; it's when the husband cannot give his wife all the time she feels entitled to demand. As long as only other couples are involved, one hears women say "I don't understand Frau So-and-so. *I* wouldn't behave like that." But when she herself is involved, every woman is unreasonable to the same degree. One must understand this demandingness. A woman who loves her husband lives only for his sake. That's why, in her turn, she expects her spouse to live likewise for *her* sake. It's only after maternity that the woman discovers that other realities exist in life for her. The man on the other hand is a slave to his thoughts. The idea of his duties rules him. He necessarily has moments when he wants to throw the whole thing overboard, wife and children too.'

Henchmen in Disarray

Towards the end of 1942 Hitler's coterie of powerful ministers split into two groups competitive with each other. Martin Bormann was allied with Field Marshal Keitel and Hans Lammers (Reich Minister and chief of the Reich Chancellery) and they formed the 'Council of Three'. Goebbels, Speer, Walter Funk and Robert Ley, who all had academic university backgrounds, with Goering's support, formed a loose bloc with the object of curbing the Council of Three's increasing control of access to the Führer. Hitler's almost total preoccupation with the running of the war front meant that the political, economic and social control of the German peoples was being usurped by the Council of Three. Himmler, the most dangerous man in Germany, controlled the brutal SS activities in Germany and the occupied territories and was almost a law unto himself. Goering, still Hitler's No. 2 and successor-designate, was now drug-ridden with morphine, enormously fat (a side-effect of the morphine addiction), preferring to devote himself to his magnificent collection of looted jewellery and paintings; he was a shadow of his earlier brilliant self. As the Luftwaffe failed to protect the German cities from the RAF Goering was frequently in disgrace with Hitler.

Stalin – 'Half Beast, Half Giant'

The failure to capture Moscow had changed Hitler's attitude to Stalin. In July 1942 Hitler told his dinner guests, 'The arms and equipment of the Russian armies are the best proof of its efficiency in the handling of industrial manpower. Stalin, too, must command our unconditional respect. In his own way he is a hell of a fellow! He knows his models, Genghis Khan and the others, very well and the scope of his industrial planning is exceeded only by our own Four Year Plan.' Hitler was sure that Stalin would create total employment unlike such 'capitalist States such as the USA'. A month later, on 9 August 1942, he was telling three Gauleiters over the evening meal, that 'had it not been for the mud and rain last October we should have been in Moscow in no time. We have now learnt that the moment rain comes, we must stop everything ... Stalin is half beast, half giant. To the social side of life he is utterly indifferent. The people can rot for all he cares. If we had given him another ten years, Europe would have been swept away ... Without the German Wehrmacht it would have been all up with Europe even now.'[61]

Hitler's Party Treasurer and Book Keeper

Franz Xaver Schwarz (1875-1947) joined the Nazi party in 1922 and as he was an accountant in the Munich city government, he became party treasurer four years later. This short, plump, bald, pedantic man was one of Hitler's 'old comrades' and a member of the close circle. In February 1925 he became party treasurer and controlled membership subscriptions. He was the quintessential book keeper. In April 1929 Hitler wrote a very explicit letter to his niece Geli Raubal, which fell into a blackmailer's hands. Schwarz arranged the required pay-off. In the 1934 'thank you notes' Schwarz came second, behind Hess in Hitler's list of thirteen main supporters, although Martin Bormann started to take control of Hitler's personal finances. On a February evening in 1942 Hitler told Himmler, 'It's unbelievable what the Party owes Schwarz. It was thanks to the good order in which he kept our finances that we were able to develop so rapidly and wipe out the other parties. Schwarz only reports to me once a year.' Hitler was delighted that he need not bother about affairs of administration. Three years later Schwarz burned all party financial documents in the Munich Brown House.[29]

Hans Heinrich Lammers (1879-1962), centre.

Hitler: 'Extraordinarily Humane' to Jews

The special guests for lunch with their Führer on 23 January 1942 were Himmler, Hans Heinrich Lammers (1879-1962), Head of Administration in the Reich Chancellery, and Colonel Kurt von Zeitzler, Chief of Staff of Army (OKH). Hitler told them, 'The Jew must clear out of Europe. Otherwise no understanding will be possible between Europeans. It's the Jew who prevents everything. When I think about it, I realise that I'm extraordinarily humane ... For my part, I restrict myself to telling them they must go away ... But if they refuse to go voluntarily, I see no other solution but extermination ... Why did the Jew provoke this war?'

The Wannsee Conference – to discuss 'the Jew' – had been held just three days before.[61]

The Wannsee Conference

In the SS RSHA headquarters at a villa in Wannsee, Berlin one of the most infamous meetings of the twentieth century took place. On 20 January 1942 most of Hitler's henchmen were gathered together to plan the 'Final Solution',

The villa at 56-58 Am Grossen in the Berlin suburb of Wannsee where the Conference was held on 20 January 1942.

Operation Anthropoid was the code name for the assassination of Heydrich. The operation was carried out in Prague on 27 May 1942 by Czech operatives after having been prepared by the British Special Operations Executive. Heydrich died from his injuries on 4 June 1942.

the extermination of the Jewish population of the Third Reich. It was carefully managed. Hitler passed the buck to his No. 2, Hermann Goering, who passed the buck to Himmler, head of the SS, who in turn ducked out and made Reinhard Heydrich chairman of the meeting. Adolf Eichmann, the RSHA deportation expert, took the minutes. The Gestapo chief, Heinrich Mueller was there, Otto Lange, Karl Schoengarth, Josef Buehler, the State Secretary, Dr Stuckart, Minister of the Interior, and Dr Roland Freiser, Minister of Justice – fifteen in all. Himmler's plan was to spread the responsibility across as many departments as possible. At no point was killing mentioned. Directives were agreed to move all Jews to the east as part of the 'territorial solution'. Heydrich's view was that the vast labour pool created by the deportations to the east would be used for road building and construction projects (with a high death rate).

The Wannsee Conference was a key stepping stone to the 'Final Solution'. All fifteen representatives of the Third Reich were thus guilty of orchestrating mass murder.

Nuclear Research, Stage Two

Goebbels' diary of 21 March 1942 noted, 'Research into the realm of atomic destruction has now proceeded to a point where results may possibly be used in the present war. It is essential that we should keep ahead of everybody.'

General Friedrich Fromm, Chief of Army Armaments, suggested to Albert Speer in April 1942 that the only chance of Germany winning the war lay in developing a weapon with totally new effects. From 1937 to 1940 the army had spent 550 million marks on the development of a large rocket which produced at Peenemunde the first V for Vengeance weapons. On 6 May 1942 Speer proposed to Hitler that Goering be placed at the head of the Reich Research Council, thus emphasizing its importance. Speer chaired a meeting at Harnack House, the Berlin centre of the Kaiser Wilhelm Gesellschaft, with Field Marshal Erhard Milch, armaments chief of the Luftwaffe, General Fromm, Admiral Karl Witzell and various scientists, including Nobel Prize-winners Otto Hahn and Werner Heisenberg. Professor Heisenberg was bitter about the lack of support for nuclear research in Germany.

Hitler Denies his Roots

Driving from Budweis to Krems in 1942 Speer noticed a large plaque on a house in the village of Spital, close to the Czech border. The wording on it read

'The Führer lived here in his youth'. Speer later mentioned this to Hitler, who flew into a rage and shouted for Martin Bormann, who hurried up, scared. Hitler snarled at him, 'How many times had he said that this village [Spital] must never be mentioned. That idiot of a Gauleiter had gone and put up a plaque. It must be removed at once.' Hitler was ashamed of his father and of his early upbringing. Linz and Braunau 'roots' were fine, but not Spital where Alois Schicklgruber, born illegitimately, had lived.

A few years later, Hitler's legal advisor and a Nazi Party member, Hans Frank, passed the time before his execution for crimes against humanity by writing an account of his life. In it he alleged that in 1930 Hitler had commissioned him to investigate his unknown grandfather. Frank claimed to have discovered that the grandfather was a young Austrian Jew named Frankenberger for whose family Hitler's grandmother, Maria Anna Schicklgruber, worked as a housemaid. She had given birth on 7 June 1837 in House 13, Strones, in the Austrian Walviertel region, to Alois, who would become Hitler's father. Maria subsequently married Johann Georg Hiedler, but it was not until 1876 that Alois Schicklgruber, aged nearly 40, took his birth certificate to the local priest, who agreed to make an illegal entry in the blank space, spelling the required name of Hiedler as Hitler. He was now officially Alois Hitler. There is, however, no concrete evidence of Frank having passed his 'discoveries' on to Hitler, or of any connection with a family called Frankenberger.

Johann Georg himself could have been the father – or perhaps his married brother, Johann Nepomuk Hiedler, with whom Alois went to live ... in Spital. Adolf's mother – Alois's third wife – was Johann Nepomuk's granddaughter.

It seems certain that Hitler was worried that something damaging might be found out about his ancestry – at worst that his grandfather had been Jewish; or that he was born of an incestuous relationship, which, combined with accounts of insanity in the family, had serious implications. Altogether an embarrassment for the leader of a party whose aim was to 'maintain the purity of the German Master Race'.

Führerprotokoll

During the twelve years of the Third Reich, Hitler issued 94 *Führerprotokolle* with a total of 2,222 points of discussion. Usually Bormann and Speer would write up the minutes afterwards. The decisions would be either 'The Führer has decided ...' crisp and clear, or 'In the Führer's opinion ...' which was a neutral viewpoint not necessarily calling for action. All are to be found in the Federal Archives (Bundesarchiv) in Koblenz. At these Führer conferences Speer would produce experts to confront Hitler, very, very politely, if he had made a decision on inadequate data.

From the outbreak of war in 1939 Hitler dominated all the main static campaigns, particularly on the Russian front. There was a distinct pattern to his situation conferences. They started every day at noon and lasted two or three hours. Hitler was the only person seated, usually in an armchair with a rush seat, and the chosen participants stood around the large map table. The key generals, Keitel, Modl and Zeitler, often Himmler, all the adjutants, OKW, Army General Staff and Waffen SS staff and liaison officers attended. On the rare occasions that Goering attended he had a special strong upholstered stool to support 'der Grosse'. Desk lamps with long swinging arms illuminated the maps. Keitel presented Hitler with agendas, covering orders or reprimands for signature. First the eastern theatre of war would be discussed. Three or four strategic maps pasted together, each of them about eight feet by five feet, were laid out in front of Hitler. Every detail of the previous day was entered on the maps, every advance, even minor patrols, and the Chief of Staff explained each entry. Bit by bit the maps were pushed further up the table – longer discussions was devoted to the important situations. The 'Bohemian corporal' pushed divisions back and forth. He revelled in petty details. He thought that by scrutiny of maps and their terrain he could influence the battlefronts. And of course strategic withdrawals were never allowed. Very few of his generals dared stand up to him. Speer noted that after autumn 1942 it became much more difficult to oppose Hitler on important questions. So Bormann, Keitel and Lammers decided to act as a committee to sift all the divergent views and proposals before they were put on the protocol agenda.

Churchill Stirring up Trouble

SO1's first 'sting' was successful. Using many intermediaries Hitler had been encouraged to believe that Lord Halifax might move to oust Churchill from the Premiership and negotiate an armistice with Germany. Despite the Hess defection to seek a peaceful solution via the Duke of Hamilton, Hitler still did not know the true state of British politicians' resolve to keep on fighting. SO1 was renamed Political Warfare Executive or PWE and was now under the leadership of Churchill's staunch friend, Brendan Bracken. Their main activities were to try to lure Himmler via his trusted Schellenberg, to sue for peace and perhaps overthrow Hitler in the process. Himmler made half a dozen efforts via Stockholm and Madrid to establish a 'concordat'; Churchill, of course, and the PWE had no intention of signing a peace agreement. But the PWE tried to stir up trouble amongst the Führer's top brass.[3]

Hitler with Speer and Keitel, 15 March 1942.

Nuclear Research, Stage Three

The Nobel Prize-winning physicist Professor Werner Heisenberg reported in 1942 on 'Atom smashing' and the development of the uranium machine and the cyclotron – a particle accelerator or atom-smashing machine. He declared that Germany had found the scientific solution of nuclear fission and that theoretically, building an atomic bomb was possible, *but* there was a lack of funds and materials and scientific men should be drafted into the nuclear research services. There was only one cyclotron in Europe – it was in Paris and had minimal capacity. Speer said that ample funds were available and General Fromm offered to release several hundred scientists from the services. However, it was clear to Speer that they could not count on anything for three or four years and the war would certainly have been decided long before then.[58]

Hitler's Bedtime Story

The ebullient piano-playing Putzi Hanfstaengl was exiled by Hitler and managed to reach London where he was interned. Eventually he reached the USA via Canada. As a valuable prisoner – the half-American friend of Hitler – he was asked or rather ordered to write a 68-page report covering every aspect of the Führer's life and character. A US government psychologist provided a checklist which *inter alia* included religion, women, art, music, literature, sexuality and friendships. The American G-2 military intelligence staff gave the code name 'S-Project' to Hanfstaengl's opus. The 'S' stood for Sedgwick, one of Putzi's influential family connections. They wanted to know Hitler's strengths: gift of oratory, leadership, military skills; and his weaknesses: 'divide and conquer', childhood poverty, anti-semitic, anti-communist phobias, occult sympathies. When the report was shown to President Roosevelt on 3 December 1942 he christened it 'Hitler's bedtime story'.[14]

Hitler's Information Network

Britain has always taken great pride in the success of the Bletchley Park ULTRA team who 'read' with conspicuous success the German Enigma radio codes. Hitler's intake of information was equally staggering. During 1941 Ambassador Hewell logged 1,100 different diplomatic papers passed to his Führer for information and action. In the first quarter of 1942 there were 800 more. FA (*Forschungsamt* – Himmler's 'Research Office') wiretaps were the main source, but the German Post Office was now unscrambling the radio-telephone link between London and Washington. Transcripts included top secret talks between Churchill and Roosevelt. Stalin's despatches from Moscow to Yugoslavia and Turkey were read. American telegrams from Cairo to Washington provided Rommel with key Allied plans including those of the projected invasion of north-west Africa. Allied diplomatic messages out of Madrid and Lisbon were routinely fed back to Hitler, including Mountbatten's plan for an amphibious attack on the French mainland at Dieppe. British historians have underestimated Hitler's sources of information ever since the Germany spies in the UK were rounded up in 1938-40.

The Atlantic Wall

As early as 13 August 1942, Hitler realised that the Allies in the West could not make a successful invasion unless they could capture a sizeable port somewhere on the huge French, Belgian and Dutch coastlines [*Führerprotokoll* with Speer, Keitel, Admiral Kranke, General Jacob and Dorsch].

As a precaution, in two years of intensive building, over seventeen million cubic yards of concrete-built pillboxes around every port and many thousands of bunkers were built for the coastal defenders. Hitler made each port garrison commander responsible directly to him with direct telephone lines. He planned the defensive installations down to the smallest details. During the hours of the night he designed the various types of defence with sketches executed

The Dieppe raid, 19 August 1942. Canadian wounded and abandoned Churchill tanks after the raid, with a landing craft on fire in the background.

with precision. They were accepted 'in toto' by General of Engineers Jakob. In the event Cherbourg, Brest, St Malo, Calais, Boulogne, Le Havre and the Scheldt estuary were defended with vigour and most of the ports' facilities were destroyed. Antwerp was captured in a two-day battle almost intact, but Dunkirk, Lorient and St Nazaire were corralled and survived, to surrender on VE Day.

Hitler's well-planned Atlantic Wall was torpedoed by the two extraordinary Mulberry harbours on the Normandy coast.

Hitler's Charisma

Traudl Junge, aged 22 in 1942, was the youngest and last of Hitler's secretaries. She wrote in her book *Until the Final Hour*, 'It is hard to recreate or imagine the mesmeric effect Hitler had on everyone he encountered. Even people bitterly opposed to him commented on the power he radiated, how they felt irresistibly drawn to him even though it made them feel troubled and guilty afterwards. This phenomenon is often present in extremely powerful men when they choose to exert their charm – and charm – or even more dangerously, charisma, rather than the emanation of evil, was Hitler's most obvious characteristic.' Traudl Junge felt that when Hitler went away from her and her colleagues 'some essential element was missing, even oxygen, an awareness of being alive – there was a – vacuum.'[38]

A typical Normandy reinforced concrete pill box in Hitler's Atlantic Wall.

Stalingrad – 'The Old Mistakes Again'

The Soviet armies encircling Stalingrad smashed through the Romanian divisions and Hitler made slighting remarks about the fighting qualities of his allies. Shortly afterwards, on 19 November 1942, the Soviets began overwhelming German divisions as well. Goering promised solemnly to supply the German troops in the pocket by air. Hitler's generals, Zeitzler and Keitel tried to persuade him that the Sixth Army under von Paulus should fight their way out to freedom, i.e. retreat, but Hitler, who was in the Berghof, simply did not understand the gravity of the situation and said, 'Our generals are making their old mistakes again. They always over-estimate the strength of the Russians. According to all the frontline reports the enemy's human material is no longer sufficient. They are weakened. They have lost far too much blood. But of course nobody wants to accept such reports. Besides how badly Russian officers are trained. No offensive can be organized with such officers. We know what it takes! In the short or long run the Russians will simply come to a halt. They'll run down. Meanwhile we shall throw in a few fresh divisions – that will put things right.' Hitler had been right over the 1940 blitzkrieg in the Low Countries and France and his doubting generals had been proved wrong. This time they were right and he was wrong. On 30 January 1943 Field Marshal von Paulus with twenty-four generals and 90,000 surviving German soldiers surrendered. A catastrophe for the Third Reich.

German panzers on the way to Stalingrad.

No Napoleonic Debacle

In the first years of campaigning in Operation Barbarossa, Hitler's Wehrmacht suffered over a million casualties, a third of the magnificent armies which had burst into Russia in June 1941. Of the sixty-eight German divisions that started Barbarossa, forty-eight had been reconstructed with replaced manpower, and seventeen partly heavily reinforced. Nevertheless the territorial gains were impressive with three Russian armies destroyed and millions of Russians captured. Hitler told a hundred or so of the party faithful – the *Reichsleiter* and the *Gauleiter* – in the Berlin Chancellery in June 1942: 'My determination and willpower have prevented a Napoleonic debacle ... in the past winter we have won the war ...'

Hitler's Table Talk

On 7 July 1941 a Party official, Heinrich Heim, was asked by Hitler to sit discreetly in a corner and take brief shorthand notes of the Führer's monologues. The typed record was then handed to Martin Bormann who read through the day's offering, making comments, clarifying various points and then initialled it and filed it. From 11 March 1942 Heim was temporarily replaced for a four-month period by Dr Henry Picker. Altogether 328 'sessions' were recorded, the last being on 29-30 November 1944. Eventually 1,045

Stalingrad in ruins.

typed pages were completed and kept in Bormann's personal custody. Of the two eventual copies made, one was passed to party archives in Munich, which were later destroyed by fire, and the other survived with Frau Bormann, and was known as 'Bormann – *Vermeke* [Notes]'. Eventually this was passed to François Genoud, a Swiss. Despite a court case against Henry Picker, who authorized a French edition, Genoud sold the English copyright to Weidenfeld and Nicolson. Edited by Hugh Trevor-Roper, it was duly published as a book in 1953 under the title *Hitler's Table Talk*.[61]

Hitler's Carte Blanche

Addressing the Reichstag on 26 April 1942, Hitler asked for total *carte blanche*. 'I do however expect one thing: that the nation give me the right to take immediate action in any way I see fit, wherever I do not find the obedience unconditionally called for by service of the greater cause. This is a matter of life and death to us [wild applause]. At the front and at home, in transport, civil service and the judiciary there must be obedience to only one idea, namely the fight for victory' [wild applause]. It was the last time the Reichstag would ever meet. Hitler was the law.

Field Marshal
Friedrich Wilhelm
Ernst Paulus
photographed in
January 1942.
He surrendered
to the Russians,
30 January 1943.

Hitler's Favourite Painters

Some of Hitler's favourite painters were:

Franz von Stuck (1863-1928) who painted erotic oils with big-busted women, grotesque devils, snakes, dwarfs, *Salome*, *Siren with a Harp*, and many others;

Eduard Grützner (1846-1925) whose pictures of tipsy monks and butlers fascinated Hitler. 'Look at these details, Grützner is greatly under-rated. It's simply that he hasn't been discovered yet [1933]. Some day he'll be worth as much as a Rembrandt.' Hitler claimed to have the largest collection of Grützner in Germany;

Carl Spitzweg (1808-85) was another favourite who mocked the small-town Munich of his period. *The Poet*, *Nepal* and *Serenade* were amongst thirty Spitzwegs owned by Hitler.

Adolf Ziegler (1829-1959), Friedrich Stahl, Hans Thoma (1839-1924) and Wilhelm Leibl (1844-1900) were long-forgotten painters rediscovered and acquired in considerable numbers by the Führer. From the dealer Karl Haberstock he purchased a Rubens, a Watteau, a Canaletto, a Bordone, a van Dyke and a Boecklin.[63]

Goebbels Sang for his Supper

Joseph Goebbels (1897-1945) became an ardent admirer of Hitler during the 1923 putsch trial. Goebbels was short, unattractive and embittered by his disabilities: his crippled left leg made him unfit for war service. He was a university graduate, which was unusual in the Hitler circles and wrote for the *Völkischer Beobachter*. He became Gauleiter of Berlin and in 1928, Nazi party propaganda chief, and introduced the greeting 'Heil Hitler' to the party and to the nation. The Nuremberg rallies and all other major Nazi military rallies were stage-managed by Goebbels. Soon he controlled all film, radio, theatre, music, painting, dance and sculpture in the Third Reich and in March 1935 he introduced the world's first regular television service and sponsored a cheap 'people's' radio set. It was he who issued the order for the Kristallnacht anti-semitic riots. He also engaged William Joyce, 'Lord Haw-Haw' to make anti-British radio broadcasts. Goebbels enjoyed a luxurious lifestyle but also supported his wife, many children and various mistresses.

One evening in mid-March 1943 he and Speer supped with Hitler, who had had a fire lit in the fireplace. An orderly brought in a bottle of wine, and Fachinger mineral water for Hitler. Speer observed how Goebbels knew how to entertain. He spoke in brilliant polished phrases, with irony in the right place and admiration where Hitler expected it, with sentimentality when the moment and subject required it, with gossip and the love-affairs of his actress friends. He mixed everything in a masterly brew – movies, theatre, old times, details of the Goebbels family and children. Stories of their games and innocent remarks distracted Hitler from his cares of state; his self assurance was strengthened and his vanity flattered. Perhaps surprisingly, Hitler reciprocated by magnifying his Propaganda Minister's achievements; Goebbels certainly sang for his supper. Speer noted, a trifle sourly, 'The leaders of the Third Reich were fond of mutual praise'.

Chickens in Sicily

Herr von Neurath reported on 20 May 1943 to Hitler and Generals Keitel and Rommel on conditions in Sicily nine weeks before Operation Husky: 'The Italian General Roatta, commander of their Sixth Army garrisoning Sicily. Roatta complained that the RAF had destroyed the railway locomotives on the island and five of the six ferries to the mainland. Moreover the German soldiers are cursed by the Sicilian peasants in the streets. The Germans have brought war with them to a peaceful country, and the sooner they go away the better. Moreover they have eaten up all our chickens.'

Hitler and the Secret Weapons (1)

The Peenemünde scientists, under Wernher von Braun's genius, had developed a remote-controlled flying bomb; a rocket plane much faster than a jet plane; a rocket missile that homed in on an enemy plane by tracking the heat rays from

Hitler at table with Magda and Joseph Goebbels.

its engines; a torpedo that reacted to sound and could pursue a fleeing ship; and a ground-to-air missile to destroy Allied bombers. Hitler had to make a crucial decision as there was only the industrial capacity to make one of these. Should it be the A-4 (the V-2), a 46-foot long rocket weighing thirteen metric tonnes which could rain terror on England? Or should they develop the Waterfall, a 25-foot long anti-aircraft missile with 500-pound warhead, which flew along a directional beam up to 50,000 feet and had a near certainty of destroying an Allied bomber? Hitler wavered: 2,210 scientists and engineers worked at Peenemünde on the V-2s and only 220 on Waterfall. London and the southeast of England survived the V-2s and the Allied bombers survived the very few Waterfalls.[58]

Hitler's Duty

Frau Henriette Schirach, wife of Baldur Benedikt von Schirach, head of the Hitler Youth and Reich Governor of Vienna, confronted Hitler on Good Friday 1943. A few days earlier in Amsterdam she heard from her hotel a

Cheerful African-American soldiers with Easter gifts for Hitler.

loud disturbance; and from her window had seen some weeping women being ordered over a bridge and disappearing into the night. She was told that it was a deportation of Jewish women. Hitler answered when she brought up that terrible occurrence: 'Be silent, Frau von Schirach, you understand nothing about it. You are sentimental. What does it matter to you what happens to female Jews? Every day tens of thousands of my most valuable men fall while the inferior survive. In that way the balance in Europe is being undermined. And what will become of Europe in one hundred, in one thousand years? I am committed by duty to my people alone, to nobody else.'

Rich Trove of Knowledge

Hitler's secret was that he trained and expanded his unusual memory – every day. When he was reading he tried to grasp the essence, the key points, and fix them in his mind. During his tea breaks with his secretaries he would chat about a subject he had been reading about in order to anchor it more firmly in his memory. Hitler often surprised people with his rich trove of knowledge, and to show his superiority he made sure never to let them know the sources of this knowledge. He convinced his listeners that everything he said was the result of his deliberations and critical thinking.

Nearly everyone was convinced that Hitler was a profound thinker and had a wonderfully sharp analytical spirit. In the book *Hitler's Table Talk 1941-1944* there are nearly 1,500 different subjects in the Index, from Baroness Abegg to Professor Zwiedeneck – a rich trove indeed.

A camp in 1942 with the sexes carefully segregated *c*. 1942.

The Spent Old Man

Nearly fifty-four and under immense pressure after defeats in Russia and North Africa, in March 1943 Hitler appeared to be 'a spent old man ... He stared fixedly into space through bulging eyes, his cheeks were blotchy and his spine was twisted by kyphosis and a light scoliosis. His left arm and leg twitched and he dragged his feet. He became increasingly excitable, reacted violently to criticism and stuck obstinately to his own opinions however ludicrous. He spoke in a dull monotone, repeated himself and liked to harp on his childhood and early career.' His doctors convinced him to try to take three months' rest. He did in fact spend two five-week periods away from the Wolfsschanze and Werwolf (Russian HQ near Vinnitsa in the Ukraine) and back at the Berghof retreat.[49]

'Whoever Rules Europe ...'

Just after von Paulus surrendered a German army at Stalingrad and while a similar disaster was happening in North Africa, Goebbels noted in his diary on 8 May 1943, 'The Führer expresses his unshakeable conviction that the Reich will one day rule all of Europe. We will have to survive a great many conflicts but they will doubtless lead to the most glorious triumphs. And from then on the road to world domination is practically spread out before us. For whoever rules Europe will be able to seize the leadership of the world.' On 24 June Hitler told his supper companions, 'I feel equally at home anywhere in the Reich and my love for all Germans [85 millions of them] is equal as long as they do not range themselves against the interests of the Reich of which I am the guardian. I behave as if I am in the midst of my family.'[52]

Hitler's Doctor

Theodor Morell (1890-1948) was Hitler's doctor for nine years until 1944. His original diagnosis of the hypochondriac Führer was 'intestinal exhaustion', which appealed to the health crank in Hitler. Morell specialized in all kinds of strange treatments: items such as 'bull's testicles' and, more dangerous, amphetamines and opium-based painkillers. Morell's treatments may have contributed to Hitler's later condition of a form of Parkinson's disease. On Sunday 18 July 1943 Hitler planned to meet Mussolini. According to Morell, 'Führer had me sent for at ten-thirty a.m., said he has had the most violent stomach pains since three a.m. and hasn't slept a wink. His abdomen is as taut as a board, full of gas, with no palpation pains anywhere. Looking *very* pale and exceptionally jumpy: facing a vital conference with the Duce in Italy tomorrow. Diagnosis: *Spastic constipation* caused by overwork over the last few days – three days with virtually no sleep, one conference after another and working far into the night. – Last night he ate white cheese and roll-ups (*Rolladen*) with spinach and peas.

'As he can't duck out of some important conferences and decisions before his departure at three-thirty p.m., no narcotics can be given him; I can only give him an intravenous injection of one ampoule of Eurpaverin, [a muscle relaxant], some gentle stomach massage, two Euflat pills [for heartburn/ stomach or intestinal complaints] and three spoons of olive oil. Last night he took five Leo pills [a laxative]. Before leaving for the airfield I gave him an intramuscular injection of an ampoule of Eukodal [morphine-based painkiller]. He was looking very bad and rather faint.'[1]

Hitler's Ownership of Books

Timothy Ryback's masterful *Hitler's Private Library* has revealed that on Hitler's death his library comprised about 16,000 volumes. He considered William Shakespeare superior to Schiller and Goethe, and he frequently

Happier days for Hitler in North Africa; Sepp Dietrich, Hitler's favourite soldier; with an Italian commander and a captured British officer.

quoted the Bard. The German translation of Shakespeare's collected works was published in 1925 by Georg Müller.

Hitler ranked *Don Quixote, Robinson Crusoe, Uncle Tom's Cabin, and Gulliver's Travels* among the great works of world literature. His library's military section, divided up by country, contained some 7,000 volumes including the Napoleonic campaigns and the Prussian Kings. There were 1,500 books covering artistic subjects such as architecture, painting, theatre and sculpture. The third category was works on spiritualism and astrology.

Hitler's libraries were in a private residence in the Obersalzburg near Berchtesgaden, Berlin and Munich. Twelve hundred of his books are now in the Thomas Jefferson building in Washington. There is clear evidence that he never looked at two-thirds of the vast collection.

The Secret German-Russian Peace Moves

The Allies were anxious to keep Stalin fighting Hitler's 'Barbarossa' armies, as the Russian losses had been catastrophic. Stalin was equally worried in case the Allies made a negotiated peace with Hitler. Crafty and devious, Stalin played cat and mouse throughout 1943 with Churchill and Roosevelt. In the same period Ribbentrop wanted to broker a peace with the Russians. In June, according to Basil Liddell-Hart, he met Molotov at Kirovograd inside the German lines and other German intermediaries met Alexandrov, a senior Soviet official. When Hitler got to hear of these talks he dismissed them as a 'Jewish provocation'. After the huge tank battle at Kursk which exhausted the Germans, with Hitler's permission the intermediaries, Peter Kleist (of the Dienstelle) and Edgar Klauss were again encouraged. The sticking points seemed to be agreement on frontiers. Dekanozov, former Soviet minister and now Deputy Foreign Minister, had talks in September with Kleist in Stockholm. Ribbentrop's diary recalled, 'This time Hitler was not as obstinate as in the past. He walked over to a map and drew a demarcation on which he could compromise with the Russians.' Mussolini, now a refugee, having been rescued from Allied captivity in November, at Hitler's instigation, now arrived at Hitler's HQ. Hitler told the Duce that he wanted to settle with Russia, but he then said to Ribbentrop, 'You know if I settled with Russia today I would only come to blows with her again tomorrow – I just can't help it.' Stalin was in fact, quite serious. When in May 1943, Churchill and Roosevelt postponed the invasion of northern Europe for a year, the Soviet leader was known to be absolutely furious. He revealed the Klauss–Kleist meeting at the Teheran Conference in November to embarrass the Allies.

The Broken Treaties

Gauleiter Erich Koch of East Prussia – a friend of Goering's and *no* friend of Ribbentrop – presented the latter on his successful visit to Moscow in August 1939 with a beautiful amber casket. It was given to 'the greatest European Foreign Minister since Bismark' (according to Hitler), as something in which to preserve *all* the treaties, he (Ribbentrop) had signed on Hitler's behalf.

The Nazi-Soviet pact was the eighteenth, of which seventeen were eventually broken. The only one not broken was the International Sugar Agreement which had been suspended at the outbreak of war in 1939. On Ribbentrop's fiftieth birthday in 1943 he was given another opulent casket adorned with semi-precious stones. It was empty. Hitler was convulsed with laughter.[43]

Strychnine Poisoning

Hitler had a number of doctors, among them Brandt, Morell and Giesing. Morell had specialized since 1931 in diseases of the urinary system and in venereal diseases. He treated Hitler's meteorism (gas in the abdomen) with Dr Koster's Antigas pills, sometimes up to sixteen a day. These did little good and in 1944 Dr Giesing discovered that these pills contained almost the maximum amount of strychnine – the Führer was being systematically poisoned. But Hitler's perverse reaction was to fire Dr Giesing and continue with Morell, who was by all accounts a charlatan.[45]

Our Long-Legged Slender Women

Early in 1944 it was clear to Hitler that Germany had to raise more than four million *new* workers for the immense manufacturing demands of armaments,

Mussolini, an unidentified general, Hitler, Keitel and others looking at a map of Europe.

munitions, submarines, aircraft, tanks and rockets. A major conference took place on 4 January with Keitel, Speer, Milch, Backe (the Agricultural Minister) and with Himmler and Fritz Sauckel (the manpower supremos). Italian forced labour could not be used as four new Italian divisions had been formed from the prisoners of war taken by the Germans after Italy's surrender to the Allies in 1943. Hitler was most reluctant to use female workers, 'Our long-legged slender women' cannot be compared with the 'stocky primitive Russian women'. After four years of total war the fraus' and frauleins' place was not in noisy factories. The fact that Britain, USA and Russia employed millions of women in factories or on the land carried no weight at all with Hitler's romantic views.

The Widening Gulf

After the catastrophes of Tunis and Stalingrad, Hitler distrusted his generals – Field Marshal von Paulus had surrendered; the indomitable Rommel had been defeated in Africa – and spent much more time distancing himself from the citizens of the Third Reich, indeed from most of his senior staff.

In 1940 Hitler had made nine big public addresses, in 1941 seven, in 1942 five and in 1943 only two. Most of the time he spent at his military field Head Quarters, or in the Berghof above Berchtesgaden.

Once his armoured train *Amerika* stopped beside a troop train filled with weary, dispirited Wehrmacht. So he pulled down the blind in his carriage to avoid looking at them.

Hitler's Pusillanimity

In January 1944 Albert Speer, Hitler's favourite architect and Minister for Armaments, was taken to hospital with violent pain in his chest and back. 'My illness had removed me too far from the true face of power: Hitler. He reacted neither negatively nor positively to all my suggestions, demands and complaints. I was addressing the empty air. He sent me no answer. I was no longer counted as Hitler's favourite minister and one of his possible successors ... This was due to Hitler's peculiarity of simply writing off anyone who vanished from his sight for a considerable time. It disillusioned me and snapped some of my ties of personal feeling towards Hitler. In unpleasant situations Hitler always tried to avoid confrontations. He did not dare send for me and request me to leave my post ... pusillanimity.'

Hitler arriving with senior officers at the Berghof.

Albert Speer, Erhard Milch and Willy Messerschmitt, May 1944.

Hygiene

Christa Schroeder spent twelve years as one of the Führer's three secretaries and was described by Dr Karl Brandt, Hitler's emergency surgeon, as 'clever, critical and intelligent ... after spending several days and nights without a break taking dictation she would always express her opinion openly and in time became critical of Hitler himself. Her boldness undoubtedly put her life in great danger.' She wrote: 'Hitler set great store on hygiene. He bathed daily, often several times a day particularly after meetings and speeches from which he would return sweating ... He would reject tiredness and would call upon endless reserves of energy ... The knowledge from 1944 onwards that he was no longer master of his own body was a heavy burden. Yet to the end he remained master of his emotions.' Well, yes and no. The Hitler rages were well known. He frightened even Reichsmarshal Hermann Goering. One of his entourage told Shirer: 'He lives a spartan personal life. He is vegetarian, a teetotaller, a non-smoker and a celibate.'

Speer the Pure Technician

The British newspaper *The Observer* of 9 April 1944 carried an article about Speer which he, rather courageously, showed to Hitler. Part of the article read:

> Speer is, in a sense, more important for Germany today than Hitler, Himmler, Goering, Goebbels or the generals. They all have, in a way, become the mere auxiliaries of the man who actually directs the giant power machine ... Speer is not one of the flamboyant and picturesque Nazis ... Much less than any of the other German leaders does he stand for anything particularly German or

Eva Braun with Hitler at the Berghof.

particularly Nazi ... He is the pure technician, the classless bright young man without background ... This is their age; the Hitlers and Himmlers we may get rid of, but the Speers, whatever happens to this particular special man will long be with us.

Hitler might have thrown a tantrum and sent Speer to a concentration camp or worse. He read the long article carefully and handed it back to Speer without a word, but with great respect.[58]

The Unusual Birthday Party

Hitler's fifty-fifth birthday on 20 April 1944 was celebrated in the Berghof with champagne and a *geburtstagstisch* (birthday table) covered with presents. There were several unusual happenings. Blondi, Hitler's beloved dog, sang with his master – Hitler howled, the dog howled and the duet went on for much of the evening. Usually totally abstinent, Hitler sipped a very sweet white wine. Amongst the scores of presents for the Führer were cakes, chocolates, fruit and various other food products, which were all destroyed on Hitler's orders in case they had been poisoned. He no longer trusted the German *hausfrauen* who had so adored him for fifteen years.[45]

Medals Galore

Military dictatorships adore medals and decorations and the Third Reich was no exception. During Hitler's years of power, 1933-45, more than 450 political and civil decorations were created, many based on their Weimar and Imperial predecessors. In 1939 Hitler reinstated the Iron Cross for bravery with a First class; the Knight's Cross (*Ritterkreuz*); with oak leaves; with oak leaves and swords; with oak leaves, swords and diamonds; and finally with golden oak leaves. Goering made sure that he received every possible decoration, including Italian medals. Hitler gave him – only him – a Grand Cross of the Iron Cross.

Political and civil awards included the Blood Order for the original participants of the Beer Hall Putsch, the Eagle Shield of Germany for intellectual achievement, and the 1929 Nuremberg Party Day Badge. Hitler sometimes wore his Great War Iron Cross, which he was awarded as a corporal regimental messenger/runner.

A calmly smoking, arrogant-looking Lieutenant-General Otto Elfeldt of the 84th Army Corps, taken prisoner on 20 August 1944.

Hitler's Lucky Star

At the end of June 1944 the Third Reich was losing the war on three fronts – the Russians in the East and to the Allies in Normandy, while the Luftwaffe had been swept from the skies. Hitler displayed steady nerves and an astonishing capacity for perseverance. Speer thought that the 'time of struggle', *Kampfzeit*, with its many setbacks had strengthened his will to continue the fight. In spite of his rapid aging and constant illness (despite Dr Morell's treatment), by auto-suggestion Hitler made himself believe in ultimate victory. Perhaps his new vicious V-weapons would do the trick; perhaps the Allies would fall out with each other. Although Hitler soberly understood the harsh military facts, Speer wrote that 'his expectation that at the last moment Fate would undoubtedly turn the tide in his favour. If there was any fundamental insanity in Hitler, it was this unshakable belief in his lucky star.'[58]

Führer Headquarters

Felsennest (Cliff Nest) at Bad Munstereiffel (1940), 30 miles from the Belgian border.

Adlerhorst (Eagle Eyrie) at Ziegerberg near the Ardennes (1940 and again 1944).

Wolfsschlucht (Wolfs' Gorge) at Bruly-le-Peche, France (June 1940).

Tannenberg named after the 1914 victory over the Russians in the Black Forest (1940).

Wolfsschanze (Wolfs' Lair), Rastenburg, East Prussia (1941-44).

Werwolf (Werewolf), Vinnitsa, Ukraine (July 1942).

Führerbunker, in the Reich Chancellery, Berlin (1945).

The Wolfsschanze

Hitler spent more than 800 days and nights in his Wolf's Lair HQ during the Second World War. The huge HQ bunker complex at Rastenberg was a purely military base. Nearly 50 staff including Hitler's four female secretaries lived like rats – the food was indifferent, the air stale and foetid, there was high humidity in the summer and it was beastly cold in the winter. The thick pine forests were sinister and claustrophobic and the tormenting mosquitoes were so pervasive that Hitler had to wear a special protective helmet like a beekeeper's for protection.[45]

Hitler and the Secret Weapons (2)

The most valuable secret weapons were the jet fighters developed by Professor Ernst Heinkel in the Rostock plant and and the design team of Lippisch and Bolkow. These included the He-162 and the Me-262 (called the *Schwalbe*, 'Swallow') with two *jet* engines, a speed of over 500 mph and a fighting capacity superior to the Allied fighter. The Me-262 was the first fully operational jet fighter, well ahead of the Gloster Meteor.

Hitler, a Great War infantry soldier, could not see its potential until in January 1944 he read an article about British success in developing jet engines. So, with Speer's agreement, he ordered Field Marshal Milch to increase production of the secret Me-262, which could help destroy the American and British bombers. But he was under a misapprehension – he thought the 262 was being developed as a bomber, and Milch had to tell him that this was not the case, quite late in its development. Speer, Jodl, Guderian, Model, Dietrich, as well as Milch and all the Luftwaffe generals, were adamant that the Me-262 was a superb fighter aircraft, not a bomber. But Hitler thought he knew best and insisted that it should be turned into a fighter-bomber – so a system allowing it to carry two 250-kg bombs was hurriedly lashed together. As an aircraft it was underpowered, its advanced airframe far outstripping the development of its engines. Although fast, it was not a very stable gun platform, its engines were unreliable, and it was, like all turbojets before the development of the afterburner, very slow to accelerate, with a long take-off run. In the end, flak batteries and conventional (i.e. piston-engined) fighters had to be deployed at airfields to protect 262s during take-off. The engines tended to ignite tarmac

Hitler with his bodyguards.

In addition to the Me-262 there was another jet, a single engine fighter, the He-162 which first flew 6 December 1944. In this photograph, partly completed Heinkel He-162s sit on the assembly line in the underground Junkers factory at Tarthun, April 1945.

runways, so the aircraft were further restricted to airfields with concrete runways. All in all, the 262 was insufficiently developed; there were too few of the aircraft operational, and it was tricky to fly, even for highly experienced pilots, while the logistical problems of supplying and servicing aircraft proved almost in surmountable. In addition, it came into service too ate – the Allies had by now invaded Europe and thereby won almost complete domination in the air.[58]

The Kreisau Circle

Count Helmet von Moltke (1907-1945) was descended from one of Germany's most distinguished families with estates in Silesia but he also had a British mother. He was a well-known lawyer and legal adviser to the counter-intelligence department of the OKW (German High Command). In 1933 he formed the Kreisau circle, named after his estate, consisting of high-minded aristocratic members of all parties who discussed and planned for a new social order when Hitler's Nazi Reich eventually came to an end. They had no plans to overthrow Hitler or the Nazis and were essentially Christian and pacifist. In 1939 and 1940 von Moltke had secret meetings with Kirk, the US Chargé at the US Embassy in Berlin. After hearing of the latest Nazi atrocities, he

Claus Schenk Graf von Stauffenberg
(1907-1944), Admiral Karl-Jesco Otto
Robert von Puttkamer (1900-1981),
and Friedrich Fromm with Hitler at the
Wolf's Lair.

wrote to his wife Freya in October 1941, 'What shall I say when I am asked
"And what did you do during this time? [massacres of civilians in Serbia and
Greece]. Since Saturday the Berlin Jews are being rounded up ... only 20 per
cent of prisoners or Jews arrive: there is starvation in the POW camps, typhoid
and other epidemics have broken out ... How can anyone know these things
and still walk around free?"'

Six months later von Moltke was arrested and died horribly in Plötzensee
prison, Berlin on 23 January 1945. Before his death von Moltke wrote to a
friend in Stockholm, 'At least nine-tenths of the population [in Germany] do
not know that we have murdered hundreds of thousands of Jews.'[45]

The Bomb Plot and Blutrache

Colonel Claudius Philipp Maria Schenk, Graf (Count) von Stauffenberg,
(1907-44), a brave soldier who been severely wounded in Tunisia, where
he had lost a hand, was appointed Chief of Staff to Colonel-General Fritz
Fromm. This presented a golden opportunity, for although a member of the
largely pacifist Kreisau Circle, he was also leader of a widespread conspiracy
to assassinate the 'Master of Vermin in the Third Reich', i.e. Hitler, and form
a new government. At 12.10 p.m. on 20 July 1944 Stauffenberg, attending
the Führer's daily conference in the Wolfsschanze, carefully placed a briefcase
containing a time bomb under the table near Hitler and then left the room to
make a phone call. Unfortunately, another officer probably then moved the
briefcase to the other side of a solid oak table. Stauffenberg waited outside

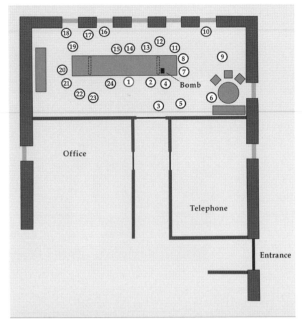

The temporary Briefing Room at Hitler's Wolf's Lair in Rastenburg, East Prussia as it was on 20 July 1944 when the bomb exploded. 1. Hitler; 2. Heusinger; 3. Korten; 4. Brandt; 5. Bodenschatz; 6. Waizenegger; 7. Schmundt; 8. Borgmann; 9. Buhle; 10. Puttkammer; 11. Berger; 12. Assmann; 13. John; 14. Scherf; 15. Voss; 16. Guensche; 17. Below; 18. Fegelein; 19. Buechs; 20. Sonnleithner; 21. Warlimont; 22. Jodl; 23. Keitel and 24. Stauffenberg.

Goering is shown the scene of the bomb blast.

until, at 12.42, the time bomb blew up. There were a number of casualties, including four deaths, but Hitler survived, with his uniform in tatters, his ear drums burst, his right arm, legs, hands and face lacerated. That afternoon Mussolini and Marshal Graziani arrived for a scheduled meeting. Goering, Himmler, Ribbentrop and Admiral Doenitz attended and the witch-hunt for the conspirators started, with Goebbels and Himmler rounding up, by means of the dreaded Gestapo, anybody they thought might be involved. This operation was named *Blutrache* ('blood vengeance') by Himmler. Over 7,000 arrests were made and the Gestapo used diabolical torture to extract names and more names. Over time, almost 5,000 souls were executed (accounts vary as to the exact number); arrests and executions continued till the end of the Nazi era, many being arrested and executed on trumped-up charges, among them Graf von Moltke. Stauffenberg and the main army conspirators were shot, most of them within hours of the bombing; and as for many of the other executions – Goebbels sent cameramen to film them taking place. The famous Field Marshal Rommel committed suicide. Hitler, Doenitz and Goering addressed the nation on the radio. Hitler said, 'It was a crime without parallel in German history ... I was spared a fate that holds no terror for me, but would have had terrible consequences for the German people. I regard this as a sign that I should continue the task imposed on me by Providence.'

Eva and Adolf – A Loving Couple

After the Stauffenberg bomb assassination plot, Eva Braun wrote to Hitler in July 1944 'Right after our very first meeting I promised myself I would follow you everywhere, even unto death. You know I live only for the love I can give you.' Hitler presented her with a book of poetry by Ludwig Thoma entitled

A photograph taken shortly after the assassination attempt had failed. From the left: Wilhelm Keitel, chief of the supreme high command; Goering, Hitler and Bormann.

Josef Filser's Gesamelter Briefwexel. He inscribed it 'Meine liebe, Eva herzlichst Adolf Hitler, Berlin, an 19/Jan 1940', which translates as 'My darling Eva. A gift of love from the heart'. Before her suicide in the Berlin bunker in May 1945 Eva made various bequests of her worldly goods and this book went to her friend Herta Schneider. It is valued at about £100,000.[67]

Nuclear Research, Stage Four

Hitler's principle of scattering responsibility meant that scientific research teams in the Third Reich were divided and often at odds with each other. According to the 'office journal' of 17 August 1944, not only all three branches of the armed forces, but also the SS and even the postal system had *separate* research facilities. Thus progress on the development of nuclear fission was negligible. In the USA all the atomic physicists were grouped in one organization. Speer, the Minister for Armaments, had 2,200 recorded points and subjects in his conferences with Hitler. Nuclear fission came up once – Führer Protocol 23 June 1942, point 15. Of course the Great War soldier was never likely to want to understand the awful potential that led to Hiroshima.[58]

Hitler with Eva at the Berghof, 1944.

A Tavern in the Town

Alois Hitler, half brother of the Nazi dictator of Germany, ran a pub in the great square of the Wittenbergerplatz in Berlin. He was remembered as 'a harmless-enough fellow, grown portly on good beer, whose chief fear was that his half brother would fly into a rage and order him to close shop since the Führer did not like to have people reminded of the lower-middle-class origins of the Hitler family.' Abstinent as he was, the Führer was unlikely to approve of a tavern in the family.[57]

Hitler's Spider

Churchill wrote just after Mussolini's death: 'At this time Hitler made a crowning error in strategy and war direction. The defection of Italy, the victorious advance of Russia and the evident preparations for a cross-channel attack by Britain and the United States should have led him to concentrate and develop the most powerful German army as a central reserve, with its interior lines and remarkable communications. Hitler however had in fact made a spider's web and forgotten the spider!'

German soldiers surrender to Canadians, 19 August 1944.

Hitler's Wacht am Rhein

Towards the end of November 1944 Hitler made it plain to his key henchmen that 'Wacht am Rhein', the codename for the great December counter-attack in the Ardennes was his last effort. He told Speer in particular 'This will be the great blow which must succeed. If it does not succeed, I no longer see any possibility for ending the war well ... But we will come through ... A single breakthrough on the Western Front! You'll see! It will lead to collapse and panic among the Americans. We'll drive right through their middle and take Antwerp. Then they'll have lost their supply port. And a tremendous pocket will encircle the entire English army with hundreds of thousands of prisoners. As we used to do in Russia.'

Secretly three huge armies, two of them SS, unleashed a terrific onslaught in mid-December. Fog, mist and snow kept the Allied airforces grounded. Savage fighting between the disorganized Americans and Hitler's armies around St Vith and Bastogne lasted until late January 1945. The American General Patton wrote in his diary, 'We can still lose this war' and Churchill was forced to ask Joseph Stalin in Moscow to bring forward his spring offensive. It was touch and go. Hitler had masterminded a huge secret offensive that not even Bletchley Park's ULTRA operation could detect.

A *Hitlerjugend* boy soldier surrenders to a GI in Cherbourg.

Right: Guderian shows Hitler the plan for the Ardennes counter-attack.

Below: An American Jeep destroyed during the Battle of the Bulge, December 1944.

Permanent Euphoria

New Year's Eve 1944 found Hitler and his entourage of adjutants, doctors, secretaries and Bormann, of course, drinking champagne. Hitler's western HQ from which he had been directing the Ardennes offensive was a series of bunkers, camouflaged as blockhouses, hidden in woods at the end of a grassy valley near Bad Nauheim, just north of Ziegenberg. The audacious drive from the Ardennes to seize Antwerp was noticeably failing. But Hitler, as usual, was making optimistic forecasts for the New Year. 'In the end we will be victorious,' he declared to his circle, who took these prophecies in silence. The alcohol had relaxed everyone but the atmosphere was very subdued. Hitler was the only one who was drunk without having taken any alcoholic drink; Albert Speer wrote that he was in the grip of a permanent euphoria.[58]

American reinforcements after the tide had turned during the Battle of the Bulge.

Atom Bombs Against England?

Hitler did sometimes comment on the prospects of nuclear fission. He was not happy with the possibility that the Third Reich might be transformed into a glowing star and joked that the scientists in their urge to uncover all the secrets under heaven might some day set the globe on fire. But Hitler was confident that he would certainly not be alive to see it. Speer was certain that Hitler would not have hesitated for a moment to employ atom bombs against England.[58]

The Nuclear Story – A Near Run Thing

Dresden was battered and burned on 14 February 1945 by the RAF and USAAF. Hitler was beside himself with fury and spoke to Dr Giesing in the Berlin Chancellery. 'I'm going to start using my Victory weapon [*siegwaffe*] and then the war will come to a glorious end. Some time ago we solved the problem of nuclear fission and we have developed it so far that we can exploit the energy for armaments purposes [*rüstungszwecke*]. They won't even know what hit them! It's the weapon of the future. With it Germany's future is assured.' Albert Speer had visited the Krupp works and was shown parts of Germany's first cyclotron. And at Heidelberg in the summer of 1944 he was shown 'our first cyclotron splitting an atomic nucleus' by Professor Walter Bothe. Professor Walther Gerlach was the Reich chief of nuclear research trying to finalize the research work done by Professors Werner Heisenberg and Carl-Friedrich von Weisacker. They had started in 1939 and were developing an experimental atomic pile at Haigerlock. So Hitler's boast – ten weeks before the end of the Third Reich – was perfectly valid!

Hitler's Paranoia

The hunt for the July Bomb Plot conspirators, known as *Genitteraktion* (storm action), had resulted in an appalling cull of the Wehrmacht senior officers involved in Operation Valkerie. In the last year of his life Hitler was paranoid about his generals: Rommel, von Witzleben, von Wartenburg, von Tresckow, Hopner, von Trof zu Solz, Bech and Admiral Canaris had been butchered, or if they were lucky, had committed suicide. So in February 1945 Hitler sent an order to all divisional commanders, bypassing the usual channels of

Dresden after the bombing of 13-15 February 1945.

Volkssturm being trained to use the Panzerfaust anti-tank weapon, February or March 1945.

command: 'You are personally responsible for reporting to me in good time – every attack planned in divisional strength *or above*; every offensive in quiet sectors of *battalion* strength *or above*; every plan for withdrawing forces; every plan to surrender a local strong point ... every report to me should contain nothing but the truth. I shall impose draconian punishments on any attempt at concealment from carelessness, oversight or deliberate action.' The Third Reich was disintegrating by 1945. Hitler's new orders ensured that the disintegration would be rapid – such was his acute paranoia over the loyalty of the Reich officer class.

Germany – 'A Wasteland'

In the last few months of countdown to *Götterdämmerung* – the end of the Third Reich – Hitler sent out several decrees (the first was on 19 March) ordering a 'scorched earth' policy: the destruction of factories, bridges, radio stations, railway tracks, canal locks, locomotives, passenger cars, freight cars, cargo vessels and barges. Rivers and canals would be blocked by sinking ships in them. Every type of explosive and ammunition would be used. Dated

Admiral Wilhelm Canaris in happier times. Canaris had always played a double game, but was found out and after being subjected to humiliation was executed on 9 April 1945.

29 March 1945, the last decree read, 'Aim is creation of a transportation wasteland in abandoned [surrendered] territory.' Hitler had previously ordered the commanders of all the Channel port fortresses (Brest, St Malo, Cherbourg, Calais, Boulogne, Le Havre, Ostend, Zeebrugge and the Scheldt harbours) to be totally destroyed on surrender. This had been done, but the destruction had been outside Germany. Now Hitler had ordered the same thing to happen to his own country, in Operation Nero. It was only due to Albert Speer's constant intervention, risking his neck in the process, that the Hitler edict was watered down and in most cases, ignored. He made a long, brilliant speech on the radio on 16 April, which undoubtedly prevented further damage to the infrastructure of Germany.[58]

Frederick the Great – Hitler's Hero

In 1934 Hitler purchased an oil painting of Frederick the Great by Anton Graff for 34,000 marks – a huge sum. It travelled with him everywhere. His *Chefpilot* Hans Bauer ensured that packed in a special bulky crate, handled with care, it travelled in the Führer's plane with precedence over the passengers! Shortly before his suicide in the bunker Hitler gave the painting to Bauer as a parting gift. Rochus Misch, a telephone operator in Hitler's bunker recalled, 'Very late one night I went into the study. There was Der Chef gazing at the painting by candlelight, sitting there motionless, his chin buried in his hand, as if he were in a trance. Hitler was staring at the King [Frederick]. The King seemed to be staring right back ... It was like stumbling upon someone at prayer.' In *Hitler's Table Talk* Frederick the Great is mentioned admiringly twenty-two times. 'When one reflects that Frederick the Great held out against forces twelve times greater than his, one gets the impression "What a grand fellow he must have been!"'[4]

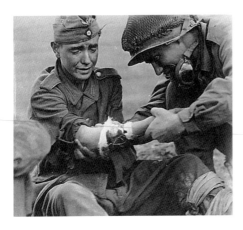

A chastened *Hitlerjugend* being attended by an American medic.

Hitler's Miracle?

On 12 April 1945 the American President Roosevelt, architect of Allied victory together with Winston Churchill and Josef Stalin, died. Goebbels, listening to American news agencies, was the first to hear it and telephoned Hitler in excitement. In the Berlin command bunker a delighted Adolf Hitler, with considerable animation, shouted out to the entourage (Bormann, Ley, Schaub, adjutants and orderlies). He held a newspaper cutting in his hand. 'Here, read it! You never wanted to believe it. Here we have the miracle I always predicted! Who was right? The war isn't lost. Read it! Roosevelt is dead!'

Goebbels and the henchmen were bubbling over with delight. Their Führer was convinced the tide would turn. History was repeating itself. The hopelessly beaten Frederick the Great had a last-minute victory. The House of Brandenburg had a last-minute miracle. Innumerable fantasies burgeoned in the bunker as the group of defeated Nazi leaders clutched at straws. Perhaps Mr Truman, the new American president, would wave a magic wand of honourable peace. But a few weeks later Stalin's Russian hordes overwhelmed Berlin. There was no miracle!

'Europe Will Never be Russian'

On 15 April 1945 Hitler issued his final proclamation to his armies fighting the Russian hordes: 'For the last time, the Jewish-Bolshevik mortal enemy has set out with its masses on the attack. He is attempting to demolish Germany and to exterminate our people. You soldiers from the East know yourselves what fate threatens all German women, girls and children. While old men and children are murdered, women and girls are denigrated to barrack-whores. The rest are marched off to Siberia.'

Hitlerjugend in Belgium, 1945; hatred and fanaticism visible in their eyes.

Hitler congratulating boy soldiers in Berlin, April 1945.

Liberation of Concentration camp survivors, April 1945.

And finally: 'Berlin stays German, Vienna will be German again and Europe will never be Russian.'

Then he issued an order that if (and when) the Reich was split in two between the Russians in the north and the Allies in the south, Field Marshal Kesselring would command the southern sector, and Great-Admiral Doenitz the northern zone.

The Isle of the Departed

In the last weeks of his life in the Berlin bunker, Hitler gave the impression of a man whose whole purpose in life had been destroyed. He was shrivelling up like an old man. His limbs trembled and his signature on papers and decrees was illegible. He walked with a stoop and dragging footsteps. His voice quavered. The old masterful Hitler had vanished. Speer recalled that his tantrums were no longer childish but those of an old man. His complexion was sallow, his face swollen. His uniform, which had always been scrupulously clean and tidy was now dirty and stained with food. He was diminished and had become senile. His three cronies towards the end were the faithful Martin Bormann, Goebbels and Robert Ley. He was still touchingly fond of his long-term secretaries, Frau Wolf and Frau Christian, and also of Frau Junge, the widow of his servant who had been killed at the Front. Eva Braun had determined to be with her man at the finish. And Goebbels had declared 'My wife and family are not to survive me. The Americans would only coach them to make propaganda against me.' The discipline in Hitler's entourage had gone and it was like a tomb in the concrete bunker isolated from the appalling tragedies as the Russian smashed their way into Berlin. In Speer's words the unreal world of the Hitler bunker was the 'isle of the departed'.[58]

Letter from the Bunker

On 23 April 1945 Hitler admitted to Ribbentrop that the war was lost, and dictated to him four secret negotiation points to put to the British. If the European continent was to survive against Bolshevik domination then Germany and Britain 'must bury the hatchet'. He ordered Ribbentrop to write immediately and secretly to Churchill. 'You will see. My spirit will arise from

Berlin, May 1945.

the grave. One day people will see that I was right.' This letter to Churchill was circulated as a memorandum to the British Cabinet. Churchill sent the letter to Stalin on 12 July 1945 saying 'it is exceptionally long and tedious'. Hitler had said to Ribbentrop, 'I actually came to power ten years too soon. Another ten years and I would have kneaded the Party into shape.' In their last discussion the Führer, quite calmly, told Ribbentrop that he had never wanted any harm to come to Britain. The big handshake with 'Germanic' England – that had always been his goal.[69]

Chocolate Cake and Puppies

In the final days in the bunker Hitler gave orders to the troops trying to defend Berlin, rarely allowing any retreat. He appointed officers, sacked others, had some executed. It was a dream world as the Russian bombardment thundered down. The Führer ate immense quantities of chocolate cake and played with Blondi and her five puppies who lived in one of the bunker's bathrooms. It is almost certain, judging by Hitler's mood swings, that his doctor, Morell, himself probably a morphine addict, had been injecting his Führer with morphine (and he left a provision behind when he departed from the bunker). Eva Braun meanwhile fantasized about starring in a movie based on her life.[18]

Messenger of Death

After Albert Speer had encountered Eva Braun in the sordid Berlin bunker he wrote: 'Figuratively and in reality, with her presence a messenger of death moved into the bunker.' Amongst the macabre witness statements was that there had been discussion about 'the best way to die'. Eva Braun was reputed to have said, 'I want to be a beautiful corpse. I will take poison.' Himmler had supplied Dr Ludwig Stumpfegger, the only doctor left in the bunker, with ampoules of hydrocyanic acid, a liquid clear as water with a scent of bitter almonds.

Speer's Farewell to Hitler

Albert Speer determined to see Hitler one last time in the Berlin bunker as the Soviets reached the suburbs. His plane landed by the Brandenburg Gate. 'Was this to be the end of our many [twelve] years of association? For many days, month after month we had sat together over our joint [architectural] plans,

Waldenburg in Baden-Württemberg was destroyed during intense fighting in April 1945.

almost like co-workers and friends. For many years he had received my family and me at Obersalzberg and had shown himself a friendly, often solicitous host.' Speer had an emotional bond with his Führer, who had promoted him to the highest levels of authority in the Reich. Bormann and Adjutant Schaub greeted Speer. They wanted him to advise Hitler to get out of Berlin, fly to Berchtesgaden and take over command in South Germany and Hitler did in fact ask Speer for advice on two key issues. The first question was whether he should stay in Berlin or move out. Speer answered 'End your life as Führer in the capital'. The second question, surprisingly, was who should be Hitler's successor. Speer thought that Admiral Doenitz was infinitely preferable to Hermann Goering, the deputy Führer, to Goebbels or Martin Bormann and advised Hitler that the Admiral would be the best choice. In any case Bormann promptly sabotaged Goering's claim and Goebbels, with Himmler, committed suicide. The Admiral was the Reich Führer for three weeks in Flensberg, and the government was nicknamed the 'operetta government'.[58]

Hitler's 'Travel Marshal'

Julius Schaub was Hitler's personal servant and part of the Osteria Bavaria social circle. He negotiated 'fees' for Hitler at NSDAP meetings and rallies. The

Russian infantry in a suburban mansion.

'fees' were paid as 'expenses'. Schaub was described as 'chief adjutant', and shortly after his master's assumption of power he assumed responsibility for Hitler's tax affairs, all his travel arrangements and all the day-to-day monetary needs. Finally, Schaub guarded Hitler's private papers. Having served time in Landsberg prison with his master, Schaub was a dedicated, loyal servant who was eventually made an SS Colonel-General (*Obergruppenführer*) and ADC to the Führer. He took part in the 'blood purge' of the SA alongside Hitler and was also his bodyguard, chauffeur and valet for over twenty years, which were rewarded with a legacy in Hitler's will of 1938. The Hitler circle nicknamed Schaub the *Reisemarshall*, *Reise* meaning 'travel'. Eventually, immediately before Hitler's suicide in the bunker, Schaub destroyed most, perhaps all of Hitler's personal papers in the Chancellery garden. He himself left the bunker on the night of 25-26 April and was sent to the Berghof to destroy the rest of his master's papers. He arrived there drunk, to hand over a letter from Eva to her sister Gretl Braun. All his world had been destroyed. What did he have to live for? But live he did until 1967.

Hitler's Intrepid Lady Flier

Hanna Reitsch (1912-1979) was Germany's most famous test pilot and held the women's gliding records in the 1930s. She was devoted to Hitler and her

The Berghof in ruins following bombing and fire. In late April 1945 the house was damaged by British aerial bombs, set on fire by retreating SS troops in early May, and looted by Allied troops. The burnt out shell was demolished by the West German government in 1952.

A dead boy soldier with grenade still in hand; a book with a front cover portrait of Hitler to his left-hand side.

war service earned her the Iron Cross, First and Second Class – the only woman with that distinction. Hanna Reitsch had volunteered a project for her to pilot and man a V-1 rocket and crash it into the British Houses of Parliament. Air Marshal Milch refused it. This diminutive fearless woman flew through Russian AA fire into Berlin on 26 April 1945. With her was General von Greim whom Hitler had just promoted to command what was left of the Luftwaffe. On the way he had been wounded by the Russian fire and Hanna had piloted the damaged plane. On arrival at Hitler's bunker, being an old friend, she said 'My Führer, why do you stay? Why do you deprive Germany of your life?' Unfortunately Hitler was manic. His trusted Himmler had without permission offered the Allies unconditional surrender of Hitler's Third Reich. Goering was negotiating to take Hitler's place as Chancellor. The Russians were shelling the bunker. So Hitler ordered Hanna to fly von Greim back to Plön and put Himmler under arrest. She also took back to relative safety letters of farewell from poor doomed Eva Braun and the Goebbels family. Hitler gave the two fliers a cyanide pill each – just in case!

The Battle for the Führer's Succession

The Shakespearian drama unfolded. The king who was about to die in the Berlin bunker had two 'prime suspects': Field Marshal Hermann Goering (urgent tasks in southern Germany) and Himmler (wheeling and dealing with the Swedish Red Cross' Count Bernadotte for a negotiated surrender).

Hitler had always trusted Himmler, whom he called 'Trevor Heinrich', who had been his powerful, evil lynch-pin holding the Third Reich together by terror. Now he was acting unilaterally and therefore 'betraying' him. Goering's offer 'to take on the total leadership of the Reich as your deputy ...' was translated by Martin Bormann as 'treachery'. So Hitler declared that 'Goering and Himmler had brought irreparable shame on the country and the whole nation by secretly negotiating with the enemy without my knowledge and against my will'. He expelled them from the Nazi party and named his successor to the Fourth Reich, Grand Admiral Doenitz, as President of the Reich and Supreme Commander of the Wehrmacht.

Hitler's Will and Testament

At midnight on 28-29 April in the Führerbunker, Hitler dictated to his secretary Traudl Junge his personal and political testament. His personal testament ended, 'Myself and my wife choose death to escape the disgrace of being forced

Russian soldiers entering the Frankfurter Allee station in Berlin.

to resign or surrender. It is our wish to be cremated immediately at the place where I have done the greatest part of my work during the twelve years of service to my people.' But his political testament was a long, rambling blend of *Mein Kampf* and *Hitler's Second Book* and took Traudl Junge until six o'clock in the morning to complete. She wrote, 'I thought how undignified it all was. Just the same phrases, in the same quiet tone and then, at the end of it, those terrible words about the Jews. After all the despair, all the suffering, not one word of sorrow, of compassion. I remember thinking, he has left us with nothing. A nothing.' Dated 29 April 1945 4 a.m., four copies of the testament were entrusted to his adjutant and press chief. For a few hours, by deed of Hitler's will, he was succeeded by Reich Chancellor Paul Joseph Goebbels

Hitler's will and marriage certificate are in the Munich Photoarchiv Hoffmann T474, 10861, 10863, and with his signature, 13502.

Hitler's Field Marshals – A Dangerous Honour

The highest rank in the German Army and entirely in Hitler's control, was Field Marshal – a rather dangerous honour.

Von Brauchitsch resigned in 1941; Keitel was hanged in 1946; von Manstein was fired in 1944; von Rundstedt was fired in 1944; von Reichenau was killed in an air crash in 1942; von Bock was killed in an air raid in 1945; von Leeb was fired in 1942; von Kluge committed suicide in 1944; von Witzleben was executed in 1944; Rommel committed suicide in 1944; von Paulus was captured by the Russians in 1943; von Busch was fired in 1944; von Kleist died in captivity in Russia; and Model committed suicide in 1945.

The Luftwaffe Field Marshals included Goering who committed suicide in 1946.

The Political Testament, April 1945

'It is untrue that I, or anybody else in Germany wanted war in 1938. It was wanted and provoked exclusively by those international politicians who either came of Jewish stock, or worked for Jewish interests. After all my offers of disarmament, posterity cannot place the responsibility on me.

Before my death, I expel from the Party the former Reich Marshal, Hermann Goering and withdraw from him all the rights conferred upon him by the Decree of 29 June 1941 and by my Reichstag speech of 1 September 1939. In his place I appoint Grand Admiral Doenitz as Reich President and Supreme Commander of the Armed Forces.

Before my death I expel from the Party and from all his offices the former Reichsführer SS and Reich Minister of the Interior, Heinrich Himmler.'

So, more or less *in extremis* in his Berlin bunker with the Russians on the doorstep, Hitler threw out two of his greatest allies (Goebbels and Bormann were alongside him to the end). Goering and Himmler, his staunch companions since the early 1920s were casually and brutally dismissed at a moment's notice.

Eva Braun in the Berlin Bunker

About 2 a.m. on 29 April 1945 Hitler dictated to a secretary 'During my years of struggle, I believed I ought not to engage in marriage; but now my mortal span is at its end, I have resolved to take as my wife [EB] who came to this city when it was already under siege, after long years of true friendship, to link her fate with my own. It is her wish to go with me to her death as my wife. This will make up for all I could not give her because of my work on behalf of my people.' There followed a funeral wedding supper.

The Wedding in the Bunker

Hitler had dilly-dallied with Eva Braun since October 1929. She had been his loyal friend, rarely his lover, rarely his confidante but had given him her total

The end has come.

devotion for almost sixteen years. She came to join him and, as she was well aware, to die in the Berlin Führerbunker. Dressed in her elegant navy-blue dress embroidered with sequins and Ferragamo black suede shoes she married her strange, important, dying Führer. Walter Wagner, a Berlin municipal councillor, was deputed to conduct the civil ceremony. The witnesses were Goebbels and Bormann (whom Eva hated). Hitler and Eva declared that they were both of pure Aryan descent and not affected by incurable diseases that would exclude them from marriage. To add to the tension of the moment Wagner signed his name Waagner, and the bride started to write her surname with a B, then crossed it out and signed 'Eva Hitler née Braun'. The reception with champagne was held at 3.30 a.m. with no friends, no music, no flowers and only 36 hours left for friendship and some love.

Champagne in the Berlin Bunker

Hitler's death was imminent. 'I have resolved to stay here ... I shall not fight personally. There is always the danger that I would only be wounded and fall into the hands of the Russians alive. I don't want my enemies to disgrace my body either. I've given orders that I be cremated. Fraulein Braun wants to depart this life with me and I'll shoot Blondi [his dog] beforehand. Believe me Speer, it is easy for me to end my life. A brief moment and I'm freed of everything, liberated from this painful existence.' Later, towards midnight, Eva Braun sent an SS orderly to invite Speer, who had been almost a confidant over the years, to have a drink with him. 'How about a bottle of champagne for our farewell? and some sweets. I'm sure you haven't eaten in a long time.' So Moët et Chandon it was with cake and sweets and the two chatted away about Goebbels, Bormann and the Russians. At three o'clock on the morning of 30 April Speer said farewell to his Führer, who simply said, 'So, you're leaving? Good. *Auf Wiedersehen.*' Hitler retired to bed at four a.m.

Later that day, after a light lunch, Hitler bade farewell to his inner circle and to members of staff. He and Eva then retired to his study. In the outer chamber clustered members of the old guard – among them, Bormann, Goebbels, Artur Axmann, (founder and official of the Hitler Youth), Ambassador Hewel, Hitler's adjutant Otto Guensche, Hitler's valet Heinz Linge and Hitler's chauffeur Erich Kempka. Later, in the little green and white study Eva Hitler crushed and swallowed her cyanide pill and her husband put the 7.65 mm Walther pistol in his mouth, bit his capsule, fired and died. *Götterdämmerung* had come and gone.[58]

Eva Braun's Art Collection

Obviously funded by Hitler, Eva Braun possessed a significant art collection: landscapes by Fischbach, Baskon, Midgard, Wax, Gradl, others from Gallegos and Franke, and portraits by Rosl, Popp and Hugo Kauffmann. Eva's favourites were a watercolour by Hitler, 'The Asian Church', a portrait of Hitler by Bohnen Berger and a north Italian landscape by Bamberger. Martin Bormann gave her as a birthday present a head of a young girl and Hitler gave her a painting from the 'school' of Titian which Mussolini had given him. The collection included a portrait of the Führer by Knirr, a portrait of Eva by Bohnenberger, a landscape of Rimini, some old watercolours of Venice and canvases by Tiedgen, Hoberg, Krauss and Hengeler Hilbakt. The fate of this collection is not known.[25]

Martin Bormann's Death

After the bodies of Hitler, Eva Braun, Goebbels and his wife Magda (who had just murdered her six children) were doused with petrol and set alight by SS guards, there was a helterskelter rush for the door by the survivors. Three of them, General Hans Krebs, General Wilhelm Burgdorf and SS Hauptsturmführer Schedle stayed behind and shot themselves. Hitler's secretaries managed to escape safely to the West. Martin Bormann and his companion, Dr Stumpfegger also escaped – but not far. For many years rumours abounded concerning Bormann, with flight to South America as a possibility. But they got as far as Lehrter railway station, came under Russian fire, were wounded and took their cyanide capsules. Their bodies were buried under the rubble and were not discovered and identified until many years later. So Hitler's Mephistopholes probably went to Hades.[53]

Right: General Helmuth Weidling (left) was given the last command of Berlin by Hitler, but surrendered to the Russians 2 May 1945.

Below: Paratroopers from the 101st Airborne at Unterstein, loading recovered art treasures stolen by Goering, April 1945.

The Russians take the Reichstag, 2 May 1945.

Hitler's Death

On 1 May 1945 at a political dinner party with Churchill, Lord Beaverbrook, Oliver Lyttelton and others Jock Colville brought in the sensational announcement broadcast by the Nazi wireless that Hitler had been killed at his post in the Reichs Chancery in Berlin and that Admiral Doenitz was taking his place. It was thought that Hitler might have been dead for several days, but 1 May is a symbolic date in the Nazi calender and no doubt the circumstances ('fighting with his last breath against Bolshevism') were carefully invented with an eye to the future Hitler myth and legend. Churchill thought that Hitler was perfectly right to die like that![13]

Hitler's Huge Purchases of Art

One of Hitler's keenest ambitions was to plan and endow a huge art complex with a museum in his favourite home town of Linz. During 1943 and 1944 he purchased some three thousand paintings at a cost of 150 million Reichsmarks. A further eight million Reichsmarks were spent in the last twelve months of the war. In late 1945 American troops found 6,755 paintings owned by Hitler in the salt mines of Alt-Ausee, destined for the Linz museum.[57]

On 8 May 1945, Doenitz authorised Field Marshal Wilhelm Keitel to sign an unconditional surrender in Berlin. Although Germany had surrendered to the Allies a day earlier, Stalin had insisted on a second surrender ceremony in Berlin.

The Ashes of the Third Reich

Hitler was dead. So were his wife Eva Braun and the whole Goebbels family. SS Brigadier Wilhelm Mohnke, commandant of the Berlin bunker citadel had given orders for a mass breakout on the evening of 1 May. Of the key witnesses, Bormann was discovered dead much later, and his doctor Stumpfegger had taken poison on 2 May in the Invalidstrasse. The secretaries, most fortunately, escaped to safety – Gerda Christian, Traudl Junge and Else Kruger. SS officers Otto Guensche and Heinz Linge, Hitler's valet, were soon captured by the Russians and imprisoned in Moscow.

The Russians arrived at the bunker on 2 May and immediately began to search for the bodies of Hitler and his associates. On 11 May they showed Hitler's dental technician, Fritz Echtman, a cigar box containing part of a jawbone and two dental bridges. From his records he identified the jawbone and a bridge as belonging to Hitler and the other bridge to Eva Braun.

The ashes of the Third Reich were to be found in a cigar box.

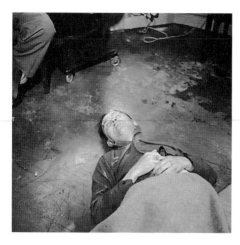

The body of Heinrich Himmler,
23 May 1945.

Sippenhaft

Heinrich Himmler had almost total physical control over Germany and the occupied territories. His SS and Gestapo were feared all round Europe for their savagery and brutality. The many concentration and extermination camps were under his control, run by the *Totenkopfverbände* (Death's Head branch of the SS). His *Einsatzgruppen* SS special action groups, four units each of 3,000 men murdered about three-quarters of a million Jews and Russian political commissars in Russia. The word 'resettled' was a euphemism for extermination. Himmler was Hitler's appalling henchman who carried out the 'Final Solution' on his Führer's instructions. A highly intelligent man, he was responsible for planning methods of murder such as mobile gas vans. After the Stauffenberg July 1944 bomb plot failed Himmler reintroduced the medieval custom of *sippenhalf* or 'blood guilt' whereby treachery was a manifestation of diseased blood and thus the *entire* families of the suspected assassins or traitors must be exterminated.

On 22 May 1945 Himmler, a fugitive, was arrested by a British soldier in this author's divisional area around Flensberg in Schleswig Holstein; the following day, before he could be interrogated, he used his cyanide pill to avoid the hangman.

The Fourth Reich – Hitler's Legacy

When Adolf Hitler via Martin Bormann ousted Hermann Goering from his role as his successor in mid-April 1945, by default Grand Admiral Doenitz, Commander of the German Navy from 1943, on Hitler's grisly, macabre death in the sordid Berlin bunker, became 'de facto' Führer of the Fourth Reich.

The Allied high command in the West had several very difficult decisions to make. Festung Holland, under the iniquitous Gauleiter Seyss-Inquart and General Blaskovitch were still full of fight. Almost 200,000 German and Dutch SS troops were penned into the Grebbe and Ems river enclave and threats had been made to smash all the dykes and return the country into the North Sea again. In Denmark 172,000 Wehrmacht, kriegsmarines and Luftwaffe, plus 40,000 naval personnel were undefeated. But in Norway the problem was much worse. Over 400,000 well-armed troops across the three services were clamouring for a fight. Reichskommissar Joseph Terboven, SS General Riedess and Jonas Lie, head of the Norwegian SS, plus the infamous Vidkun Quisling had no intention of surrendering. However Admiral Doenitz, as Führer of the Fourth Reich, realised that the threat from Stalin's brutal marauding hordes was a far greater threat, and acted accordingly.

From his small centre of power in and around Flensburg on the Danish frontier, he told the German nation over Radio Hamburg: 'I take over the command of all branches of the German Wehrmacht in the determination to continue the struggle against Bolshevism ...' He then ordered the Gauleiter of Hamburg (unwillingly) to surrender, summoned Seyss-Inquart, the Governor of Denmark Lindemann and Terboven, and convinced and ordered them to surrender without a final *Götterdämmerung*.

Finally, in Operation Blackout on 23 May the British 11th Armoured Division sent its Hussar Comet tanks and motorised infantry into the Fourth Reich and

The author, right, RHA lieutenant, Kiel, May 1945.

captured 8,500 Germans including Admiral Doenitz, General Jodl, Reinbecke, Dethleffson and Reich Minister Alfred Speer. And the British Liberation Army and Royal Navy in swift but complicated operations, captured nearly a million well-equipped and mildly belligerent armed survivors of the Third Reich during the months of May and June 1945.

Operation Eclipse

This secret plan was the end-game of the Third Reich, encompassing the capture of Hitler's armed forces penned into Schleswig-Holstein, and those in Holland, Denmark and Norway, in effect the complete destruction of the German war potential. Admiral Doenitz, as Fuhrer of the Fourth Reich, was between the devil and the deep blue sea. Stalin's cossack millions were pushing their way towards the Baltic and Field Marshal Montgomery's troops, including the 11th Armoured Division in which the author fought, only just reached Kiel and the Danish borders before the Russian Marshal Konstantin Rokossovsky's troops arrived at Wismar. Doenitz played for time to allow as many German citizens and troops as possible to escape to the West, since the Allies were more likely to respect the Geneva Convention than the Russians. Although Montgomery had signed the Instrument of Surrender on 4 May, the diehard Governors of Holland (Seyss-Inquart), Norway (Terboven) and Denmark (Lindemann) had between them nearly a million men under arms and longing to fight for the Fatherland.

Operation Eclipse was a miracle of improvisation involving the Royal Navy, British Army, Airborne troops and the RAF co-ordinating with the local Freedom fighters.

Many of Hitler's Reichkommissars committed suicide, many more faced the death penalty from local courts. By October 1946 Hitler's million undefeated troops were back in Schleswig Holstein, disarmed and awaiting screening to separate the goats (dangerous) from the sheep (less dangerous).

Retribution

The Allies agreed that there should be a grand showcase trial of all the captured Nazi hierarchy. This started in November 1945 in Nuremberg and lasted for nine months; in the end, using careful, thorough Anglo-American judicial procedures, justice was done and seen to be done. The Russians and French demanded the death penalty for every defendant with the minimum of legal 'fuss'. 'Crimes against humanity' were fairly easily established. For instance, the extermination camp at Mauthausen had seven volumes of Totenbucher (death books) in red leather, handsomely tooled. The name, sex, age, nationality, camp number, death number and cause of death for the 35,318 men, women and children who were exterminated in five years. The victims all apparently died of the same ailment, heart failure. They died in alphabetical order. They died at brief intervals.

The SS (camp commandants were usually SS colonels), the Waffen SS, the Gestapo, the SD (the Nazi party's security and intelligence body) were all declared guilty organisations.

Adolf Eichmann, who was put in charge of 'The Final Solution' by Hitler, estimated that his policies killed six million Jews – four million in the extermination camps, three million Poles, two million Russians and one million Germans.

Bergen-Belsen was the largest concentration camp – the author's battlegroup was the first to go in at 10 a.m. on 14 April 1945. The trial of 44 camp guards and the camp doctor took place in Luneberg and on 16 November, 30 of them were declared guilty. There were also half a dozen smaller camps, mainly clustered around Hamburg. This author was the junior officer of the judge/jury at Hamburg in 1945 and in Oldenburg in 1946. All the trials were supervised by a Judge Advocate General, a top-ranking British barrister, to ensure fair play, such as efficient interpreters for the Crown and defendant and efficient counsel for the accused. The author was one of the official witnesses when Mr Albert Pierrepoint, the last British hangman, executed thirteen war criminals at

Alfred Jodl and a dejected-looking Alfred Rosenberg at Nuremberg, 1946.

First row: Goering, Hess, Ribbentrop, Keitel. Second row: Doenitz, Raeder, Schirac and Sauckel; December 1945.

Hameln on 12 December 1945 – before lunch! Altogether Pierrepoint hanged about 240 war criminals on his fifteen three-day working visits to the British zone in a two-year period.

It took five long years of fighting to bring Hitler's Third Reich to its knees and peace. Nevertheless several million Russian POWs in Germany were deemed by Stalin to be traitors and on their return to Russia were either shot or sent to the gulags. A million or more German POWs in Russia never returned to their Fatherland.

Bibliography

1. Aldrich, Richard *Witness to War,* Corgi 2005
2. Allen, Peter *Crown and Swastika,* Robert Hale 1983
3. Allen, Martin *Himmler's Secret War,* Robson 2005
4. Baur, Hans *Hitler's Pilot,* Frederick Muller, 1958
5. Bloch, Michael *Ribbentrop,* Abacus 2003
6. Bryant, Arthur *Turn of the Tide,* Reprint Society 1958
7. Bullock, Alan *Hitler,* Penguin 1967
8. Burleigh, Michael *Third Reich,* Pan Books 2001
9. Burleigh, Michael *Germany turns Eastwards,* Pan Books 2002
10. Chant, C. *Warfare & the Third Reich,* Salamander 1998
11. Chesnoff, Richard *Pack of Thieves,* Weidenfeld and Nicolson 2001
12. Churchill, Winston *The Gathering Storm,* Reprint Society 1950
13. Colville, John *Fringes of Power,* Lyons Press 2002
14. Conradi, Peter *Hitler's Piano Player,* Duckworth 2005
15. Delaforce, Patrick *Invasion of the Third Reich* (Amberley 2011)
16. Delaforce, Patrick *The Hitler File* (O'Mara Books 2007)
17. Dodd, M. *My years in Germany,* Gollanz 1939
18. Fest, Joachim *Hitler,* Weidenfeld and Nicolson 1974
19. Fest, Joachim *Inside Hitler's Bunker,* Pan 2005
20. Fitzgerald, Michael, *Adolf Hitler: A Portrait,* Spellmount 2007
21. Gilbert, G. M., *The Psychology of Dictatorship,* Ronald Press 1950
22. Gisevius, H. B. *To the Bitter End,* Boston 1947
23. *Goebbels' Diaries* (Hamish Hamilton 1948, L. Lochner Ed.)
24. Greiner, Joseph *Das Ende des Hitler-Mythos,* Amalthea 1947
25. Gunn, Nerin *Eva Braun: Hitler's Mistress,* Bantam 1969
26. Halder, Franz *War Diary,* Munich 1949
27. Hamann, Brigitte *Hitler's Vienna,* OUP 1999
28. Hanfstaeng, Ernst *Hitler, the Missing Years,* Eyre & Spottiswood 1957
29. Heiden, Konrad *The Fuhrer,* Carroll & Graf, NY 1999
30. Hoffman, Heinrich *Hitler was my Friend,* Burke 1955
31. Hibbert, C. *Mussolini,* Longman 1962
32. Hitler, Adolf *Mein Kampf,* Hurst & Blackett 1939
33. Hitler, Adolf *Second Book,* Enigma 2003
34. Irons, Roy *Hitler's Terror Weapons,* Collins 2002

35. Jetzinger, Franz *Hitler's Youth*, Hutchinson 1953
36. Jones, Nigel *Birth of the Nazis* (Carroll & Graf 2004)
37. Jörgensen, C. *Hitler's Espionage Machine*, Lyons Press 2004
38. Junge, Trudl *Until the Final Hour*, Weidenfeld & Nicholson 2003
39. Kershaw, Ian *Hitler – Hubris*, Penguin 2001
40. Kershaw, Ian *Hitler – Nemesis*, Penguin 2001
41. Kershaw, Ian *Making Friends with Hitler*, Allan Lane 2004
42. King, Francis *Satan and Swastika*, Mayflower 1976
43. Kordt, Erich *Nicht aus den akten*, Stuttgart 1950
44. Kubizek, A. *The Young Hitler I knew*, Allen Wingate 1954
45. Lambert, Angela *The Lost Life of Eva Braun*, Centruy 2006
46. Lovell, Mary *Mitford Girls*, Abacus 2002
47. Macksey, Kenneth *Hitler Options*, Wrens Park 1995
48. Magenheimer, Heinz *Hitler's War*, Cassell 2004
49. Maser, Werner *Hitler's Letters and Notes*, Allen Lane 1973
50. Matthews, Rupert *Hitler: Military Commander*, Arcturus 2003
51. Pool, James *Who Financed Hitler?* Dial Press, 1978
52. Reuth, Ralf Georg *Goebbels*, Constable 1993
53. Read, Anthony *Devil's Disciples*, Jonathan Cape 2003
54. Read, Anthony and Fisher, D. *Fall of Berlin*, Pimlico 1995
55. Ryback, Timothy *Hitler's Private Library*, (Bodley Head 2008)
56. Schad, Martha *Hitler's Spy Princess*, Sutton 2004
57. Shirer, William L. *Nightmare Years 1930-40*, Birlinn 1984
58. Speer, Albert *Inside the Third Reich*, Sphere Books 1971
59. Stafford, David *Churchill and Secret Service* Abacus 2001
60. Taylor, James and Shaw, W. *The Third Reich*, Penguin 1997
61. Trevor-Roper, Hugh (ed.) *Hitler's Table Talk (1941-4)*, Enigma 2000
62. Welch, Clair *Rise and Fall of the Nazis*, (Magpie 2008)
63. Whetton, Cris *Hitler's Fortune*, Pen and Sword 2004
64. Whiting, Charles *Hitler's Secret War*, L. Cooper 2001
65. *World War II Collection*, The Stationery Office 2001

Journals

66. *Jewish Chronicle* of London, 6 September 1996
67. *The Daily Telegraph* news article, September 2006

Archives

68. Bundesarchiv Koblenz R43 II/957 p. 71
69. Cabinet Paper; CP(45) 48 to the British Cabinet File, PRO [Cabinet File] CAB66/66.
70. FO 837/593, National Archives, Kew
71. FO 371/26542, National Archives, Kew
72. German Foreign Policy Document 5740/HO 30995-031018
73. German Foreign Policy Document 5740/HO 31457-61
74. Goebbels 'Tagebucher', Bundesarchiv, Munich 1987

Dramatis Personæ

These mini-biographies are short sketches of the main characters who marched on and off the stage of the Third Reich and who are also mentioned in this book. In particular, focus is given on how they met their end. Where a character is prominently illustrated in the text, no head-shot is provided. Appropriate illustrations are not available for every person mentioned.

Amann: Max Amann (1891-1957)

Amann was an official with the honorary rank of SS-Obergruppenführer. He was Hitler's sergeant during the First World War and became his literary agent, publisher – he published Mein Kampf – financial adviser and almost, but not quite, a friend. Arrested after the War, Amann was deemed a Hauptschuldiger ('main guilty one') and sentenced, in 1948, to ten years in a labour camp, but was released in 1953. Stripped of his property, pension rights and practically all of his fortune, he died in poverty on 30 March 1957.

Axmann: Artur Axmann (1913-1996)

Axmann succeeded Baldur von Schirach as Reich Youth Leader (Reichsjugendführer) of the Nazi Party in 1940. In 1941, he was severely wounded on the Eastern Front, losing an arm. During the last weeks of the War his units consisted mostly of children and adolescents. In May 1949, a Nuremberg de-Nazification court classified him as a 'major offender', sentencing him to prison for three years and three months. Axmann became a prosperous businessman after the War.

Bechstein: Helene Bechstein (1876-1951)

Helene, with her husband Edwin (d. 1934), of the famous piano manufacturing firm, was a close friend of Hitler's. She bestowed many gifts on him including his first luxury car, a red Mercedes costing 26,000 marks, and frequently invited him to Berchtesgaden, her family's villa. It was always Helene expectation that Hitler would marry her daughter, Lotte.

Beck: Ludwig August Theodor Beck (1880-1944)

A German general and Chief of Staff between 1935-38, Beck became increasingly disillusioned with the Nazi Party, standing in opposition to the increasing authoritarianism of the regime and Hitler's aggressive foreign policy; he resigned from his post in August 1938. In 1943, he planned two abortive attempts to kill Hitler by means of a bomb. In 1944, he was one of the driving forces behind the 20 July assassination plot. It was proposed that Beck would become the head of the provisional government that would assume power in Germany after Hitler had been eliminated. The plot failed, and by the next morning Beck was in the custody of General Friedrich Fromm. He offered to commit suicide and shot himself, but in severe distress, he succeeded only in severely wounding himself; a sergeant was brought in to administer the coup de grâce.

Blomberg: Werner Eduard Fritz von Blomberg (1878-1946)

Blomberg was a German Field Marshal, Minister of War and Commander-in-Chief of the Armed Forces until January 1938. He advised Hitler to allow Germany more time to re-arm before pursuing a high-risk strategy of localized wars likely to trigger a much larger conflict. Goering and Himmler tried to discredit Blomberg by accusing him of being a homosexual; he and his wife were subsequently exiled for a year to the isle of Capri. Having spent the War in obscurity, Blomberg was captured by the Allies in 1945 and gave evidence at the Nuremberg Trials. In March 1946, while at Nuremberg, he died of cancer.

Bormann: Martin Ludwig Bormann (1900-1945)

In May 1941, Hess's flight to Britain cleared the way for Bormann to become head of the Party Chancellery. Bormann was a master of intricate political infighting; as Hitler's private secretary, his proximity to the Führer made him the enemy of Goebbels, Goering, Himmler, Rosenberg, Ley, Speer and a plethora of other high-ranking officers and officials, both public and private. Bormann took charge of all of Hitler's paperwork, appointments and personal finances. Hitler came to have complete trust in Bormann, giving the latter tremendous influence. He died attempting to escape from Berlin in May 1945.

Brandmayer: Balthaser Brandmayer (1892-1960)

Balthaser was a war comrade of Hitler's in the Bavarian Reserve Infantry Regiment 16. After the War he worked as a bricklayer in Bruckmühl. In 1932, together with the publisher Heinz Bayer, Brandmayer wrote Two Messengers, a book on the experiences shared with Hitler during the War. In the same year he joined the party and in 1934, as Hitler's former comrade, he was employed by the Deutsche Reichsbahn. In 1937 Hitler gave him 5,000 Reichsmarks 'to clarify his economic circumstances'. After the War he returned to bricklaying.

Brandt: Karl Brandt (1904-1948)

Brandt was SS-Gruppenführer in the Allgemeine-SS and SS-Brigadeführer in the Waffen-SS. Among other positions, he headed the administration of the euthanasia programme from 1939 and was selected as Hitler's personal physician in August 1934. Along with his deputy Werner Heyde and others, Brandt was involved in criminal human experimentation. He was convicted of crimes against humanity and hanged on 2 June 1948.

Brauchitsch: Heinrich Alfred Walther von Brauchitsch (1881-1948)

Brauchitsch was promoted to Field Marshal in 1940 and was a prominent architect of Hitler's 'blitzkrieg' war, making modifications to the original plan to overrun France. In 1941, the army's failure to take Moscow earned him Hitler's enmity, and after suffering a serious heart attack, he was relieved of his command on 10 December 1941. At the end of the War, Brauchitsch was arrested and charged with war crimes, but he died in Hamburg in 1948 before he could be prosecuted.

Braun: Eva Braun (1912-1945)

Eva Braun first met Hitler in 1929 while she was assistant to the beer-loving Heinrich Hoffmann, the Third Reich's official photographer. Eva attended the Nuremberg Rally in 1936, and Hitler's Berghof villa became her gilded cage. The staff referred to her as 'EB', addressed her as 'Madame' and kissed her hand. She referred to Hitler as 'Chief' and he called her 'Patscherl'. Over the years they exchanged hundreds of letters and Hitler paid her monthly wages to the Hoffmann studios until the end of their lives. She committed suicide with Hitler on 30 April 1945 in his underground bunker in the Reich Chancellery gardens in Berlin.

Braun: Wernher Magnus Maximilian, Freiherr von Braun (1912-1977)

Braun was one of the leading figures in the development of rocket technology. In his twenties and early thirties he was the central figure in Germany's rocket development programme, responsible for the V-2 combat rocket. After the War, he and some of his rocket team were taken to the United States as part of the secret Operation Paperclip. Braun was the chief architect of the Saturn V launch vehicle, the superbooster that propelled the Apollo spacecraft to the moon.

Brueckner: Wilhelm Brueckner (1884-1954)

On 9 November 1923, Brueckner took part in the Beer Hall Putsch in Munich and was sentenced to a year and a half in prison. In 1930 he became Adolf Hitler's adjutant and bodyguard, later rising to Chief Adjutant, one of Hitler's closest confidants next to Goebbels and Dietrich. On 18 October 1940, he was suddenly relieved of his position for having an argument with Hitler's house manager, Arthur Kannenberg; an event probably manipulated by Bormann. Julius Schaub succeeded Brueckner, who joined the Wehrmacht, becoming a colonel by the end of the War.

Bruckmann: Elsa Bruckmann (1865-1946)

Born as Princess Cantacuzene of Romania, Elsa was the wife of publisher Hugo Bruckmann. She managed the 'Salon Bruckmann' and made it her mission to introduce Adolf Hitler to leading industrialists.

Buch: Walter Buch (1883-1949)

Buch was an early member of the NSDAP. Following the abortive Beer Hall Putsch, Buch maintained contact between Hitler, imprisoned in Landsberg, and the illegal party leadership in Austria. He was instrumental in Roehm's downfall, and as a jurist he was also responsible for the 'legalisation' of the anti-Semitic vandalism carried out by party members during the so-called Kristallnacht (9 November 1938). After the War, Buch was seized and sentenced to five years in a labour camp. In July 1949, in the course of yet another wave of de-Nazification, he was classified as a 'Hauptschuldiger' ('main guilty one'), meaning that he was considered to be an especially culpable war criminal. On 12 November, he ended his own life by slitting his wrists and throwing himself into the Ammersee.

Buechner: Bruno Buechner (1871-1943)

Buechner was a famous bicycle road racer and pioneer pilot in German Africa. With his wife Elisabeth he bought the Moritz Pension in Obersalzburg which he renamed Platterdorf Hotel. The Buechners were friends of Hitler, and Elisabeth, a towering Brünhilde type, gave the Hitler a rhinoceros-hide dog whip.

Buehler: Josef Buehler (1904-1948)

Buehler joined the NSDAP in 1922 and was one of the members of the attempted putsch in Munich on 9 November 1923. He was appointed Minister of Justice for Bavaria in 1933 and was secretary and deputy governor to the Nazi-controlled General Government in Kraków. Buehler attended the Wannsee Conference on 20 January 1942 as the representative from the Governor General's office. After the War he was tried before the Supreme National Tribunal of Poland for crimes against humanity; he was condemned to death, and executed in Kraków.

Burgdorf: Wilhelm Burgdorf (1895-1945)

Burgdorf was a Wehrmacht general. He was promoted to Chief of the Army Personnel Office and Chief Adjutant to Hitler in October 1944. At that time, he was further promoted in rank to Lieutenant General. On 14 October 1944, Burgdorf arrived at the Rommel home. He had been instructed to offer Rommel a choice – take poison, receive a state funeral, and obtain immunity for his family and staff, or face a trial for treason. Rommel drove away with Burgdorf and Maisel; Rommel's family received a telephone call 10 minutes later saying that he had died. On 29 April 1945, Burgdorf, Krebs, Joseph Goebbels, and Martin Bormann witnessed and signed Hitler's last will and testament. On 2 May, following the earlier suicides of Hitler and Goebbels, Burgdorf and his colleague, Chief of Staff Hans Krebs, also committed suicide by gunshot to the head.

Canaris: Wilhelm Franz Canaris (1887-1945)

Canaris joined the German Imperial Navy in 1905 and served during the First World War. In 1935, Canaris was made head of the Abwehr, Germany's official military intelligence agency. Later that year, he was promoted to Rear Admiral. In 1938, with the support of MI6, Canaris devised a plan to assassinate Hitler, precipitating the dissolution of the entire Nazi Party before the invasion of Czechoslovakia, but nothing came of this. The assassination of Heydrich in Prague, organised by MI6, was done in part to preserve Canaris in his important position. Evidence mounted that he was playing a double game, and at the insistence of Himmler, who had suspected him for a long time, Hitler dismissed Canaris in February 1944, replacing him with Schellenberg. Canaris was put under house arrest, preventing him from taking any direct part in the 20 July plot. Himmler kept Canaris alive for some time because he planned to use him secretly as a future contact with the British. When Himmler's plan failed to materialise, he received Hitler's approval to send Canaris to his death. He was humiliated before witnesses and then led to the gallows barefoot and naked on 9 April 1945.

Christian: Gerda Christian (1913-1997)

Gerda Christian was one of Hitler's secretaries. She had been engaged to Hitler's driver Erich Kempka, but this fell apart and she later married Luftwaffe officer Eckhard Christian in 1943. In April 1945, after his promotion to the Luftwaffe Command Staff, Eckhard Christian was stationed in Berlin at the Führerbunker HQ. He left the bunker complex on 22 April 1945 to become Chief of the Liaison Staff of the Luftwaffe to OKW Command Staff North. Gerda and Traudl Junge both volunteered to remain with Hitler in the Führerbunker. After Hitler's death, Gerda tried to escape Berlin, but she was captured by the Russians the following day. She was a committed Hitler loyalist, and divorced Eckhard Christian in 1946 because he did not remain with her in the Führerbunker until after Hitler's death. Gerda moved to Düsseldorf, where she worked at a hotel and died at the age of 83 in 1997.

Ciano: Galeazzo Ciano (1903-1944)

Count Ciano held diplomatic posts in South America before marrying Edda Mussolini in 1930. In 1936, he was appointed by Mussolini as Minister of Foreign Affairs. Ciano was a supporter of the German alliance, but objected to the way that Hitler ordered the invasion of Poland without consulting Italy. Mussolini followed Ciano's advice to keep out of the Second World War until the fall of France in May 1940. In 1942 Ciano became increasingly dissatisfied with Mussolini and in February 1943, after a series of heated arguments, he resigned as Foreign Minister. Ciano left Rome after Mussolini was overthrown, but he was captured by the Germans. On 11 January 1944, on Mussolini's order, Ciano was given a mock trial and executed by a shot to the head while tied to a chair.

Darré: Richard Walther Oscar Darré (1895-1953)

In 1933, Darré became Reich Minister of Food and Agriculture, serving from June 1933 to May 1942. He developed a plan for Rasse und Raum (Race and Space) which provided the ideological background for the Nazi expansionist policy, called Drang nach Osten and Lebensraum (Drive to the East and Living space). Darré strongly influenced Himmler in his goal to create a German racial aristocracy based on selective breeding. He was forced to resign in 1942. At Nuremberg he was sentenced to seven years, but was released in 1950 and died of cancer in 1953.

Dietrich: Josef 'Sepp' Dietrich (1892-1966)

Prior to 1929, Dietrich was Adolf Hitler's chauffeur and bodyguard but received rapid promotion after his participation in the murder of Hitler's political opponents during the 'Night of the Long Knives'. Hitler promoted him within the Wehrmacht and he fought in France, Greece and Yugoslavia before taking command of the I.SS-Panzerkorps, attached to Army Group Centre on the Eastern Front. In 1943, Dietrich was sent to Italy to recover Benito Mussolini's mistress Clara Petacci. He commanded the 6.SS-Panzer-Armee in the Battle of the Bulge in 1944 and received numerous German military medals, but also became notorious for his mistreatment of prisoners of war. He was sentenced to life imprisonment, but this was later reduced to twenty-five years. He was eventually released in 1958. Dietrich died of a heart attack in 1966.

Dodd: Martha Eccles Dodd (1908-1990)

Martha was the vivacious young daughter of US Ambassador Professor William E. Dodd. She was very attracted to Hitler and was invited to have tea with him at the Kaiserhof Hotel on a number of occasions. She once declared that she was in love with him and wanted to organise him a tour of the United States. This did not meet with the approval of Goering, who spread the rumour that Martha was a Soviet agent; Hitler refused to see her again and banned her from all future diplomatic receptions. Soon after, reports circulated that she had attempted suicide by slashing her wrists. In 1938 she married American millionaire investment broker, Alfred Kaufman Stern, and became active in left-wing politics.

Doenitz: Karl Doenitz (1891-1980)

At the start of the Second World War, Doenitz was the senior submarine officer in the German Navy. In January 1943, he replaced Grand Admiral Erich Raeder as Commander-in-Chief of the German Navy. On 30 April 1945, after the death of Adolf Hitler and in accordance with Hitler's last will and testament, Doenitz was named Hitler's successor as Staatsoberhaupt (Head of State), with the title of Reichspräsident (President) and Supreme Commander of the Armed Forces. On 7 May 1945, he ordered Alfred Jodl to sign an official German surrender in Rheims, France. Doenitz remained as head of the temporary Flensburg Government until it was dissolved by the Allied powers on 23 May 1945. Doenitz was imprisoned for ten years in Spandau and released October 1956.

Drexler: Anton Drexler (1884-1942)

Drexler was instrumental in the formation of the anti-communist German Workers' Party. The German Workers' Party was the precedent for the Nazi Party; Drexler served as mentor to Hitler during his early days in politics. Drexler changed the name of the party to the National Socialist German Workers' Party early in 1920. By 1921, Hitler was rapidly becoming the undisputed leader of the party and Drexler was thereafter reduced to the purely symbolic position of honorary president; he left the party in 1923. He had no part in the NSDAP's re-founding in 1925, and he rejoined the party only after Hitler had come to power in 1933. He received the party's Blood Order in 1934 and was still occasionally used as a propaganda tool until about 1937, but was largely forgotten by the time of his death.

Eckhart: Dietrich Eckhart (1868-1923)

Dietrich Eckhart, a nationalist poet, founded the Deutsche Arbeiterpartei with Gottfried Feder and Anton Drexler, which later became the NSDAP. Eckhart met Adolf Hitler when Hitler gave a speech before party members in 1919. He introduced Hitler to Erich Ludendorff, who was later imprisoned with Hitler in Landsberg, and Alfred Rosenberg. On 9 November 1923, Eckhart participated in the failed Beer Hall Putsch; he was arrested and placed in Landsberg Prison along with Hitler and other party officials, but was released and died of a heart attack in Berchtesgaden on 26 December 1923.

Eichmann: Adolf Eichmann (1900-1962)

Eichmann was an SS-Obersturmbannführer and one of the major organisers of the extermination camps in German-occupied Eastern Europe. After the War, he fled to Argentina and lived under a false identity. He was captured there by Mossad operatives and taken to Israel to face trial, where he was found guilty and executed by hanging in 1962.

Elser: (1903-1945)

Elser was an opponent of Nazism. He planned and carried out an assassination attempt on Hitler on 8 November 1939 in Munich at Hitler's annual speech on the anniversary of the failed Beer Hall Putsch. Hitler left the beer hall at about 13 minutes before Elser's bomb exploded as planned at 21:20. Elser was arrested by chance at 20:45, about 35 minutes before the bomb exploded, by the customs border police in Konstanz when he tried to cross the border into Switzerland. After his confession to the crime in Munich, Elser was taken to the Berlin headquarters of the Gestapo where he was severely tortured. He was imprisoned in Sachsenhausen and Dachau concentration camps, and just three weeks before Hitler's own suicide, the Führer ordered Elser to be executed.

Epp: Franz Ritter von Epp (1868-1946)

Epp served during the First World War and subsequently formed the Freikorps Epp, a right-wing paramilitary formation mostly made up of war veterans, of which future leader of the SA, Ernst Roehm, was a member. Epp became a member of the party and then of the Reichstag in 1928, holding this position until 1945. He served as the NSDAP's head of its Military-Political Office from 1928 to 1945, and later as leader of the German Colonial Society, an organisation devoted to regaining Germany's lost colonies. At the end of the War, he was imprisoned by the Americans and died in a prison camp in 1946.

Esser: Hermann Esser (1900-1981)

Esser entered the Nazi Party with Hitler in 1920 and became the editor of the Nazi paper Völkischer Beobachter and a Nazi member of the Reichstag. In the early days of the party, he was Hitler's de facto deputy. Esser was a renowned pervert; after a scandal whereby he sexually assaulted the underage daughter of a businessman, he was suspended from the party. Even Hitler said of him: 'I know Esser is a scoundrel, but I shall hold on to him as long as he is useful to me.' From 1939 to the end of the War he served as the Under-Secretary for Tourism in the Reich Propaganda Ministry. He was imprisoned twice and died in 1981.

Feder: Gottfried Feder (1883-1941)

Feder was an economist, an important early member of the Nazi Party, and the party's economic theoretician. Initially, it was his lecture in 1919 that drew Hitler into the party. Hitler eventually decided to move away from Feder's economic views; when he became Chancellor in 1933, he appointed Feder as Under-Secretary at the Ministry of Economics. After the 'Night of the Long Knives', Feder began to withdraw from the government, finally becoming a professor at the Technische Hochschule in Berlin in 1936, where he stayed until his death in 1941.

Freiser: Roland Freiser (1893-1945)

Freiser joined the Nazi Party in 1925. He rose to become Reich Minister of Justice 1934-42 and was at Wannsee Conference. In 1942 he became President of the People's Court; the number of death sentences rose sharply under his stewardship and he was known for humiliating defendants and shouting at them. He was killed during an American bombing raid in February 1945.

Fritsch: Werner Thomas Ludwig Freiherr von Fritsch (1880-1939)

Fritsch was a prominent Wehrmacht officer and a member of the German High Command. Himmler and Goering accused him of being homosexual, but Fritsch had never been a womaniser and had preferred to concentrate on his army career. He was forced to resign on 4 February 1938. It soon became known that the charges were false, and Fritsch was acquitted on 18 March, but the damage to his name had been done. He was the second German general to be killed during the Second World War – by a Polish bullet on 10 September 1939.

Fromm: Friedrich Fromm (1888-1945)

Fromm was Commander-in-Chief of the Reserve Army, responsible for training recruits and replacing personnel in the Wehrmacht. Though he was aware that Stauffenberg was planning an assassination attempt against Hitler, he remained quiet. When the plot failed, Fromm immediately had the conspirators executed to cover up potential allegations that he himself was involved. These actions did not save him, and he was eventually executed by firing squad on 12 March 1945.

Gansser: Emil Gansser (1874-1941)

Gansser was a pharmacy and chemical engineer. He joined the party in 1921 and mediated between the NSDAP and Siemens. Through his party and Siemens connections, he acquired wealth which he salted away in Swiss Banks.

Goebbels: Joseph Goebbels (1897-1945)

Goebbels came into contact with the Nazi Party in 1923 during the French occupation of the Ruhr, and became a member in 1924. He rose to power in 1933 along with Hitler and was appointed Propaganda Minister. One of his first acts was the burning of books. He exerted totalitarian control over the media, arts and information in Germany. Goebbels remained with Hitler in Berlin to the end; after Hitler's suicide, Goebbels succeeded him as Chancellor, but along with his wife Magda, he killed their six young children and then committed suicide.

Goering: Hermann Goering (1893-1946)

Goering fought in the First World War, initially in the infantry and then as a fighter pilot, finally commanding the famous Richthofen Squadron. A member of the party from its early days, he was wounded in 1923 during the failed Beer Hall Putsch. He suffered from a lifelong addiction to morphine after being treated with the drug for his injuries. He founded the Gestapo in 1933 and was appointed Commander-in-Chief of the Luftwaffe in 1935. At Nuremberg he was sentenced to death by hanging, but committed suicide by taking cyanide the night before his execution.

Graf: Ulrich Graf (1878-1950)

Graf became Hitler's personal bodyguard from 1920 to 1923. He was present at the Beer Hall Putsch, where, with Rudolf Hess, he cleared Hitler's way to the platform. In a mêlée at a subsequent march, Graf shielded Hitler with his body, receiving several bullets and probably saving Hitler's life. He was elected to the Reichstag in 1936, became an Oberführer in the SS in 1937 and on 20 April 1943, Hitler's birthday, he became an SS Brigadeführer. Graf survived the War and died in 1950.

Grynszpan: Herschel Grynszpan (1921-1944?)

Herschel was a German-born Jewish refugee of Polish parents. In Paris on 7 November 1938 he shot and killed Ernst vom Rath, a junior German Embassy official, saying he was acting in the name of 12,000 persecuted Jews. Grynszpan made no attempt to resist or escape, and identified himself correctly to the French police. Grynszpan was seized by the Gestapo after the German invasion of France and brought to Germany where he was last heard of in prison in 1944. His eventual fate is not known, but may be guessed at. He was eventually declared dead in 1960.

Guderian: Heinz Guderian (1885-1954)

General Guderian was a pioneer in the development of armoured warfare, and was the leading proponent of tanks and mechanisation in the Wehrmacht. He became Inspector-General of Armoured Troops, rose to the rank of Colonel General (Generaloberst), and was Chief of the General Staff of the Heer in the last year of the War. Guderian surrendered to American troops on 10 May 1945 and remained in US custody as a prisoner of war until his release on 17 June 1948. Despite Russian and Polish government protests, he was not charged with any war crimes.

Guensche: Otto Guensche (1917-2003)

Guensche first met Hitler in 1936 and was his SS orderly officer from 1940 to 1941. He then had front-line combat service until January 1943 when he became a personal adjutant for Hitler. In 1944, Guensche fought on the Eastern Front and then in France until March, when he again was appointed as a personal adjutant for Hitler. He was present at the 20 July 1944 assassination attempt on Hitler at the Wolf's Lair in Rastenburg. Guensche was entrusted by Hitler to ensure that his body was cremated after his death on 30 April 1945. He stood guard outside the room as Hitler and Eva Braun committed suicide. He was captured by Russian troops and after various prisons and labour camps he was released from Bautzen Penitentiary in 1956.

Gutmann: Hugo Gutmann (1880-1971)

Gutmann was a German-Jewish officer and Hitler's superior officer during the First World War. In 1938, Guttman was arrested by the Gestapo but released due to sympathetic SS personnel, who knew his history. In 1939, he and his family escaped to Belgium and in 1940, he emigrated to the USA just prior to the invasion. Guttman eventually settled in the city of St Louis, Missouri, where he changed his name to Henry G. Grant. He died in 1971.

Haase: Werner Haase (1900-1945)

In 1935 Haase began serving as Hitler's deputy personal physician. In the last days of the fighting in Berlin in late April 1945, Haase, with Ernst Guenther Schenck, was working to save the lives of wounded Nazis in an emergency casualty station located in the large cellar of the Reich Chancellery. On 29 April, Hitler expressed doubts about the cyanide capsules he had received through Himmler's SS. To verify the capsules' potency, Haase was summoned to the Führerbunker to test one on Hitler's dog Blondi. A cyanide capsule was crushed in the mouth of the dog, which died as a result. Haase was made a Russian prisoner, but died in captivity in 1945.

Halder: Franz Halder (1884-1972)

General Halder was Chief of the Army General Staff from 1938 until September 1942, when he was dismissed after frequent disagreements with Adolf Hitler. During the summer of 1942, Halder had told Hitler that he was underestimating the number of Russian military units, while Hitler argued that the Russians were nearly broken. Hitler concluded that the General no longer possessed an aggressive war mentality. Following a speech in which Hitler announced his plan to find a replacement for Halder, Halder walked out stating 'I am leaving' and was retired into the 'Führer Reserve' on 24 September 1942. Hitler had him imprisoned in early 1945 and he was turned over to US troops on 4 May 1945, spending the next two years in an Allied prisoner of war camp.

Hanfstaengl: Ernst 'Putzi' Hanfstaengl (1887-1976)

Hanfstaengl had an American mother and was brought up and educated in the USA where, in 1920, he married Helene Elise Adelheid Niemeyer. He returned to Germany in 1922 and soon became one of Hitler's most intimate followers. For much of the 1920s, Hanfstaengl introduced Hitler to Munich's high society and helped polish his image. He also helped to finance the publication of Mein Kampf, and the party's official newspaper, the Völkischer Beobachter. Hanfstaengl wrote both Brownshirt and Hitler Youth marches, based on his memories of Harvard football songs; he later claimed that he devised the chant 'Sieg Heil'. Several disputes arose between Hanfstaengl and Goebbels which led to him being removed from Hitler's staff in 1933. He and Helene divorced in 1936. Hanfstaengl fell completely out of Hitler's favour after he was denounced by Unity Mitford, a close friend of both the Hanfstaengls and Hitler. He moved to England where he was imprisoned as an enemy alien after the outbreak of the Second World War. In 1942 he was turned over to the US and worked for President Roosevelt's 'S-Project', revealing information on approximately 400 Nazi leaders.

Hanisch: Reinhold Hanisch (1884-1937?)

In 1909 Hanisch came to Vienna, where he met Hitler. In 1910 he lived with Hitler in the Meldemannstrasse men's dormitory. They created an informal partnership: while Hitler painted postcards and pictures, mostly watercolours, Hanisch would sell them. The men shared equally the sums received, but they later fell out. Hanisch served in the First World War and in 1918 he married. He was imprisoned for theft in 1923 and divorced in 1928. After 1930, to earn a basic living, he produced watercolours, which he sold as alleged works of Hitler from their years in Vienna. His fraud was discovered and in 1932 he was sentenced to three days in jail. He continued to forge Hitler pictures until a major prison sentence in 1936. After Hitler's rise to power, Hanisch made money from numerous interviews with national and international newspapers. His memoir of Hitler posthumously appeared in 1939 in The New Republic. He appears to have died in prison in 1937, but it is unknown how he died.

Hanke: Karl Hanke (1903-1945)

Hanke joined the party in 1928 and the SA in 1929. In 1932 he was made Chief Gau Organisational Director and personal adjutant to Goebbels. Hanke was the first party official to establish contact with the young architect Albert Speer and they became close friends. Hanke rose within the party but came unstuck in 1938 due to a liaison with Magda Goebbels who intended to leave her husband for him. He then joined the army and SS, rising to Reichsführer-SS. In May 1945, he escaped to Prague, but was captured and executed by Czech partisans.

Hanussen: Erik Jan Hanussen (1889-1933)

Hanussen was an Austrian Jewish publicist and clairvoyant performer acclaimed in his lifetime as a hypnotist, mentalist, occultist, and astrologer; he taught Hitler a great deal about the importance of dramatic effect. Predicting the Reichstag fire was his most famous feat of clairvoyance. After a miscalculated use of inside information, he was assassinated on 25 March 1933, most likely by a group of SA men.

Haushofer: Karl Haushofer (1869-1946)

Following the First World War, Haushofer forged a friendship with Hess who became his scientific assistant. In 1919 he became Privatdozent for political geography at Munich University and professor in 1933. After the establishment of the Nazi regime, Haushofer remained friendly with Hess, who protected him and his wife from the racial laws. After the plot of 20 July 1944, Haushofer's son Albrecht was arrested and later shot. From 24 September 1945 onwards, Haushofer was informally interrogated to determine whether he should stand trial at Nuremberg. On 10 March 1946 he and his wife committed suicide.

Heiden: Erhard Heiden (1901-1933)

Heiden was an early member of the party and in 1925 he joined a small stormtrooper bodyguard unit known as the Schutzstaffel (the SS). Heiden was an early advocate of separating the SS from its master organisation, the Sturmabteilung (SA). Heiden hired Himmler to serve as his deputy, regarding him as a 'keen young clerk'; he was soon dismissed by Hitler and succeeded by Himmler as Reichsführer-SS. In April 1933 he was arrested on Himmler's orders and killed shortly after.

Heines: Edmund Heines (1897-1934)

Heines joined the party and the SA. From 1931 to 1934, he served as an SA leader in Silesia and as Ernst Roehm's deputy. He was arrested during the 'Night of the Long Knives' and was caught in bed with an 18-year-old youth. He refused to cooperate and get dressed. When this was reported to Hitler, he went to the room and ordered him to get dressed within five minutes or risk being shot. Heines still refused to cooperate and Hitler became so furious that he ordered some SS men to take him and the boy outside to be executed.

Hess: Rudolf Hess (1894-1987)

After hearing Hitler speak for the first time in May 1920, Hess became completely devoted to him. He joined the fledgling Nazi Party in 1920 as one of its first members and commanded an SA battalion during the Beer Hall Putch. Hess served seven and a half months in Landsberg Prison and acted as Hitler's private secretary there, transcribing and partially editing Mein Kampf. He rose in Hitler's estimation and on the eve of the invasion of Poland, Hitler announced that should anything happen to both him and Goering, Hess would be next in the line of succession. On 10 May 1941 he flew solo to Scotland in an attempt to negotiate peace with the United Kingdom, where he was arrested and became a prisoner of war. Hess was tried at Nuremberg and sentenced to life imprisonment, which he served at Spandau Prison, Berlin.

Hettlage: Karl Maria Hettlage (1902-1995)

Hettlage was an SS captain and one the founding members of the National Socialist German Law Academy. From 1934 to 1938 he was city treasurer of Berlin and from 1938 to 1951 he served as a board member of Commerz and Private Bank. Until 1945, Hettlage was one of Speer's representatives and remained very close to him. Surprisingly, he was able to resume his career after the War without much difficulty, although the stain of his former position in the SS could not be completely erased. He served in Konrad Adenauer's post-war government.

Hewel: Walther Hewel (1904-1945)

Hewel was one of the earliest members of the party, joining as a teenager. After Hitler's imprisonment following the Beer Hall Putsch, Hewel stayed in Landsberg Prison with him and acted as his valet for several months. He served as a diplomat in the Foreign Ministry, and on 15 March 1939, he transcribed the conference between Hitler and Czech president, Emil Hácha. However, he spent most of the War without an official portfolio. Hewel usually ended up dealing with situations and events that Hitler could not handle; he remained in his inner circle right up to Hitler's suicide on 30 April 1945. Hewel was the last individual to engage in a long, personal conversation with Hitler, and was said to have tried to cheer him up. He killed himself on 2 May 1945, biting down on a cyanide capsule while shooting himself in the head.

Heydrich: Reinhard Tristan Heydrich (1904-1942)

Heydrich was one of the main architects of the Holocaust. He was an SS-Obergruppenführer, General der Polizei, Chief of the Reich Main Security Office and Stellvertretender Reichsprotektor of Bohemia and Moravia. Heydrich chaired the January 1942 Wannsee Conference, which laid out plans for the 'Final Solution' to the 'Jewish Question'. He helped organise Kristallnacht, a series of co-ordinated attacks against Jews throughout Germany and Austria. In Operation Anthropoid on 27 May 1942, Heydrich was attacked in Prague by a British-trained team who had been sent by the Czechoslovak government-in-exile to kill him. He died from his injuries a week later.

Himmler: Heinrich Luitpold Himmler (1900-1945)

Himmler joined the party in 1923 and the SS in 1925. In 1929 he was appointed Reichsführer-SS by Hitler. Himmler developed the SS into a powerful group with its own military. Following Hitler's orders, he set up and controlled the Nazi concentration camps. From 1943 onwards, he was both Chief of German Police and Minister of the Interior, overseeing all internal and external police and security forces, including the Gestapo. On Hitler's behalf, Himmler formed the Einsatzgruppen and built extermination camps. Late in the War, Hitler gave Himmler command of the Army Group Upper Rhine and the Army Group Vistula; he failed to achieve his assigned objectives and Hitler replaced him in these posts. Shortly before the end of the War, without Hitler's knowledge, Himmler attempted to open peace talks with the Western Allies. Hearing of this, Hitler dismissed him from all his posts in April 1945. Himmler was arrested by British forces and he committed suicide on 23 May 1945.

Hindenberg: Paul Ludwig Hans Anton von Beneckendorff und von Hindenburg (1847-1934)

After a long career in the Prussian Army, Hindenburg retired in 1911 but was recalled in 1914, becoming Chief of the General Staff from 1916. He was recalled to public life in 1925 to be elected as the second President of Germany. Hindenburg despised Hitler and condescendingly referred to him as that 'Bohemian corporal'. He dissolved the parliament twice in 1932 and eventually was forced by circumstances to appoint Hitler as Chancellor in January 1933. He died the following year.

Hitler: Paula Hitler (1896-1960)

Paula was seven years younger than her brother. At one time she worked as a secretary for a group of doctors in a military hospital, but she kept her identity a secret. Whenever she saw a small chapel when travelling in the mountains, she would go in and say a silent prayer for her brother. In March 1941, Hitler was staying at the Imperial Hotel in Vienna and it was here that Paula met him for the last time. Hitler never mentioned her in his writings because of his embarrassment at her weak mental state. After the War, she lived unmarried in a two-bedroom flat near Berchtesgaden. Her main interest was the Catholic Church. She died on 1 June 1960.

Hoesch: Leopold von Hoesch (1881-1936)

Hoesch was a career diplomat who began his political career in France in 1923. In 1932, Hoesch was transferred to London, where he remained until his death. He was well liked by most British statesmen, including Sir Anthony Eden. By 1934, Hoesch was beginning to challenge Hitler indirectly, sending communiqués to Konstantin von Neurath, Foreign Minister, detailing Hoesch's distrust of Ribbentrop whom Hitler had appointed to serve as Commissioner of Disarmament Questions. The relationship between Hoesch and Hitler continued to sour as Ribbentrop gained more power within the German government. By 1936, Hoesch was quickly becoming a thorn in Hitler's side. Before Hitler could take action against him, he died of a heart attack on 11 April 1936.

Hoffmann: Heinrich Hoffmann (1885-1957)

Hoffmann worked in his father's photographic shop and as a photographer in Munich from 1908. He joined the party in 1920 and was chosen by its new leader, Hitler, as his official photographer. Hitler and Hoffman became close friends. Hoffmann's photographs were published as postage stamps, postcards, posters and picture books. Following Hoffmann's suggestion, both he and Hitler received royalties from all uses of Hitler's image, making Hoffman a wealthy man. In 1933 he was elected to the Reichstag and in 1938 Hitler appointed him a 'Professor'. He was arrested on 10 May 1945 and sentenced to four years imprisonment for Nazi profiteering.

Hohenlohe: Stephanie Julianne von Hohenlohe (1891-1972)

Stephanie married Friedrich Franz von Hohenlohe-Waldenburg-Schillingsfürst in 1914, but the couple divorced in 1920. Despite being Jewish, she became friendly with Hitler who called her his 'dear princess'. She developed a very close friendship with Goering, and Himmler even declared her an 'honorary Aryan'. In a 1938 MI6 report, British intelligence said that 'she is frequently summoned by the Führer who appreciates her intelligence and good advice. She is perhaps the only woman who can exercise any influence on him.' She also befriended Lord Rothermere and was able to get him to pay her a £5,000 annual retainer, which ceased in 1939 leading to a court case. On the outbreak of war she returned to England, and then moved to the USA. After the War she rebuilt influential connections in Germany. She died in Geneva in 1972.

Hossbach: Friedrich Wilhelm Ludwig Hossbach (1894-1980)

Hossbach served on the Eastern Front in the First World War, rising to the rank of Senior Lieutenant (Oberleutnant). He remained in the army and is best known for the 'Hossbach Memorandum', a report of a meeting held on 5 November 1937 between Hitler, Blomberg, Fritsch, Raeder, Goering, Neurath and Hossbach. In May 1945, Hossbach (who was largely opposed to the Nazi regime) was warned by friends to expect a visit from the Gestapo. They arrived at his house an hour before the Americans; Hossbach, armed with a pistol, engaged his visitors in a firefight until they fled. He was taken into American custody.

Jodl: Alfred Josef Ferdinand Jodl (1890-1946)

Jodl served during the First World War and remained in the army. He was nominally assigned as an artillery commander from 1938 to August 1939 during the Anschluss, but from then until the end of the War he was Chief of Operation Staff OKW. Jodl acted as a Chief of Staff during the swift occupation of Denmark and Norway. He was injured during the 20 July 1944 plot to assassinate Hitler and was awarded the special wounded badge alongside several other leading Nazi figures. He was found guilty at Nuremberg and hanged on 16 October 1946.

Junge: Gertraud Junge (1920-2002)

Gertraud (Traudl) was the youngest of Hitler's three secretaries. At the age of 22 she worked at Hitler's HQ at Rastenburg in East Prussia and later in the Berlin Bunker. In June 1943, she married Hans Junge, Aide-de-Camp to the Führer, who was killed a year later when a Spitfire strafed his company on the Normandy Front. Gertraud Junge survived the last chaotic days in Berlin, typing Hitler's last will and testament. She was arrested by the Russians and then the Americans and interrogated for hours. She died childless in 2002.

Kahr: Gustav Ritter von Kahr (1862-1934)

Kahr became Prime Minister of Bavaria in 1920 and was instrumental in the failure of Hitler's Beer Hall Putsch. Hitler and Ludendorff sought Kahr's support, but he had his own plan with Seisser and Lossow to install a nationalist dictatorship without Hitler. On 30 June 1934 – the 'Night of the Long Knives' – Kahr was punished for his 'treason' during the Beer Hall Putsch. He was abducted in Munich and hacked to death with axes by SS members and then thrown into a swamp near Dachau.

Keitel: Wilhelm Bodewin Johann Gustav Keitel (1882-1946)

Keitel served on the Western Front during the First World War. He remained within the army after the War and by 1938 he was promoted to the Supreme Command of the Armed Forces, effectively making him War Minister. Soon after his appointment at OKW, he convinced Hitler to appoint his close friend, Walter von Brauchitsch, as Commander-in-Chief of the Army. During the Second World War, Keitel was one of the primary planners of the Wehrmacht campaigns and operations on the western and the eastern fronts. In 1940, after the French campaign, he was promoted to Field Marshal along with several other generals. After the failed plot of 20 July 1944, Keitel sat on the army court that handed over many officers to Freisler's notorious People's Court. Following the Nuremberg trials he was executed by hanging.

Kempka: Erich Kempka (1910-1975)

Kempka joined the Nazi Party in 1930 and two years later was one of eight founding members of the SS-Begleit-Kommando. He was present at the arrest of Ernst Roehm in 1934, and in 1936 he replaced Julius Schreck as Hitler's primary chauffeur and chief of his car fleet. Unless in the company of an important personality, Hitler would sit in the front, next to Kempka, with his valet behind him. In April 1945, Kempka accompanied Hitler to the Führerbunker. He was one of those responsible for the burning of Hitler and Eva Braun's corpses after they committed suicide together on the afternoon of 30 April 1945. On 20 June 1945, he was captured by US troops at Berchtesgaden and eventually released in 1947. He died in 1975.

Kesselring: Albert Kesselring (1885-1960)

Kesselring served on both the western and eastern fronts during the First World War and remained in the army until 1933, when he was discharged to become head of the Department of Administration at the Reich Commissariat for Aviation. During the Second World War, Kesselring commanded air forces in the invasions of Poland and France, the Battle of Britain and Operation Barbarossa. As Commander-in-Chief South, he was overall commander in the Mediterranean theatre including North Africa. In the final campaign of the War, he commanded German forces in Western Europe. Kesselring was sentenced to death at Nuremberg, but the sentence was subsequently commuted. He was released in 1952 and died in 1960.

Klausener: Erich Klausener (1885-1934)

Klausener served as an ordnance officer on the western and eastern fronts during the First World War; he was later imprisoned for a short time for participating in boycotts during the French occupation of the Ruhr in 1923 and 1924. Beginning in 1928, Klausener became head of the Catholic Action group and prior to 1933 he energetically supported the police battle against unlawful Nazi activities. After the 'Night of the Long Knives', a squad of SS men, apparently acting on the orders of Goering and Heydrich, entered his office at the Transportation Ministry and shot him dead at his desk.

Kluge: Guenther Adolf Ferdinand 'Hans' von Kluge (1882-1944)

Kluge was a staff officer during the First World War, and in 1916 he fought at the Battle of Verdun. By 1936 he was a lieutenant general, and in 1937 he took command of the Sixth Army Group. He led the Sixth into battle in Poland in 1939. In October 1943 he was badly injured in a car accident and was unable to return to duty until July 1944, when he became Rundstedt's replacement as commander of the German forces in the West. When Stauffenberg attempted to assassinate Hitler on 20 July 1944, Kluge was with him in his headquarters in La Roche-Guyon. On 17 August 1944 he was replaced by Model and recalled to Berlin for a meeting with Hitler. Thinking that Hitler would punish him as a conspirator, he committed suicide by taking cyanide near Metz that same day.

Kordt: Erich Kordt (1903-1969)

Kordt spoke perfect English and joined the German Foreign Office in 1928, later serving in the London Embassy under Ribbentrop, for whom he developed a personal dislike. Despite this, he became a member of the Nazi Party in November 1937, and in February 1938, when Ribbentrop became Foreign Minister, he was appointed head of the Foreign Office's 'Ministerial Bureau'. In June 1939, Kordt went to London to warn Robert Vansittart, the diplomatic advisor to the British government, of the secret negotiations between Germany and the Soviet Union. He was dismayed that all approaches made by the German Resistance Movement within the German Foreign Office were ignored by the British. In April 1941, Kordt was posted to Tokyo as the German Embassy's First Secretary, and later to Nanking as German Consul, where he worked as an agent for the Russians until 1944. From 1951, Kordt was a professor of international law at the University of Cologne.

Krebs: Hans Krebs (1898-1945)

Krebs remained in the army after the First World War, rising to become a general of infantry. As Chief of the Army General Staff (OKH), Krebs was in the Führerbunker below the Reich Chancellery garden during the Battle of Berlin. On 28 April 1945, Krebs made his last telephone call to Field Marshal Wilhelm Keitel at the new Supreme Command HQ in Fürstenberg. He told Keitel that, if relief did not arrive within 48 hours, all was lost. The following day Krebs, Burgdorf, Goebbels, and Bormann witnessed Hitler signing his will. Late that evening, a somewhat delusional Krebs radioed Jodl with the following demands: 'Request immediate report. Firstly, of the whereabouts of Wenck's spearheads. Secondly, of time intended to attack. Thirdly, of the location of the 9th Army. Fourthly, of the precise place in which the 9th Army will break through. Fifthly, of the whereabouts of General Holste's spearhead.' The following day Hitler committed suicide at around 3.30 p.m. After a bungled attempt to surrender, Krebs committed suicide on 2 May 1945.

Kriebel: Hermann Kriebel (1876-1941)

Kriebel was a retired lieutenant colonel; he fought with the Freikorps during the White counter-revolution and in 1923 became the military leader of the Kampfbund. Kriebel was a key figure in the Beer Hall Putsch of 8-9 November 1923, and was convicted with Hitler in 1924, serving his sentence in Landsberg Prison just outside Munich. Kriebel maintained his ties with the party, but he did not benefit from Hitler's rise to power. He later became Consul General in Shanghai.

Kubizek: August 'Gustl' Kubizek (1888-1956)

Kubizek and Hitler first met while competing for standing room in the Landestheater in Linz, Austria. They quickly became close friends; the two shared a small room from February to July 1908. Kubizek was accepted into the Vienna Conservatory where he quickly made a name for himself. In 1908 Hitler abruptly broke off the friendship and drifted into homelessness. Kubizek did not attempt to contact Hitler until 1933, when he wrote to congratulate him on having become Chancellor of Germany; they eventually met in 1938, the last meeting being in 1940. Kubizek was arrested and his home was searched by US forces in 1945, but the Hitler correspondence and drawings were not found. He was released from prison on 8 April 1947.

Lammers: Hans Heinrich Lammers (1879-1962)

Having served in the First World War, Lammers resumed his career as a lawyer, becoming an Under-Secretary at the Ministry of the Interior by 1922. In 1932 he joined the party and by 1937 he was Reich Minister without portfolio. On 30 November 1939 he became a member of the Council of Ministers for the Defence of the Reich. Following the battle of Stalingrad, Lammers, Bormann and Keitel attempted to create a three-man junta representing the Nazi Party. Goebbels, Speer, Goering and Himmler all saw this proposal as a power grab and Lammers eventually lost influence as the continuation of the War rendered his post irrelevant. In April 1945, Hitler ordered SS troops to shoot Lammers, but he was rescued when he was captured by US forces. His wife, however, committed suicide. At Nuremberg he was sentenced to ten years' imprisonment, but he was released in 1952.

Lange: Martin Franz Erwin Rudolf Lange (1910-1945?)

Lange went to the University of Jena and received a doctorate in law in 1933. He joined the SA in November of that year, and the SS in 1936. He worked for the Gestapo in Berlin, Vienna, Riga and Stuttgart. In November 1941 he was deeply involved in planning and executing the murder of 24,000 Latvian Jews from the Riga ghetto. He was called to the Wannsee Conference by Heydrich where, as an SS-Major along with Eichmann, the recording secretary of the conference, Lange was the lowest ranking of the SS officers present. Heydrich, however, viewed his first-hand experience in conducting the mass murder of Jews as valuable for the conference. He was said to be killed in action in February 1945; he may have committed suicide, but the records are unclear.

Lenard: Philipp Eduard Anton von Lenard (1862-1947)

Lenard was a distinguished scientist and won the Nobel Prize in 1905. He was a strong German nationalist who despised English physics, which he considered as having stolen its ideas from Germany. He joined the Nazi Party and was an outspoken proponent of the idea that Germany should rely on 'Deutsche Physik' and ignore what he considered the fallacious and deliberately misleading ideas of 'Jewish physics', by which he meant chiefly the theories of Albert Einstein. As an advisor to Hitler, Lenard became Chief of Aryan Physics under the Nazis. He was expelled from his Heidelberg post by Allied occupation forces in 1945, and he died in 1947.

Ley: Inge Ley (d. 1942)

Gossip circulated throughout Germany about the beautiful Inge's (Inga) relationship with Hitler and the cause of her suicide. She and her husband, Robert Ley, had three children, but she was troubled by her husband's acute alcoholism. She was well known to have had a passion for Hitler. She was an exceptionally beautiful woman and Ley commissioned a life size portrait of her in the nude which he displayed prominently in his house. According to Robert Ley's private secretary, Inge shot herself on 29 December 1942, suffering depression following complications during childbirth which had left her drug-dependent.

Ley: Robert Ley (1890-1945)

Ley served as an aviator during the First World War. After the War he gained a doctorate at university and joined the party having read Hitler's speech at his trial following the Beer Hall Putsch. When Hitler became Chancellor in January 1933, Ley accompanied him to Berlin. In April, when the trade union movement was taken over by the State, Hitler appointed him as head of the German Labour Front (DAF), where he freely embezzled funds. In 1942, his second wife Inge shot herself after a drunken brawl. Ley's subordinates took their lead from him, and the DAF became a notorious centre of corruption. Despite his failings, Ley retained Hitler's favour; until the last months of the War he was part of Hitler's inner circle along with Bormann and Goebbels. He was captured on 16 May 1945 and indicted at Nuremberg. Three days later he strangled himself using a noose made by fastening strips of his towel to the toilet pipe in his cell.

Linge: Heinz Linge (1913-1980)

Linge was an SS officer and worked as Hitler's valet from 1935 until Hitler shot himself on 30 April 1945. Linge was one of the last people to leave the bunker and was subsequently arrested by the Russians who interrogated him about the circumstances of Hitler's death. He was eventually released from Russian captivity in 1955 and then gave numerous television interviews. He died in Bremen in March 1980.

Lossow: Otto von Lossow (1868-1938)

Lossow was a lieutenant colonel during the First World War and remained in the army, becoming a commander in Bavaria. By 1923 he was politically aligned with Kahr and Seisser and the three had their own plans for a nationalist government without Hitler. At the Beer Hall Putsch they ostensibly supported Hitler, but seeing the way matters were heading they went over to General von Seeckt and helped put down the coup.

Lubbe: Marinus van der Lubbe (1909-1934)

Lubbe joined the Dutch Communist Party in 1925. After an injury at a building site where he worked, he moved to Leiden in 1927 where he learned to speak some German and founded the Lenin House, where he organised political meetings. According to the Berlin police, Lubbe claimed to have set the Reichstag building on fire as a cry to rally the German workers against fascist rule. Under torture, he confessed again and was brought to trial along with the leaders of the opposition Communist Party. He was guillotined on 10 January 1934.

Ludendorff: Erich Friedrich Wilhelm Ludendorff (1865-1937)

Ludendorff was a general during the First World War. Convinced that the German Army had been betrayed by Marxists and Republicans in the Versailles Treaty, he joined Hitler in the unsuccessful Beer Hall Putsch. In 1925 he ran for president against his former colleague, Paul von Hindenburg. After 1928, Ludendorff went into retirement, having fallen out with the Nazi Party. He no longer approved of Hitler and began to regard him as just another manipulative politician. In an attempt to regain Ludendorff's favour, Hitler paid him an unannounced visit on his birthday in 1935 and offered to make him a Field Marshal if he came back into politics. Ludendorff did not welcome Hitler or his offer.

Maurice: Emil Maurice (1897-1972)

Maurice was an early member of the party and became the SA commander of the newly established Stabswache, a special SA company responsible for guarding Hitler at political rallies. He was imprisoned with Hitler after the Beer Hall Putsch. In 1925, Hitler refounded the Stabswache as the SS and Maurice became SS member No. 2, after Hitler himself. He reportedly had a brief relationship with Geli Raubal, Hitler's niece, and therefore lost his job as Hitler's chauffeur. Himmler later recommended that Maurice be expelled from the SS, along with other members of his family due to their Jewish ancestry, but to Himmler's annoyance, Hitler stood by his old friend. In 1948 Maurice was sentenced to four years in a labour camp.

Milch: Erhard Milch (1892-1972)

Milch commanded a fighter wing, Jagdgruppe 6, at the end of the First World War. In 1933, following an early career at Junkers, he took up a position as State Secretary of the Reich Aviation Ministry, answering directly to Goering. In this capacity he was instrumental in establishing the Luftwaffe. In 1944 Milch sided with Goebbels and Himmler in attempting to convince Hitler to remove Goering from command of the Luftwaffe. When Hitler refused, Goering retaliated by forcing Milch out of his position. For the remainder of the War, he worked under Speer. He was sentenced to life imprisonment at Landsberg Prison by the Allies, but his sentence was commuted to fifteen years in 1951. He was released in 1954.

Mitford: Diana Mitford (1910-2003); Unity Valkyrie Mitford (1914-1948)

Diana was the third daughter of Lord Redesdale. She was married first to Bryan Walter Guinness, heir to the barony of Moyne, and secondly to Sir Oswald Mosley, 6th Baronet of Ancoats, leader of the British Union of Fascists. Her second marriage, in 1936, took place at the home of Goebbels, with Hitler as guest of honour. She was interned for three years during the Second World War and later moved to Paris. Unity was the fourth daughter of Lord Redesdale. Along with her sister Diana she was a prominent public supporter of Nazism, and from 1936, a part of Hitler's inner circle of friends for five years. Following the declaration of war, she attempted suicide and Hitler arranged for her to be sent home to England. She never fully recovered and died in 1948.

Model: Otto Moritz Walter Model (1891-1945)

Model served during the First World War and remained in the army. He was a supporter of the Nazi regime and served throughout the War. At various times in 1944 he commanded each of the three major army groups on the Eastern Front. By August 1944 Model was transferred to defence in the west where he successfully held the Arnhem bridge. Three months later, following a joint plan developed with Runstedt, led the push for Antwerp, culminating in the Battle of the Bulge. The failure of this attack marked the end of Model's special relationship with Hitler. He shot himself in the head on 21 April 1945.

Moltke: Helmuth James Graf von Moltke (1907-1945)

Moltke studied legal and political sciences. In 1935, he declined the chance to become a judge because he would have been obliged to join the Nazi Party. He helped victims of Hitler's regime emigrate, and between 1935 and 1938, he regularly visited Britain. He was drafted into the High Command of the Armed Forces (OKW), Counter-Intelligence Service, Foreign Division under Admiral Canaris. Moltke led the 'Kreisau Circle' but opposed the assassination of Hitler. He was not involved in the 29 July 1944 plot, but he was arrested, and in January 1945 he stood along with several of his fellow regime opponents before the People's Court of Roland Freisler. Because no evidence could be found, Freisler had to invent a charge de novo. Moltke was sentenced to death on 11 January 1945 and executed twelve days later.

Morell: Theodor Gilbert Morell (1886-1948)

Morell served as a medical officer during the First World War. He joined the Nazi Party in 1933 and later met Hitler at an event at the Berghof. He was constantly recommended to other members of the Nazi leadership, but most of them, including Goering and Himmler, dismissed him as a quack. By April 1945, Hitler was taking twenty-eight different pills a day, along with numerous injections every few hours and intravenous injections of methamphetamine almost every day. On 22 April 1945, about a week before committing suicide, Hitler dismissed Morell from the Führerbunker in Berlin, saying that he did not need any more medical help. Morell was captured, but was never charged with any crimes. He died in 1948 after a stroke.

Mueller: Renate Mueller (1906-1937)

Mueller was a popular actress in Berlin in the late 1920s. A blue-eyed blonde, she was considered to be one of the great beauties of her day. She starred in more than twenty German films, including Viktor und Viktoria (1933). With the rise of the Nazi Party, Mueller came to be regarded as an ideal Aryan woman and was courted and promoted as Germany's leading film actress. A meeting with Adolf Hitler in the mid-1930s resulted in Mueller being offered parts in films that promoted Nazi ideals. She died after a fall from her hotel window – presumably suicide, but this is not clear.

Mueller: Heinrich Mueller (1900-1945?)

At the end of the First World War, Mueller served as a pilot for an artillery spotting unit. He was later employed in the political department of the police headquarters and rose quickly through the ranks of the SS. During the Second World War, he was heavily involved in espionage and counter-espionage. After the assassination attempt against Hitler on 20 July 1944, Mueller was placed in charge of the arrest and interrogation of all those suspected of involvement in the resistance. Over 5,000 people were arrested and about 200 were executed, including Canaris. In the last months of the War, Mueller remained at his post, apparently still confident of a German victory. He remains the most senior figure of the Nazi regime who was never captured or confirmed to have died.

Mussolini: Benito Amilcare Andrea Mussolini (1883-1945)

Mussolini created the Fasci di Combattimento in 1919 and following the 'March on Rome' in October 1922, he became Prime Minister of Italy. He began using the title 'Il Duce' in 1925. He inaugurated public works programmes which included the 'taming of the Pontine Marshes'. He was also dedicated to the improvement of job opportunities and public transports. On 10 June 1940, Mussolini led Italy into the Second World War, but after the 1943 Allied invasion of Italy, King Victor Emmanuel had him arrested. On 12 September 1943, Mussolini was rescued from prison in the daring Gran Sasso raid by German special forces. On 28 April 1945 he was captured and summarily executed near Lake Como by Italian partisans. His body was then taken to Milan where it was hung upside down at a petrol station. Two days later Hitler shot himself. The war in Europe came to an end just ten days after his death.

Neurath: Konstantin von Neurath (1873-1956)

Neurath served as an officer during the First World War. By 1932 he was Minister of Foreign Affairs and he continued to hold that position under Chancellor von Schleicher and then under Hitler. In 1937, Neurath became a member of the Nazi Party, but Hitler sacked him in February 1938. In March 1939, Neurath was appointed Reichsprotektor of Bohemia and Moravia and Hitler chose him in part to pacify the international outrage over the German occupation of Czechoslovakia. In 1941 he was relieved of his day-to-day powers and replaced by Heydrich and Daluege. At Nuremberg he was sentenced to fifteen years' imprisonment, but was released in 1954.

Papen: Franz Joseph Hermann Michael Maria von Papen (1879-1969)

Papen was expelled from the USA during the First World War and later served as an officer, first on the Western Front and later in Palestine. He entered politics and was a member of the Parliament of Prussia in 1921-32. Hindenburg appointed him Chancellor, but the cabinet he formed with the assistance of General Kurt von Schleicher was weak; by 1933 he was replaced by Hitler, himself becoming Vice-Chancellor. Hitler and his allies quickly marginalised Papen and the rest of the cabinet. During the 'Night of the Long Knives', General von Schleicher was gunned down along with his wife, but Papen managed to survive. He was later sidelined by being made Ambassador to Austria. Hitler dismissed him from his mission in Austria in 1938, and he later served as Ambassador to Turkey in 1939-44. At Nuremberg he was acquitted, but a later de-Nazification court sentenced him to eight years' hard labour. Papen was released on appeal in 1949.

Paulus: Friedrich Wilhelm Ernst Paulus (1890-1957)

Paulus served during the First World War and after the Armistice he fought with the Freikorps in the east as a brigade adjutant. Paulus was promoted to Lieutenant General in August 1940 and named Deputy Chief of the German General Staff, in which role he helped draft the plans for Operation Barbarossa. In January 1942 he was promoted to General and became Commander of the German Sixth Army, leading the drive on Stalingrad during that summer. He fought the Soviet defenders for three months, but following a massive counter-offensive, Paulus found himself surrounded. He surrendered on 31 January 1943, a day after he was promoted to the rank of Field Marshal. In Russian captivity, Paulus became a vocal critic of the Nazi regime. He was released by the Russians in 1953.

Poetsch: Leopold Poetsch (1853-1942)

Poetsch was Hitler's teacher in geography and history from 1901 to 1904. He was a fervent believer in pan-Germanic rule and Hitler was captivated by his teachings; at this time Hitler began regularly reading a local anti-Semitic newspaper. In his later years, Hitler spoke of Poetsch as a 'great man' and he was clearly influential in Hitler's self-imposed mission to exterminate all Jews. In 1936 some teachers in Linz sent their now-famous pupil photographs to remind him of them, and they asked Poetsch to join them, but he refused, arguing that he did not agree with Hitler in his defamation of Austria as he had sworn an official oath to Austria.

Quisling: Vidkun Abraham Lauritz Jonssøn Quisling (1887-1945)

On 14 December 1939, Hitler met Quisling, a Norwegian right-wing politician, and promised to respond to any British invasion of Norway, perhaps pre-emptively, with a German counter-invasion. In the early hours of 9 April 1940, Germany invaded Norway by air and sea, intending to capture King Haakon VII and the government. In the afternoon, Quisling was told by German liaison Hans Wilhelm Scheidt that should he set up a government, it would have Hitler's personal approval. From 1942 to 1945 Quisling served as Minister-President, working with the occupying forces. His government was dominated by ministers from Nasjonal Samling, the party he founded in 1933. Quisling was put on trial during the legal purge in Norway after the War and found guilty of charges including embezzlement, murder and high treason. He was executed by firing squad on 24 October 1945.

Raeder: Erich Raeder (1876-1960)

Raeder joined the Imperial Navy in 1894 and was promoted to Admiral in 1928. As head of the German Navy, he focused all of his efforts on rebuilding the High Seas Fleet. He was a believer in battleships and was hostile towards submarines and aircraft carriers. Raeder was interested in using Norway as a base to allow the Kriegsmarine to attack the North Atlantic sea-lanes to Britain; he was instrumental in Hitler's decision to invade Norway. Raeder was opposed to Operation Sea Lion and also had doubts about Germany's ability to gain air superiority over the English Channel. In the autumn of 1942, in an attempt to limit Doenitz's power, Raeder retracted Doenitz's responsibility for training U-boat crews, only to see Doenitz ignore his orders. Raeder resigned from Kriegsmarine in May 1943 and was succeeded by Doenitz. After the War, Raeder was sentenced to life imprisonment at the Nuremberg Trials for waging a war of aggression. The sentence was later reduced and he was released in 1955.

Raubal: Angela Franziska Johanna Raubal, née Hitler (1883-1949); Angela Maria 'Geli' Raubal (1908-1931)

Angela Hitler was the second child of Alois Hitler and his second wife, Franziska Matzelsberger. Her mother died the following year. She and her brother Alois Hitler Jr were raised by their father and his third wife Klara Pölzl. Her half-brother Adolf was born six years after her, and they grew very close. She married Leo Raubal (1879-1910) and had two children, Leo and Geli. Angela lost contact with her half-brother for ten years, and then in 1928 she and Geli moved to the Berghof where she became Hitler's housekeeper. After Geli's suicide, Angela left Berchtesgaden and moved to Dresden. Hitler broke off relations with Angela and did not attend her second wedding to the architect Professor Martin Hammitzsch. Angela died of a stroke in 1949. Geli (junior) was close to her uncle Adolf from 1925 until her suicide in 1931. She moved into Hitler's Munich apartment in 1929 when she enrolled in medicine at university. Hitler was infatuated with her and refused her any freedom

or permission to go to Vienna. While Hitler was absent at a meeting, Geli shot herself in the Munich apartment with Hitler's pistol. Hitler treated Geli's room at the Berghof as a shrine and it was kept as she had left it; he hung portraits of her in his room there, and at the Chancellery in Berlin.

Reinhardt: Fritz Reinhardt (1895-1969)

Reinhardt joined the party and with his talent for speaking and his knowledge of economic and taxation systems, he quickly built up a career. From 1928 to 1930 he was the Governor of Upper Bavaria. In 1930 he became a member of the Reichstag and took the leading role in the party's financial issues. In 1933, he became an SA Gruppen-führer and a member of Hess's staff. He was the chief architect of the Tax Reconciliation Act of October 1934. He was publisher of the tax newspaper Deutsche Steuerzeitung, which along with all his other publications was made required reading for all finance officials. After the War, Reinhardt was placed in Allied custody, and in 1949 he was classified as a 'main culprit' and sentenced to four years in a labour prison. He is pictured here between Otto Skorzeny and Kurt Zschirnt.

Reitsch: Hanna Reitsch (1912-1979)

Reitsch became Germany's leading female stunt pilot and later chief test pilot for the Luftwaffe. She worshipped Hitler and the Nazi ideology and became the only woman to win the Iron Cross. Hanna Reitsch spent three days in the Führerbunker shortly before Hitler's suicide; she then flew out with the newly appointed Chief of the Luftwaffe, General Robert Ritter von Greim, whose orders were to mount a bombing attack on the Russian forces that were now approaching the Chancellery and Führerbunker. Hanna Reitsch survived the War and died in 1979.

Ribbentrop: Ulrich Friedrich Wilhelm Joachim von Ribbentrop (1893-1946)

Ribbentrop was first introduced to Hitler in 1928 and became a secret emissary between him and Papen. From the start, Ribbentrop was Hitler's favourite foreign-policy adviser. In August 1936, Hitler appointed him Ambassador to Britain with orders to negotiate the Anglo-German alliance, but this came to nothing. In 1938 he succeeded Neurath as Foreign Minister and his most successful moment came with the signing of the Non-Aggression Pact with Russia in August 1939. He was against the attack on the USSR in 1941 and passed a word to a Soviet diplomat: 'Please tell Stalin I was against this war, and that I know it will bring great misfortune to Germany.' As the War progressed, Hitler found Ribbentrop increasingly tiresome and sought to avoid him; his position weakened further when many old Foreign Office diplomats participated in the 20 July 1944 assassination attempt on Hitler. In April 1945, Ribbentrop attended Hitler's 56th birthday party in Berlin. Three days later, he attempted to meet with Hitler, only to be told to go away. This was their last meeting. He was arrested after the War, tried at Nuremberg, and executed in 1946.

Roehm: Ernst Julius Guenther Roehm (1887-1934)

Roehm joined the German Workers' Party, which soon became the Nazi Party. He also met Hitler and they became political allies and close friends. Following the Beer Hall Putsch, Roehm was found guilty, but was granted a conditional discharge. At Landsberg Prison in April 1924, Roehm was given full powers by Hitler to rebuild the SA in any way he saw fit. By August 1933, Roehm and Hitler were so close that he was the only Nazi who dared address Hitler as 'Adolf,' rather than 'mein Führer'. Despite this friendship, Roehm represented a challenge to Hitler, who by now desired the support of the army. In the 'Night of the Long Knives' on 30 June 1934, Roehm and the entire leadership of the SA was purged; Roehm was shot in the chest at point-blank range.

Rosenberg: Alfred Ernst Rosenberg (1893-1946)

Rosenberg became one of the earliest members of the German Workers Party, later to become the Nazi Party, joining in January 1919, ten months before Hitler. After the Beer Hall Putsch, Hitler appointed Rosenberg as a temporary leader of the party. He was named leader of the party's foreign political office in 1933, but he played little practical part in the role. Rosenberg reshaped Nazi racial policy over the years, but it always consisted of Aryan supremacy, extreme German nationalism and anti-Semitism. Following the invasion of Russia, he was appointed head of the Reich Ministry for the Occupied Eastern Territories. At the Nuremberg Trials he claimed to be ignorant of the Holocaust; he was sentenced to death and executed on 16 October 1946.

Rundstedt: Karl Rudolf Gerd von Rundstedt (1875-1953)

Runstedt served during the First World War and remained in the army. He commanded Army Group A during the invasion of France, and was promoted to Field Marshal on 19 July 1940. In the Russian campaign he commanded Army Group South, responsible for the encirclement and the Battle of Kiev. He was dismissed by Hitler in December 1941, but was recalled in 1942 and appointed Commander-in-Chief in the West. He was dismissed again after the defeat in Normandy in July 1944, but was again recalled as Commander-in-Chief in the West in September, and dismissed for a final time March 1945. Rundstedt was aware of the various plots to depose Hitler, but he did not support them. He was charged with war crimes but did not face trial and was released in 1949.

Saxe-Coburg: Charles Edward, Duke of Saxe-Coburg and Gotha (1884-1954)

Saxe-Coburg was a grandson of Queen Victoria and Prince Albert, and also, until 1919, the Duke of Albany and a Prince of the United Kingdom. The duke supported Germany during the First World War, but never held a major command. He joined the Nazi Party in 1935 and became a member of the SA. He also served as a member of the Reichstag representing the Nazi Party from 1937 to 1945, and as President of the German Red Cross from 1933 to 1945. The duke attended the funeral of his first cousin King George V in his SA uniform and approached the new King-Emperor, Edward VIII, about the possibility of a pact. Nothing came of these talks. Nonetheless, he continued to send Hitler encouraging reports about the strength of pro-German sentiment among the British aristocracy. After the War he lost most of his assets and died in seclusion.

Schacht: Hjalmar Horace Greeley Schacht (1877-1970)

Schacht was an economist, banker, liberal politician, and co-founder of the German Democratic Party. He served as the Currency Commissioner and President of the Reichsbank under the Weimar Republic. He was a fierce critic of Germany's reparation obligations following the Treaty of Versailles. In 1934 Hitler appointed Schacht as his Minister of Economics. Schacht supported his public works programmes, most notably the construction of autobahns to alleviate unemployment. He disagreed with what he called 'unlawful activities' against Germany's Jewish minority and in 1935 made a speech denouncing Julius Streicher. He objected to high military spending, and thereby came into conflict with Hitler and Goering. In November 1937 he resigned as Minister of Economics, but remained President of the Reichsbank until Hitler dismissed him in January 1939. He had no role during the War and was imprisoned after the 20 July 1944 plot. He was tried at Nuremberg and acquitted.

Schaub: Julius Schaub (1898-1967)

Schaub was born in Munich, and in 1925 he was hired privately by Hitler as a personal assistant. Schaub was one of Hitler's personal adjutants until 1945, and was in constant close contact. Near the end of the War, on 23 April 1945, Hitler ordered Schaub to burn all of his personal belongings and papers from the Reich Chancellery and the Führerbunker. Schaub then flew to Munich and did the same in Hitler's private apartment at Prinzregentenplatz and at the Berghof in Obersalzberg. He was arrested on 8 May 1945 and remained in custody until February 1949.

Schellenberg: Walther Friedrich Schellenberg (1910-1952)

Schellenberg joined the SS in May 1933 after graduating in Law at the University of Marburg. He met Heydrich and went to work in the counter-intelligence department of the SD. From 1939 to 1942 he was Himmler's personal aide and a deputy chief in the Reich Main Security Office under Heydrich, who answered only to Himmler. In 1940 he was charged with compiling the Informationsheft G.B., a blueprint for the occupation of Britain. A supplement to this work was the list of 2,300 prominent Britons to be arrested after a successful invasion of Britain. At the end of the War, Schellenberg persuaded Himmler to try negotiating with the Western Allies through Count Folke Bernadotte and personally went to Stockholm in April 1945 to arrange their meeting. He was taken into custody by the British in June 1945.

During the Nuremberg Trials, he testified against other Nazis. In the 1949 Ministries Trial he was sentenced to six years' imprisonment, during which time he wrote his memoirs, The Labyrinth. He was released in 1951 and died the following year.

Scheubner-Richter: Max Scheubner-Richter (1884-1923)

Scheubner-Richter was an early member of the Nazi Party and it was he, along with Rosenberg, who devised the plan to drive the German government to revolution through the Beer Hall Putsch. He was a Baltic German born in Riga and lived a large part of his life in Imperial Russia. After the First World War he was involved in the Russian counter-revolution and moved to Germany with Rosenberg in 1918. At the end of September 1923, Scheubner-Richter provided Hitler with a lengthy plan for revolution. During the Beer Hall Putsch, walking arm-in-arm with Hitler, he was shot in the lungs and died instantly. Hitler claimed Scheubner-Richter to be the only 'irreplaceable loss'.

Schirach: Baldur Benedikt von Schirach (1907-1974)

Schirach had an American mother and English was his first language. He married Henriette Hoffmann in 1932, daughter of Heinrich Hoffmann, Hitler's personal photographer and close friend. Through this relationship, Schirach became part of Hitler's inner circle. In 1931 he was a Youth Leader and in 1933 he was made head of the Hitler Youth. He fell into disfavour with Hitler in 1943, but remained at his post. He surrendered in 1945 and was one of the officials put on trial at Nuremberg. He was one of only two men to denounce Hitler. On 1 October 1946, he was found guilty of crimes against humanity for his deportation of the Viennese Jews. He was sentenced to twenty years' imprisonment at Spandau, and was released in 1966.

Schleicher: Kurt von Schleicher (1882-1934)

Schleicher entered the German Army in 1900 as a lieutenant and in his early years made two friendships that played an important role in his life; one was to Franz von Papen, and the other, to Oskar von Hindenburg. In the early 1920s, Schleicher had emerged as a leading protégé of General von Seeckt, who often gave Schleicher sensitive assignments. Between September 1923 and February 1924, the army took over much of the administration, a task in which he played a prominent role. The appointment of Groener as Defence Minister in January 1928 did much to advance his career. After a complex career with myriad political manoeuvres, Schleicher became Chancellor in 1933, but stepped down shortly afterwards when he was unable to control a government. Initially he supported Hitler, but this turned out to be a fatal mistake; seventeen months later he was shot down during the 'Night of Long Knives'.

Schoengarth: Karl Georg Eberhard Schoengarth (1903-1946)

In 1933, Schoengarth became a member of the SD Intelligence Service of the SS. During the German attack on Poland he was Senior Inspector of SiPo Security Police in Dresden. In January 1941 he was sent to Krakow, Poland, as the Senior Commander of SiPo and SS Intelligence, where he formed several Special Action Groups with the intention of perpetrating massacres. He was responsible for the murder of up to 10,000 Jewish citizens between July and September 1941. From early July 1944 until the end of the War, he worked as Commander of the Gestapo in the Netherlands. He was captured by the Allies and charged with the crime of murdering a downed Allied pilot. He was tried by a British Military Court in Burgsteinfurt and was found guilty on 11 February 1946. He was sentenced to death by hanging.

Schreck: Julius Schreck (1898-1936)

Schreck served during the First World War and joined the Nazi Party in 1920 at about the same time as Hitler; the two developed a deep friendship. In 1921 Schreck was one of the founders of the SA and also helped form the Stabswache, which was an early company of SA troops assigned as bodyguards to Hitler. In 1923 he participated in the Beer Hall Putsch. In 1925, he was asked by Emil Maurice to help establish a new bodyguard for Hitler which would be known as the Stosstrupp Adolf Hitler. Later that year, the group of eight men was renamed as the Schutzstaffel and Schreck became SS Member No. 5. He also worked as Hitler's chauffeur. In 1930 he was appointed as an SS-Standartenführer, but had little power. In 1936 he developed meningitis and died in May.

Schroeder: Christa Schroeder (1908-1984)

Schroeder was employed as a stenotypist in the Oberste SA-Führung, the SA high command. Hitler met her there in early 1933 when he had been appointed Chancellor; he took a liking to her and hired her the same year. She lived at the Wolf's Lair near Rastenburg, Hitler's initial Eastern Front headquarters. On 20 April 1945, during the Battle of Berlin, Schroeder, Bormann and several others were ordered by Hitler to leave Berlin by aircraft for the Obersalzberg. She was arrested on 28 May 1945 in Hintersee near Berchtesgaden and interrogated by the French liaison officer Albert Zoller serving in the 7th US Army. She was released on 12 May 1948.

Schwarz: Franz Xaver Schwarz (1875-1947)

Schwarz served during the First World War as a second lieutenant in the infantry. He joined the Nazi Party in 1922 and his membership number was six. He participated in the failed Beer Hall Putsch of November 1923, and with the re-establishment of party in 1925 he became full-time Treasurer. Hitler gave Schwarz full authority for the financial affairs of the party and attended his 60th birthday celebration on 27 November 1935. Schwarz's able administration of party funds insured a cash balance of one billion reichmarks by the end of the War. He was arrested by US troops and died in an Allied internment camp near Regensburg on 2 December 1947. He was posthumously classified by the Munich de-Nazification court as a 'major offender'.

Speer: Albert Speer (1905-1981)

Speer joined the Nazi Party in 1931 and reported to the party's leader for the West End of Berlin, Karl Hanke, who hired Speer to redecorate a villa he had just rented. Hanke was enthusiastic about Speer's work and launched his career within the party. He became a member of Hitler's inner circle and was commanded by him to design and construct a number of structures, including the Reich Chancellery and the Zeppelinfeld stadium in Nuremberg where party rallies were held. As Minister of Armaments, Speer was so successful that Germany's war production continued to increase despite massive and devastating bombing. He was tried at Nuremberg and sentenced to twenty years' imprisonment for his role in the Nazi regime, principally for the use of forced labour. He served his full sentence, most of it at Spandau Prison in West Berlin, and was released in 1966.

Stauffenberg: Claus Schenk Graf von Stauffenberg (1907-1944)

Stauffenberg was commissioned as second lieutenant in 1930. Following the outbreak of war in 1939, he and his regiment took part in the attack on Poland, the invasion of France and Operation Barbarossa. He was later transferred to the Tunisian campaign as part of the Afrika Korps, and was severely wounded in April 1943. While recuperating he became involved in the resistance movement. Early plans came to nothing, but in July 1944 he had an opportunity, code-named 'Operation Valkyrie'. On 20 July 1944, Stauffenberg entered the briefing room at the Wolf's Lair carrying a briefcase that contained two small bombs. Some minutes later, he excused himself and left the room. Stauffenberg had been heroic, but suffered two unfortunate set-backs which caused the plan to fail. First he only had time to arm one of the two bombs; secondly, after he had left the room, another officer moved his briefcase behind a strong oak base of the table. Hitler survived and the conspirators were tracked with appalling reprisals.

Strasser: Gregor Strasser (1892-1934)

Strasser served during the First World War, rising to the rank of First Lieutenant. In 1919 he and his brother Otto joined the right-wing Freikorps with the young Heinrich Himmler as his adjutant. In 1921, Strasser's group joined forces with Hitler's Nazi Party. His leadership qualities were quickly recognised and he took an active part in the Beer Hall Putsch. After 1925, Strasser's organisational skill helped the NSDAP to take a big step from a marginal South German splinter party to a nationwide mass party with wide appeal. In 1932 he toyed with the idea of joining Sleicher's government. On 30 June 1934, the 'Night of the Long Knives', Strasser was arrested and killed on Hitler's personal order by the Berlin Gestapo.

Streicher: Julius Streicher (1885-1946)

Streicher served during the First World War, rising to the rank of Lieutenant. In 1919 Streicher became politically active and was a supporter of Hitler after hearing him speak in 1922. He took part in the Beer Hall Putsch. Streicher was the publisher of Der Stürmer, a newspaper which promulgated anti-Semitic propaganda and orchestrated anti-Jewish campaigns. He had numerous enemies, especially Goering, and in spite of his special relationship with Hitler, he was stripped of his party offices and withdrew from the public, although he was permitted vto continue publishing Der Stürmer. At Nuremberg, he was found guilty of crimes against humanity and hanged on 16 October 1946.

Stuckart: Wilhelm Stuckart (1902-1953)

In 1922 Stuckart studied law and political economics at Munich and Frankfurt, where he also joined the Nazi Party. From 1932 to 1933 he worked as a lawyer and legal secretary for the SA in Stettin, and upon Himmler's recommendation, he joined the SS in 1933. In 1935 he was given the task, alongside Loesener and Medicus, of co-writing the anti-Semitic Law for the Protection of German Blood and German Honour and The Reich Citizenship Law, together better known as the Nuremberg Laws. Stuckart later represented Wilhelm Frick, the Interior Minister, at the Wannsee Conference on 20 January 1942. In 1945 he was tried and imprisoned for his role in formulating and carrying out anti-Jewish laws. He was eventually released in 1949. He died in a car accident in 1953, but there was suspicion of Mossad involvement.

Weber: Christian Weber (1883-1945)

Weber was an early friend of Hitler's and was among his earliest political associates. Well-known as a thug, he had the habit of carrying a riding crop with him – a habit shared by Hitler in the early years. His name became a by-word for corruption in Munich and it was regularly questioned how this former hotel bellboy had come to own a number of hotels, businesses and smart residences. Numerous Jewish businesses and assets fell into his open lap. On the 'Night of the Long Knives', Weber was among those SS men who travelled to Bad Wiessee to purge the Sturmabteilung leadership. At the end of the War he was killed by Bavarian insurrectionists.

Wessel: Horst Ludwig Wessel (1907-1930)

Wessel joined the Nazi Party in 1926 and soon impressed Goebbels, the Party Governor. In October 1929 he dropped out of university to devote himself full-time to the Nazi movement. Wessel played the schalmei, a type of oboe popular in Germany, and he founded an SA Schalmeien-kapelle, which provided music during SA events. In early 1929, Wessel wrote the lyrics for a new Nazi fight song which was first published in Goebbels's newspaper Der Angriff; this song later became known as 'Horst Wessel Song', with a tune stolen from an old Imperial Navy folk song. On the evening of 14 January 1930, Wessel answered a knock on his door and was shot in the face and fatally wounded. Albrecht Hoehler, an active member of the local Communist Party branch was sentenced to six years' imprisonment for the shooting, and was executed by the Gestapo after the Nazi accession to power in 1933. Wessel's death was a propaganda coup for Goebbels who whipped up anti-communist hysteria.

Wiedemann: Fritz Wiedemann (1891-1970)

Wiedemann served alongside Hitler during the First World War when, as regimental adjutant, he was Corporal Hitler's superior. After the War, Wiedemann left the army and became a farmer, initially refusing an offer from Hitler at the regimental reunion in 1922 to help organise the SA. However, when Hitler came to power, Wiedemann accepted a new offer to link up with his former corporal, initially in the offices of Rudolf Hess before taking up his post at Hitler's side. He became a member of the Nazi Party on 2 February 1934, and from then on Wiedemann remained constantly at Hitler's side as an adjutant. In 1939 he fell out of favour with Hitler and his rival, Julius Schaub, rose as the more important adjutant. To side-line him, he was appointed Consul General to the USA in San Francisco. Wiedemann gave evidence at Nuremberg after the War. Charges against him were dropped in 1948.

Zeitzler: Kurt Zeitzler (1895-1963)

Zeitzler served during the First World War and received an officer's commission as a reward for outstanding bravery. He was placed in command of an infantry battalion. Between 1919 and 1937 he served as a staff officer in the army, and then as a staff officer for the Oberkommando des Heeres (OKH). He served under General Siegmund List during the invasion of Poland, and under General von Kleist in the invasion of France. He was part of the German force that successfully resisted the Dieppe raid on 19 August 1942. He was promoted to General of the Infantry and simultaneously appointed Chief of Staff of the Army General Staff on 24 September 1942, replacing Franz Halder. Following the débâcle at Stalingrad, Zeitzler's relations with Hitler became strained. After a series of violent rows with Hitler, he abruptly left the Berghof on 1 July 1944. Hitler had him dismissed from the army in January 1945 and refused him the right to wear a uniform. After the War, Zeitzler was held in British captivity until February 1947. He died in 1963. In the photograph Zeitler is on Hitler's left.